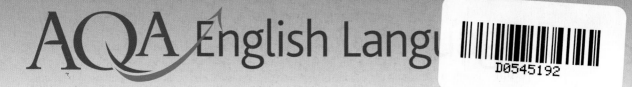

AQA English Langu...

AS

Exclusively endorsed by AQA

Marcello
Giovanelli

Dr Alan Pearce

Series editor
Mark Saunders

Nelson Thornes

Contents

AQA introduction

Nelson Thornes and AQA

Nelson Thornes has worked in collaboration with AQA to ensure that this book offers you the best support for your AS or A Level course and helps you to prepare for your exams. The partnership means that you can be confident that the range of learning, teaching and assessment practice materials has been checked by the senior examining team at AQA before formal approval, and is closely matched to the requirements of your specification.

Blended learning

Printed and electronic resources are blended: this means that links between topics and activities between the book and the electronic resources help you to work in the way that best suits you, and enable extra support to be provided online. For example, you can test yourself online and feedback from the test will direct you back to the relevant parts of the book.

Electronic resources are available in a simple-to-use online platform called Nelson Thornes *learning space*. If your school or college has a licence to use the service, you will be given a password through which you can access the materials through any internet connection.

Icons in this book indicate where there is material online related to that topic. The following icons are used:

Learning activity

These resources include a variety of interactive and non-interactive activities to support your learning.

Progress tracking

These resources include a variety of tests that you can use to check your knowledge on particular topics (Test yourself) and a range of resources that enable you to analyse and understand examination questions (On your marks…).

Research support

These resources include WebQuests, in which you are assigned a task and provided with a range of weblinks to use as source material for research.

Study skills

These resources support you and help develop a skill that is key for your course, for example planning essays.

Analysis tool

These resources feature text extracts that can be highlighted and annotated by the user according to specific objectives.

When you see an icon, go to Nelson Thornes *learning space* at **www.nelsonthornes.com/aqagce**, enter your access details and select your course. The materials are arranged in the same order as the topics in the book, so you can easily find the resources you need.

How to use this book

This book covers the specification for your course and is arranged in a sequence approved by AQA.

Its structure mirrors the specification exactly: it is split into two units (Unit 1 Categorising texts and Unit 2 Creating texts), each of which is divided into Sections A and B. Each section begins with an introduction to the topics that will be covered and concludes with exam (Unit 1) or coursework (Unit 2) preparation. At the back of the book you will find feedback on the Classroom and Extension activities, and a glossary of key terms.

The features in this book include:

Learning objectives

At the beginning of each section you will find a list of learning objectives that contain targets linked to the requirements of the specification.

Key terms

Terms that you will need to be able to define and understand.

Classroom activities

Activities that enable you to apply the knowledge introduced in the text.

Extension activities

Activities that encourage you to try out for yourself the ideas described in the text.

Links

Links to other areas in the text book which are relevant to what you are reading.

Further reading

Suggestions for other texts that will help you in your study and preparation for assessment.

AQA Examiner's tip

Hints from AQA examiners to help you with your study and to prepare for your exam.

AQA Examination-style questions

Questions in the style that you can expect in your exam. AQA examination questions are reproduced by permission of the Assessment and Qualifications Alliance.

Nelson Thornes is responsible for the solution(s) given and they may not constitute the only possible solution(s).

Web links in the book

Nelson Thornes is not responsible for third party content online, there may be some changes to this material that are beyond our control. In order for us to ensure that the links referred to are as up-to-date and stable as possible, the websites provided are usually homepages with supporting instructions on how to reach the relevant pages if necessary.

Please let us know at **webadmin@nelsonthornes.com** if you find a link that doesn't work and we will do our best to redirect the link, or to find an alternative site.

Introduction to this book

Why study English Language?

It is in fact very common to be fascinated by language. Maybe you listen with particular interest when you come across an accent that is different from your own; or you might have a young child in your family learning to talk before your very eyes (and ears); or perhaps you are intrigued by the way new words seem to appear on a weekly basis – or even by the unique histories of older words. Each of these, and many more besides, are the business of the linguist – and that is what you have officially become, now that you are studying the English language at AS Level.

I say *linguist*, as you will find that the way that you approach texts and language at Advanced Level is likely to be quite different from your previous experience of textual analysis, original writing, investigation, and discussion. You are beginning to turn your natural interest in language into the study of *linguistics*, and that can be a weird and wonderful new world.

The progression that takes place from GCSE English, through to AS Level, and then A Level study can be challenging. There are common paths that all of these qualifications share, but (to continue the metaphor) you will find that they begin to lead you into entirely new places within the language, and very often split off in several directions, as you encounter increasingly specialised subject matter.

You will be familiar with the skills of textual analysis from your GCSE work, and this remains a fundamental part of the AQA GCE AS and A Level English Language experience. However, you will find that the process becomes more sophisticated: where you would previously pick out individual words in a piece of writing at GCSE level, and maybe even define them as a noun, adjective or verb; at AS and A Level, your analysis will learn to extend its range across the spectrum of word classes, confidently taking in adverbs, conjunctions, prepositions, determiners and pronouns. In addition, your understanding of these concepts deepens: a verb is no longer just that, but takes on particular functions and attributes. It begins to present itself to you as stative or dynamic, transitive or intransitive, its tense and aspect become clear, as does its part within a wider structure of phrases, clauses, and sentence types.

Similarly, the importance of original writing is retained at AS and A Level – often a favourite element of the GCSE course. Yet it too has matured: whilst still promoting creativity and expression with language, your writing becomes a tool to help you understand, even more fluently, the way texts are crafted by their writers and producers. Writing a story is still just that, but it has also evolved to allow you to try your hand at generating particular effects – perhaps those that you have admired in another piece – with the linguistic awareness of exactly how you are seeking to manipulate language to do it. Self-reflection is an important strategy to help you to achieve this linguistic consciousness, and the practice of writing commentaries in your own style allows you to analyse your own writing. This is often a new experience for students, and is one of the ways that Advanced Level study increases your independence as a user of the English language.

But perhaps the newest experience on offer in studying English at Advanced Level is the way that language can be treated as a science. To this extent, the work you have done in the school science laboratory may well prove more familiar to you than double GCSE English on a Tuesday morning ever did – but don't let that put you off! You will debate the research of linguists trying to find the truths at the heart of the many conundrums that English poses. And they will use words like 'hypothesis', 'methodology', and 'variables'. Only now the variables aren't the amount of water and sunshine a plant gets, or the temperature of a flame, or the strength of a spring. Instead, social variables – gender, age, ethnicity, social class – and linguistic variables – the glottal stop, using complex sentences, or slang – are the measurements used. Best of all, you get to try these things out for yourself in your own investigation of language, and use it as coursework.

How is English Language B assessed?

The way that the AQA GCE English Language Specification B is structured also bears comparison with GCSE courses. There is still coursework, at AS and at A Level, and this amounts to 40 per cent of the overall grade in each case. This offers a good balance of the ways in which you will be assessed, and helps you to embark upon the sort of independent study and exploration that Advanced Level work makes possible.

That makes 60 per cent for the examinations – the good news is that there is just one paper for the AS Level and one for the A Level course. The only thing that is missing from your GCSE study is assessed speaking and listening work, although discussion and presentation is still likely to be a significant part of the way that you learn.

Assessment objectives (AOs) may well become more prominent in your life, if they haven't done so already! The way that your coursework and examinations are marked is governed by these AOs, and you'll find plenty of detail in this book to help you understand exactly what they mean for each unit. There are four AOs used in 'Spec B Lang' (as you may hear it affectionately called), and these help to emphasise the importance of communicating your ideas clearly, using linguistic approaches well, placing the language examples that you deal with in context, and developing your creative abilities. These are balanced differently across each unit, and mastering the ability to think and write in a way that best meets the demands of the AOs is often a pretty smart way of making sure you're getting the most from your course.

What does each unit cover?

The Spec B Lang units presented in this textbook are carefully designed to meet the expectations that the AQA examination board has of what you can achieve as an AS and A Level student. There are two units at AS Level, fully covered in the AS Level book, and two more at A Level, fully covered in the A2 book, and, an introduction to these will give you a good idea of what sort of material you can look forward to.

Unit 1 Categorising texts introduces you to the terminology and concepts that will underpin much of your future linguistic study. In the examination for this unit, you are shown a wide range of texts, including groupings of texts in some of the more significant and controversial areas that are closely entwined with language: power, gender, and technology.

Unit 2 Creating texts is the coursework unit for the AS Level. This encourages you to hone your skills as a writer in targeting specific audiences, for a particular purpose, within a certain context – indeed, audience, purpose and context will become an inseparable threesome for you when considering any text. The reflective skills of the commentary mentioned earlier are also a part of this unit and allow you to explain your intentions for your texts to the person who marks it – a pretty handy and novel opportunity.

Moving into the A Level, the examination, 'Developing language' covers new ground, with two major areas of linguistic study: the way that children acquire language and the way that English changes and develops over time. For language change, you will delve into several hundred years of linguistic history and chart the path of English right through to the present day: from Dr Samuel Johnson to Boris Johnson, Mayor of London, if you will! Your work on language acquisition may well illuminate a more personal history: helping you to answer the often puzzling question, by exploring how children develop their speech, reading and writing, of just how you first learned the English language.

Finally, if you've liked all that, you get the chance to investigate a particular area of the language in more detail. The coursework unit in the A Level year, 'Investigating language', stresses the independence and academic approaches that will help prepare you for the ways that you may study at university, or work on projects in a future job. The best advice for this unit is to choose something you have a real interest in – and make sure it's to do with language! As well as helping you develop these skills of independent learning, this can be an excellent way of exploring a topic that you may want to go on to study further (the language of journalism for example), or forge a career in (say, the development of literacy in schools).

Where could it take you?

So, what *does* the future hold for a linguist? English Language is certainly a subject very well regarded by Higher Education institutions, and because you are studying the thing that you will probably use the most whatever you do in life – your language – it easily complements any educational course you might follow, and provides a new perspective on most conceivable professions.

At university, there is a considerable range of English-related courses available, that directly build on one or more aspects of your work at AS and A Level, from creative writing through to speech therapy. However, outside the wider school of English, your knowledge and skills will share ground with the many subjects within the social sciences, and particularly with psychology, sociology, and law-related courses. Even further afield, it is not difficult to see the value of a sophisticated understanding of English in areas of design, business, computer science – in almost anything you could imagine, really.

When you come to begin a career, you will find linguistic study will make you an attractive, skilled and flexible employee in most services and industries. Whether it is the increased insight you can bring to analysing written or spoken language, or your ability to control and shape your own communication, abilities of this nature will prove a real benefit to you. Even some of the specific topics you will have studied may find their niche: maybe the Language and technology work you have done at AS Level will give you an overview of the impact of technology as you start out as a software designer. Or, perhaps the Language acquisition topic will help you get to grips with work in childcare and with very young children. You never know, you might even want to start teaching English yourself and passing your ideas on!

The English Language B series

All of which brings me back to the Nelson Thornes English Language series. The examination boards have all produced entirely new courses for 2008; AQA have worked exclusively with Nelson Thornes to produce a series of books designed to be an ideal companion and guide to your journey through our language. In addition to these texts, there are support materials for your teachers, and online e-learning resources, which help to create a multi-dimensional and truly blended learning experience. The work that has gone into this collection has been carried out by teachers and examiners who have taught linguistics in schools, colleges and online, with AQA and students, for many years, and have just the right mix of experience and subject knowledge to bring the course to life for you.

The English language holds something for everyone, and I am sure that the step you have taken to embark upon AS and A Level English Language is one that you will enjoy and one which will offer you genuine challenge and personal satisfaction. Use this book to help you, but be prepared to follow your nose too – language is such a tremendous and ever-changing thing, it would be impossible for one book to cover everything. Then, maybe, come back to the book to keep you right on track as you prepare for your exams, your coursework, and success. Which only leaves me to wish you the very best in your new life as a linguist – it should be fun.

Categorising texts

- **AO1** Select and apply a range of linguistic methods to communicate relevant knowledge using appropriate terminology and coherent, accurate written expression (10 per cent of the AS mark).

- **AO2** Demonstrate critical understanding of a range of concepts and issues related to the construction and analysis of meanings in spoken and written language, using knowledge of linguistic approaches (20 per cent of the AS mark).

- **AO3** Analyse and evaluate the influence of contextual factors on the production and reception of spoken and written language, showing knowledge of the key constituents of language (30 per cent of the AS mark).

Key terms

Text: an example of spoken or written language for analysis.

Discourse: a continuous stretch of language (especially spoken) that is longer than a sentence.

Transcript: an accurate written record of a conversation or monologue, including hesitations and pauses.

Script: a pre-planned and written-out speech.

Unit 1 provides you with a wide range of methods for exploring and analysing language. You will work on a wide range of written texts and also branch out into the perhaps unexplored territory of spoken texts, examining the ways in which speeches are structured and how people work together to hold meaningful conversations. In practice, this means that you will consider the whole possible range of human communication. You will be encouraged to think not only about formal language properties, but also about how, where and why they are conducted. You will also examine the relationships that exist between writers, readers and speakers.

Collecting data in a scrapbook

As you work through this unit and prepare for your examination, you will notice that many of the activities and tasks invite you to think about applying what you have learnt to real language in examples that you have collected yourself. One of the most beneficial things that you can do today, throughout this unit and the entire course, is collect your own examples of data. This will provide you with the opportunity to further develop what you have learnt in lessons, either by exemplifying some aspect of your learning or by challenging it in an unusual way. Keeping an annotated scrapbook of language examples will enable you to build up a bank of resources that you can use independently or in class. Making notes on each example and revising them as you progress through the unit will help you to become a successful student of language and to develop critical awareness. You will notice that many of the so-called rules and conventions of language are frequently broken: there is no such thing as 'correct' language in the real world!

Generally you should aim to gather as wide a range of written and spoken material as possible. It would be worth investing in some tapes, CDs or DVDs to capture data from television and radio, and remember that useful data can be found in unexpected places: don't throw away that junk-mail!

A note on terminology

The term **text** is used in this book to describe and discuss examples of written and spoken language. In the same way, **discourse** is used to refer to both written and spoken varieties. In the case of spoken language, a text may be referred to as a **transcript** (a recording of a speech or conversation that has been subsequently written down) or as a **script** (a pre-planned speech that is later spoken).

A | Text varieties

Introduction

In this section you will:

- understand the demands of Section A and the kinds of focuses you will be exploring in your studies

- explore the ways in which written and spoken texts might be grouped and the reasons for those groupings

- explore and develop your understanding of a range of language frameworks as a way of describing language in action

- have the opportunity to work on the kinds of texts that might appear in an examination question on this unit.

Section A focuses on developing your skills in descriptive linguistic analysis, focusing on a wide range of varieties of texts, produced for a number of different purposes and audiences.

This will involve revisiting some terms that will probably be familiar to you from your study of English at GCSE Level, but will also develop your expertise in using more sophisticated terminology to describe and analyse examples of language products. As a result, the range of material that you will be working on throughout your studies will be much more extensive than the range you encountered at GCSE Level. For example you will be applying your new learning to explore written texts such as advertisements, literary poems and prose extracts, websites, cartoons and newspaper headlines and a whole range of spoken material.

You will explore how language use is dependent on a number of contextual demands and how text producers use language to influence and determine meaning. One of the key requirements on the examination question for this section will be your ability to group texts and explain your reasons for those groupings using precise and accurate linguistic terminology.

With this in mind, the first topic focuses on classification and introduces you to some of the basic principles behind classification. Further topics will then allow you to learn and develop skills in linguistic analyses by presenting you with a number of language frameworks and a range of texts for you to explore.

Finally, you will be able to work on similar texts to those you will find in an examination question on this unit and look at sample answers written by an AS Level student.

An introduction to classification

In this topic you will:

- understand some of the basic principles behind classifying objects and texts

- consider some of the ways in which classification may be complex and problematic

- learn how to apply some models of classification when examining a range of texts.

Classification: some basic ideas

Classification is a way of making it easier to identify types of items based on similarities. Think about your music collection. You might organise it by type (e.g. rock, dance, indie), further sub-types (e.g. metal, thrash, nu-metal, grunge). Or you might organise it alphabetically by artist. If you have different CDs by the same artist, you might organise these by the year of release. If you have vinyl or cassettes, you might use a different system, and if you store music digitally, you might have another set of systems. If you have an MP3 player, look at the system it uses. This will give you an idea of the complexities involved, particularly if different programs group files in different ways.

Classification involves placing items into groups based on similar features and relationships between group members. It is clear that not all items in a group will share the same features; if they did, we would not be able to distinguish between them at all. What we can say is that classification gives us a mechanism for more detailed exploration. Consider the classification system in Figure 1.

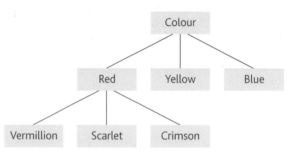

Fig. 1 *Classification of colours*

It is clear that classifying all colours as *red*, *yellow* or *blue* will not get us far if we want to be both more absolute and more exploratory in our groupings. If we move down a level, our groups will still contain a wide range of colours that are similar but also different. Even if we move down several levels, we may still be faced with some large groups. You could try this yourself and see what happens.

We can therefore make the following observations about classification:

- Classification involves finding similarities based on objective properties.
- Within groups, there will be differences between group members.
- Some items do not fit easily into groups.
- Some items may fit easily into many groups; there may be some complex overlap.

To explore classification in more detail, we will now look at data similar to what you might expect to find on Section A of the examination paper.

AQA Examiner's tip

Always look for *patterns* that emerge as you think about grouping texts and the ways in which language features stand out or are *foregrounded* in a text. Be aware of differences within groupings, of overlaps and of other potential problems.

Classroom activity 1

Look at Texts A–F. How might you group them? How would you justify your groupings? What kinds of problems arise? Read the introductory text at the start of each one when thinking about criteria for groupings.

See page 193 for feedback on this activity.

Text A

All-round
performer

Legal & General is one of the UK's leading financial services companies. Established in 1836, Legal & General is one of the UK's top 50 FTSE companies. Over 4.5 million people rely on Legal & General for life assurance, pensions, investments and savings plans. Our fund managers are responsible for investing more than £116 billion* worldwide on behalf of investors, policyholders and institutions.

For more details of the range of services available from Legal & General please visit our website at www.legalandgeneral.com

*As at 31 December 2002.
Legal & General Assurance Society Limited.
Registered in England No. 166055.
Registered Office: Temple Court, 11 Queen Victoria Street, London EC4N 4TP.
Approval Number: H11663

Legal & General

An advertisement that appeared in a theatre programme for a performance at Shakespeare's Globe in 2003

Text B

SEASONAL SPECIAL

Dorset chocolate mousse cake

Remember the classic chocolate biscuit refrigerator cake? This is a modern version using good-quality chocolate, butter biscuits and served with local blueberries and thick Dorset cream.

READY IN 1-1¼ HRS, PLUS COOLING TIME

SERVES 8 EASY

350g/12oz dark chocolate (about 70% solids),
  broken into small pieces
225g/8oz unsalted butter
5 free-range eggs
300g/10oz golden caster sugar
100g/4oz butter biscuits, or butter shortbread,
  broken into bite-size pieces
TO SERVE
284ml carton double cream
225g/8oz blueberries

1 Heat oven to 160C/fan 140C/gas 3. Line and butter a 23cm spring-form tin. Put the chocolate and butter in a pan and melt over a very low heat. Set aside. Using an electric whisk (see offer over the page), beat the eggs with the sugar until the mixture is thick, pale and doubled in volume (takes about 5 mins).
2 Pour the chocolate into the whisked egg mixture and gently, but thoroughly, fold in. Add the broken biscuits and gently fold again.
3 Pour the mixture into the prepared tin and bake for 40-45 mins until just firm. Remove from the oven and allow to cool in the tin for about ½-¾ hr. You now have a choice as to how you serve this. You can serve it while still warm and the centre is still melty and gooey, as in the picture, or you can chill it (up to a day ahead) and it will be firm and fudgy enough to cut into wedges. Serve with cream and fresh blueberries.

PER SERVING 720 kcalories, protein 9g, carbohydrate 67g, fat 48g, saturated fat 27g, fibre 3g, added sugar 52g, salt 0.22g

A recipe that appeared in a cookery magazine in 2004

Text C

Mr Bump walked up to his garden gate and looked down the lane.

Mr Muddle was passing by.

"Good afternoon," said Mr Muddle

As you and I know, it was morning. But Mr Muddle, not surprisingly, always gets things in a muddle.

"I seem to have lost my memory," said Mr Bump. "Do you know what my name is?"

"You're Mr Careful," said Mr Muddle.

"Thank you." said Mr Bump.

An extract from a children's story called Mr Bump Loses His Memory

Text D

A

BILL

TO

Make provision about research in the arts and humanities and about complaints by students against institutions providing higher education; to make provision about fees payable by students in higher education; to provide for the appointment of a Director of Fair Access to Higher Education; to make provision about grants and loans to students in higher or further education; and for connected purposes.

B E IT ENACTED by the Queen's most Excellent Majesty, by and with the advice and consent of the Lords Spiritual and Temporal, and Commons, in this present Parliament assembled, and by the authority of the same, as follows:—

An extract from the Higher Education Bill, *DfES, 2004*

Text E

A transaction in a newsagent's shop. A is the customer and B is the vendor. A has arrived to settle his newspaper account.

Key
(.) Indicates a brief pause.
(1) Indicates a longer pause with the number of seconds in brackets.
[*demonstrates*] Place actions and movements in italics and in
square brackets.
Overlaps in conversation are marked with a set of vertical lines.

A: hello there (.) I've come er need to settle my account
B: It's 135 Penny Street isn't it
A: yeah
B: OK (2) let me just check that for you [*looks for records*] I can't seem to… what paper do you have
A: er (.) The Times. It might ‖be under… ‖
B: ‖on Sundays too‖
A: no just the week
B: [*searching records*] OK er (.) here we are (1) just The Times on weekdays
A: That's right
B: I'm not getting much right today [*laughs*]
A: That's OK how much
B: right (.) that will be [*adds up figures on paper*] £15 exactly please
A: [*hands over cash*]

Text F

An extract from an IM (Instant Messaging) conversation that was posted on an Internet forum.

> *A*: (12:56:08 AM): i didn't meet him but someone else did and it's kinda a funny story
> *B*: (12:57:38 AM): TELL ME
> *A*: (12:56:17 AM): lol
> *A*: (12:57:03 AM): okkkk so my 6th grade american history teacher (who was my history day mentor/advisor throughout high school) was at a conference thing in chicago
> *A*: (12:57:27 AM): and she was with some other teachers... well the conf wasn't in chicago but it was close so one day they all decided they were going to go to chicago
> *A*: (12:57:40 AM): it's a british lady named emma
> *B*: (12:59:17 AM): okay i dont care tell me about eddie
> *A*: (12:58:10 AM): so emma and the other teachers did some touristy things around chicago and then they decided they were gonna hit up some bars/clubs
> *B*: (12:58:27 AM): oh and this was like the week after lollapalooza
> *B*: (12:59:58 AM): where they closed
> *A*: (12:59:02 AM): and so they went to a few and there was like no one there and then they walked into one but the bouncer told them they couldn't go in but they went in anyway
> *A*: (1:00:08 AM): so they went to the bar and then the bartender asked them if they were with the people from the golf tournament and they were like NO! but then the bartender told them that they were the only not rich/famous people there because it was reserved for the people that were with eddie from a golf tournament
> *A*: (1:01:04 AM): so then one of the other teachers freaked out cuz she was a huuuuge eddie vedder/pearl jam fan and she wanted to talk to him but she was too shy and thought it would be rude cuz he was having a convo with another guy (who is the owner of the company that makes/distributes the condiments for mcdonalds across the world)
> *B*: (1:02:41 AM): hahahahah
> *B*: (1:02:49 AM): i would like stumble
> *B*: (1:02:51 AM): and blabber
> *B*: (1:02:52 AM): and stutter
> *A*: (1:01:29 AM): lol yeah apparently he's short tho
> *B*: (1:02:55 AM): and then just like cry
> *B*: (1:02:57 AM): yeah kinda
> *B*: (1:03:06 AM): still a great looking dude

This exercise will have demonstrated that when working with real texts we may face a number of complexities in attempting to classify data. It also shows that key patterns are emerging in the kind of detail we might use to help us classify texts. We have identified the following as potential ways of grouping texts and exploring within these groupings. The italicised words are important terms that will be explored in the remainder of this topic.

Some essential key terms

- Whether a text is written or spoken and some of the ways in which texts may be considered to have elements of both (*Speech and writing*).

- Types of text, for example advertisements, recipes (*Genre*).

■ The importance of considering what might have influenced the writing of a text and where it might be read or spoken (*Context*).

■ For whom the text was produced (*Audience*).

■ The reason why a text has been produced (*Purpose*).

■ The language patterns and words a text uses and whether they are formal or informal (*Formality*).

■ Speech and writing

One of the basic distinctions we can make about texts is whether they belong to the spoken or written **mode**. However, such a broad differentiation can cause problems if data is not handled carefully and generalised comments about the differences between speech and writing are considered in a simplified manner. The following activity asks you to think about the problems of a simplified classification.

■ Classroom activity 2

The two lists in Table 1 represent what is known as an **oppositional view** of speech and writing. For each of the suggested features, discuss how useful you feel this kind of classification model is. Use Texts A–F on pages 5–8 and the examples of texts that you have collected for your scrapbook to support criticism of this model as an over-simplified one.

See page 194 for feedback on this activity.

■ Key terms

Mode: the medium of communication, for example speech or writing.

Oppositional view: a broad way of defining modes, which suggests that their qualities are strictly opposites, for example writing is formal, speech is informal.

Continuum: a way of representing differences by placing texts along a line showing degrees of various features.

Table 1 *An oppositional view of speech and writing*

Writing is:	Speech is:
objective	interpersonal
a monologue	a dialogue
durable	ephemeral
planned	spontaneous
highly structured	loosely structured
grammatically complex	grammatically simple
concerned with the past and future	concerned with the present
formal	informal
decontextualised	contextualised

Adapted from **Baron**, *2000, p21*

Alternatives to the oppositional view

One way to avoid this strict and awkward distinction between speech and writing is to consider the two not as opposites but as part of a **continuum**, with texts placed at different points on a line, according to their linguistic features in relation to conventional ideas about speech and writing. This is a neater way of recognising that problematic texts can contain typical elements of both speech and writing. Try placing the texts you worked with during the previous activity on the continuum in Figure 2 overleaf, and discuss whether this represents a better way of distinguishing between these modes. Two suggestions have been made for you.

Fig. 2 *Speech–writing continuum*

Another alternative to the oppositional view is the idea that the human mind classifies according to **prototypes** using a *radial structure*. A prototype represents the best example of a particular classification group. It is used as a central reference point for other examples that are considered less 'good' members, and which accordingly move outwards from the centre of the radial structure. This idea is particularly useful for considering not just the modes of speech and writing but also **sub-modes**, **genres** and **types**. It is important to remember that prototypes are not fixed entities; rather they are subject to renewal and change through experience and interaction with others and are governed by social conventions as to what might be good, less good and bad examples of a particular group. Figure 3 shows how we might distinguish between Texts C, D and F (see pages 6–8) using this model.

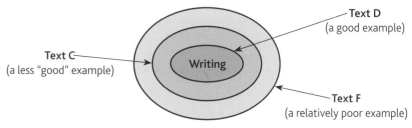

Fig. 3 *Categorising Texts C, D and F using a radial structure*

■ **Extension activity 1**

Look at the suggested hierarchy of classification below. Use the continuum and/or prototype models to help classify examples of texts from your scrapbook within this hierarchy. Think about how you arrived at your conclusions. Do your ideas of what constitutes a prototype differ from other people's? If so, why do you think that this is the case?

Mode: writing, speech

Sub-mode: poetry, prose, drama, conversation, monologue

Genre: comedy, tragedy, horror, romance

Type: sonnet, short story, play, e-mail, text message

Multimodality

Your work on mode will have demonstrated that many texts contain features of both speech and writing. In addition, **multimodal texts** can be considered those that contain multiple features: not just words but images, sounds and symbols as a way of communicating. Text C on page 6 is a simple example of a multimodal text, combining print and visual image. At a more complex level, technology has made multimodality in texts common, as in web pages, where print, image and sound are all used as part of the construction of a text.

Context and audience

The terms **context** and audience are no doubt familiar to you. Context refers to all those situations in which texts are produced (written or spoken) and received (read, heard or listened to) and contextual factors may include all of those external events and details and information about text producers and receivers that might influence the ways in which a text has been written, spoken, read or listened to. Assessment objective 3 (AO3) is an important one in Section A, and your ability to evaluate contextual factors and consider their effect on meaning will be crucial to your success in both sections of this unit. With this in mind, you should always consider context as you explore and analyse groupings and texts. Your past experience and understanding of context may have been much simpler than that which is suggested in Figure 4, which we will spend some time considering.

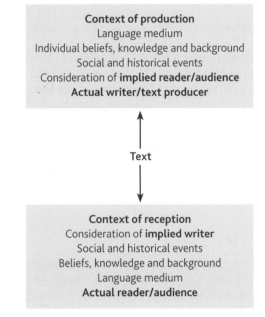

Fig. 4 *Text and context*

■ Key terms

Context: the temporal and spatial situations in which a text is produced or received, e.g. where the producer and/or receiver of the text is; what he or she is doing; who he or she is talking to; what has occurred previously.

Context of reception: the situations in which a text is read and those factors that might influence a reader's interpretation.

Context of production: the situation in which a text is produced and those factors that might influence its writing.

Actual reader: any reader who actually engages with the text.

Implied reader: the kind of reader a text producer has in mind when writing and who might be expected to 'follow' the author's point of view.

Implied writer: a constructed image of the writer a reader may have in mind.

An important point that you should keep in mind is that context in the study of language relates as much to the **context of reception** as it does to the **context of production**. This means carefully considering the situations in which texts are *received* as well as those in which they are *produced*. Central to this concept is the idea that an **actual reader's** beliefs, knowledge and communicative competence all lend themselves in some degree to establishing the *meaning* of a text in conjunction with those of the text producer and the wider social and historical contexts in which a text is produced and received. When a text is produced, it may have a defined target audience. The type of person a text producer has in mind can be considered the **implied reader**. This of course is a construct sometimes based around the kinds of values a text producer might want us to have. For example, the Legal and General advertisement on page 5 has as its implied reader someone who takes investments and legal services seriously and is looking for a 'sound deal'; this construct may of course be very different from the values and opinions held by the actual reader of this text. On the other hand, as readers we often have some idea of an **implied writer**. In the case of the Legal and General text, this may be a constructed image of someone who is experienced and

■ Key terms

Actual writer: the 'real' person behind the text.

Purpose: the reason a text is produced.

Multi-purpose: a text with more than one purpose.

Dual-purpose: a text with two clear and defined purposes.

Primary purpose: the main reason a text has been produced.

Secondary purpose: a secondary (and sometimes more subtle) reason.

AQA Examiner's tip

Context relates as much to *reception* as it does *production*. When looking at a text, always consider *where* and *how* it is likely to be read, in addition to considering the factors that would have influenced its production.

■ Link

In Unit 2, you will explore your own writing skills and produce two pieces of writing with distinct primary purposes. It would however be a gross over-simplification to suggest that any text has only one purpose, although of course some texts are less likely to have secondary or other multi-purposes.

knowledgeable in investments. In truth of course, the **actual writer** of this text works for an advertising agency!

■ Classroom activity 3

Text G is a short extract from a pop song, originally released in 1993, which was re-mixed and became a number-one single in 1994. What do you understand by these lines? Are you able to pin down their meaning?

See page 194 for feedback on this activity.

Text G

Things can only get better
Can only get better
Now I've found you

Jamie Petrie and Peter Cunnah, 'Things Can Only Get Better', 1993

The range of contexts in which these lines in Text G have been used demonstrates that not only do a wide range of contextual factors influence the ways in which texts gain meaning, but that this meaning is never fixed or established, although some meanings will become more widely accepted than others. It also shows that the reader's role is not a passive one. Rather, textual meaning is a kind of negotiation between text producer and receiver. It relies on textual cues presented and structured in an intentional way by the producer and picked up on and developed by readers, according to their own background and the contexts in which they encounter the text to generate a coherent and satisfying understanding.

Purpose

A text's **purpose** may not always be as obvious as it might seem at first. The extract from 'Things Can Only Get Better' demonstrates how a text may have a number of different purposes, depending on the context of its reception. Although it is important to consider what the original purpose may have been, in the real world and with real readers, a text's purpose may vary drastically. A good way of thinking about this is to consider purpose as what a text gets *used* for in a given and defined context, or in other terms what its *function* is.

With this in mind, another useful set of terms is **multi-purpose, dual-purpose, primary purpose** and **secondary purpose**.

■ Classroom activity 4

Revisit Texts A–F on pages 5–8. Discuss whether these could be considered multi-purpose texts and, if they can, what you feel their primary and secondary purposes might be. What functions might these texts perform? Are any of the texts problematic?

Individuals and groups

As your reading and work on context will have demonstrated, the importance of an individual's language 'make-up' cannot be underestimated.

The term **idiolect** is used to describe an individual's distinct language features. Individuals may also form groups with a distinct language style: a **sociolect**. This is the consequence of group membership of a **discourse community**, which uses language in distinctive ways. Discourse communities may be big (e.g. every secondary schoolteacher in England), or small (e.g. a group of three friends). Each discourse community will have shared ways of using language, responding to texts and, of course, the use of a particular sociolect.

Extension activity 2

Read Text H.

Using the table below, try to map your own idiolect by considering these variables and the impact they have had on you as a language user. Have there been moments in your life when one influence has been greater than another? You should also think about all of the discourse communities that you are a member of. Are there aspects of different sociolects that are a pattern of your language make-up?

Key terms

Idiolect: an individual's style of speaking or 'linguistic fingerprint'.

Sociolect: a defined use of language as a result of membership of a social group.

Discourse community: a group with shared values and approaches to reading.

Text H

Mike was born in Seattle, USA and spent most of his childhood there. He later moved to Britain with his parents and attended a school in inner London. He left school at eighteen and worked for a time as a journalist on a music magazine, often travelling across Europe. He also plays regularly in a rock band and spends his spare time editing a website where he frequently posts articles on music. He has regular contact with friends and family in the USA and his occupation means that he has large friendship groups across Europe.

Mike's personal language use (his idiolect) has been influenced by a range of factors, such as his upbringing in the USA and the fact that he later moved to the UK. In addition, his work as a music journalist and his personal interest in music mean that he will be a member of different discourse communities, each with its own language style. Mike's involvement in an online virtual community has also played a role in shaping his language 'fingerprint'.

Influence	Effect on language
Your gender	
Your place of birth	
Your parents	
Your education	
Your class	
Your extended family and friends	
Any online 'virtual communities' that you belong to	
Your political/religious and/or other strong beliefs	
Your reading/listening preferences	

Register: a variety of language appropriate to a particular purpose and context.

Field: the general purpose of an act of communication.

Tenor: the relationship between the participants in a conversation or between text producer and receiver.

Formality and register

If you look again at Texts A–F on pages 5–8, you will notice differences in terms of the **register** that each one uses. Text F uses an informal register, with words such as 'touristy', 'gonna' and 'okay', whereas Text D relies on a much more formal register, with words such as 'provision', 'enacted' and 'consent of the Lords Spiritual and Temporal' and of course, it is also highly structured. As we have noted, the level of formal and informal features, or register, is closely related to a text's context and purpose. As Text F is an instant messaging conversation between two friends who know each other well, there is no need for formal language features. In contrast, Text D needs to be in a more formal register because of its subject matter and the fact that there is no discernible close relationship between text producer and receiver. We might also say that the producer of Text D is assuming some kind of authority or power over its readers. This relationship between producer and receiver influences language use or register, as shown in Figure 5.

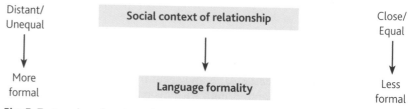

Distant/Unequal   **Social context of relationship**   Close/Equal

More formal   **Language formality**   Less formal

Fig. 5 *Text producer/receiver relationship and register*

We can therefore distinguish and define the features of a register as being dependent on:

■ the general purpose of communication – the **field**

■ the relationship between the producer and receiver – the **tenor**

■ the medium of communication, for example written or spoken, which we have defined previously as the mode.

■ Classroom activity 5

To explore the relationship between register and context in more detail, choose three of Texts A–F on pages 5–8. Rewrite them, altering the level of formality in each, either subtly or more drastically. What is the effect of your changes, given the contexts that are provided for each text? Explain any *inappropriateness* in your revisions, using the terms *field*, *tenor* and *mode*?

When considering formality, you may want to look at some of the language features listed below.

■ Vocabulary choices, including forms and terms of address.

■ Length of sentences.

■ Extended expressions of phrases.

■ Spelling conventions.

■ Layout.

■ Use of images, pictures, emoticons.

■ Paragraphing and punctuation.

See page 194 for feedback on this activity.

Dialect

Regardless of where you live, it is likely that you use some degree of **dialect** in both your written and spoken language. Although strictly speaking, this term refers to any set of variations in vocabulary and grammar, it is often used to describe regional variation. Dialectal differences, which are differences in word choice and order, should not be confused with the term **accent**, which refers to the characteristic pronunciation of sounds by inhabitants of a region. **Standard English (SE)** is just one example of dialect that has its roots in standardised forms of written English that began to appear with the advent of the printing press in the 15th century.

Today, Standard English, sometimes unfortunately referred to as 'correct English' is the dialect that is taught in schools and universities and has become acceptable as a formal and universal standard. Equally unfortunate is the fact that there is still prejudice towards, and stereotyping of, people who use certain dialects that may be considered stigmatised in wider circles such as education and the media.

Classroom activity 6

Look at the cartoons. How do these play on a stereotype by using a **representation** of a Yorkshire dialect?

See page 194 for feedback on this activity.

Specialist registers

Register can also be considered as a variety of language choices (mostly in terms of vocabulary and grammar) based on occupation. In this way, groups of individuals may use a specialist set of terms according to a defined and shared set of expectations and a shared knowledge base. Occupational variation can be difficult to understand for those with little or no specialist knowledge – think of the language of doctors, computer experts and car mechanics. Some occupational varieties are also highly formal, for example the language of the legal profession. Often a **specialist register** implies a certain kind of text receiver and may exclude those who are not members of the same discourse community.

■ Extension activity 3

As well as looking for texts that explicitly use dialectal variation for effect, you could explore some of the attitudes that exist towards certain kinds of dialect. You may have experienced negative attitudes towards your own dialect. An interesting piece of research would be to explore your teachers' attitudes towards any dialectal variation you may use or have used in pieces of your own writing. Does this tell you anything about the way in which educational establishments attach values to language use?

■ **Key terms**

Jargon: specialist terminology that may exclude others.

Colloquialism: an established set of informal terms used in everyday language.

Slang: colloquial language that is inventive and particular to individuals or groups.

■ Extension activity 4

Find three texts that feature extensive use of a specialist register or of jargon. How do they include and exclude particular groups of readers? Would you say that in some cases this use of language is necessary? Experiment with replacing words and phrases with less-specialised ones and consider the impact that this has. Ensure that you add these examples to your scrapbook.

Colloquial language and slang

Colloquialisms and **slang** are examples of informal language. Some linguists treat the two interchangeably; others argue for a clear distinction between the two, suggesting that colloquialisms are more established examples of informal words and phrases such as 'I'm gonna', whilst slang terms tend to be more original and confined to particular sets of individuals. For example, 'wicked' is often used as a slang term for 'excellent' by young people.

■ Further reading

General

Crystal, D. *The Cambridge Encyclopedia of the English Language*, Cambridge University Press, 1995

Carter, R., Goddard, A., Reah, D., Sanger, K., and Bowring, M. *Working with Texts: A Core Book for Language Analysis*, Routledge, 2001

Russell, S. *Grammar, Structure and Style*, Oxford University Press, 1993

Classification

Montgomery, M., Durant, A., Fabb, N., Furniss, T., and Mills, S. (2nd edn.) *Ways of Reading: Advanced reading skills for students of English literature*, Routledge, 2000

Speech and writing

Baron, N. S. *Alphabet to e-mail: How written English evolved and where it's heading*, Routledge, 2000

Register and dialect

Bunton, P. 'Dialect literature and literary dialect' *emagazine* 32, 2006

Stockwell, P. *Sociolinguistics: A resource book for students*, Routledge, 2002

Trousdale, G. 'Northern English – a state of mind?' *emagazine* 35, 2007

Also, visit **www.bl.uk/learning** for a range of ideas and activities on exploring dialect varieties and use.

Language frameworks

In this topic you will:

- consider why using the frameworks is an important part of your study of AS English Language

- learn important terminology and the concepts behind it, to assist you with more detailed analyses of texts

- explore how using the frameworks can help you develop your ideas on the grouping task in Section A.

What are the language frameworks?

The language frameworks provide us with a way of addressing some of the questions we have faced when trying to discuss formal textual features. Look back to your initial thoughts on Texts A–F on pages 5–8. Some of the observations we first made about language features can now be expressed using the following language frameworks.

Table 1 *Language frameworks*

Focus for topic	Language framework(s)	Key learning areas within topic/framework
What types of words does it use? What are the relationships between them?	Lexis/semantics	Word classes, lexical cohesion, lexical fields, semantic relationships, figurative language (metaphor)
How are words created? What kinds of larger structures such as phrases and sentences are used?	Grammar – morphology and syntax	Word formation, phrases, clauses, sentence types and function, grammatical cohesion
How is sound used?	Phonology	Sound production, phonemes, sound symbolism
How does context affect the text's production and reception? How do these texts operate in real life? How do they rely on social conventions, shared understanding and implied meanings?	Pragmatics	Shared and implied meanings, conversational maxims, deixis
How is the text structured?	Discourse structure	Discourse patterns, discourse types
What visual aspects of the text are present?	Graphology	Shape, signs, logos, typographical features, space

Why use them?

So far, we have concentrated on how we might classify texts and some of the potential problems inherent in that process. At the moment, however, our comments have been in general terms around issues of formality, register, dialect, audience and purpose. In order for our observations and analyses to be more detailed, another layer of description is needed: language frameworks.

Any professional body will have its own set of specialist terms. Imagine an orthopaedic surgeon who didn't use the precise names of the bones in the human leg when discussing a patient with a colleague. Using general and vague terms would not make this surgeon a very successful one, nor a very professional one! Linguists too have their own set of specialist terms to describe language features and to inform and support their own analyses and interpretations. One of the keys to success at AS Level is to be able to apply these to the texts that you will encounter. In fact, the frameworks underpin all future study at both AS and A2 Level, and your ability to use them with confidence will be crucial to your work throughout this course.

Using the frameworks for descriptive linguistic analysis

The language frameworks provide a useful tool to help you analyse texts and explore your ideas. Although you may be able to identify some general language features and comment on aspects of meaning, using the frameworks will provide a way of moving beyond intuitive comments into close and precise linguistic analysis. It is important to remember in Section A that you should always think of terminology as a means of enabling your comments to be rigorous and systematic. In this way, using terminology consistently and accurately will:

- allow you to draw attention to linguistic features in a scientific and precise manner as a way of showing not just *what* a text means but *how* it expresses its meaning
- allow other students, teachers and examiners to see how you have arrived at a particular interpretation through using a common set of linguistic terms
- show that you have a command of linguistic **metalanguage** and are able to select frameworks and apply them to texts appropriately.

But be warned: you will get little credit for mere feature-spotting, that is, just drawing attention to language features with little or no interpretative comment. You should always consider the likely effect of language features on a reader and how they help you to make sense of a text as a whole, using contextual information to inform your ideas.

Key terms

Metalanguage: a set of technical terms used to describe how language operates.

AQA Examiner's tip

Always think about the effect that language features have on a reader/receiver and how these have been shaped by **contextual factors**.

Lexis and semantics

Key terms

Lexis: the framework that deals with the vocabulary system of a language.

Semantics: the framework that deals with meaning and how that is generated within texts.

Textual cohesion: the term used to describe how a text is logically structured to create a coherent sense of meaning.

What is lexis? What is semantics?

Lexis is the term that linguists use to describe the vocabulary system of a language. The number of words available to text producers is huge, and words are generally chosen carefully to help generate meaning. **Semantics** refers to the study of meaning and how meaning is created within texts. Semantics is also concerned with the relationships between lexical items and how these create **textual cohesion**.

Categorising words – word classes

One of the most basic ways that we can distinguish between words or lexical items is to consider their form by placing them into word classes. A word class will typically consist of lexical items that share the same behavioural properties, that is they perform *specific roles* that distinguish them from other items in a different word class.

Classroom activity 7

1. Construct 10 sentences using the words below, for example: 'His teacher is very angry'.

2. Taking each sentence individually, classify each word depending on its role within your sentence, as indicated in Table 2 below (some examples have been completed for you).

a(n)	teacher	is	computer	rather
appears	dignified	large	short	moves
becomes	door	moderately	this	slowly
shop	bedroom	every	old	shouts
harbour	outstandingly	very	lawnmower	her
enormous	sells	frightening	immensely	apple
rather	untidy	his	my	dark
slow	helpful	angry	cake	guitars

Table 2 *Word classes*

Word class	Description/function	Example
Noun	Names of objects, feelings, attitudes, people or places	cottage
Verb	Shows actions, events or states of being, feeling or thinking	seems
Adjective	Adds detail to nouns	bleak
Adverb	Adds detail to verbs or other adverbs	extraordinarily
Determiner	Positioned in front of nouns to add detail or to clarify	the, a, an

In addition to these, the three word classes in Table 3 make up the basic set that you need to know at AS Level.

Table 3 *The basic word classes needed for AS level*

Word class	Description/function	Example
Conjunction	Links words, phrases and clauses together	and, but, or, although, because
Preposition	Shows relation in terms of time or place	in, at, by, on
Pronoun	Replaces nouns and can also refer forwards and backwards to them in longer stretches of text	I, me, you, his, our

Pronouns can be further classified as shown in Table 4.

Table 4 *Further classification of pronouns*

Type of pronoun	Example
Person	I, you, she, they
Possessive	My, his, our, their
Reflexive	Myself, himself, themselves
Demonstrative	this, these, that, those
Relative	who, whom, which

Personal pronouns change their form depending on their number and their function within a sentence as **subject**, **object** or **possessive**.

Table 5 *Personal pronouns*

		Subject	Object	Possessive
Singular	First person	I	Me	My
	Second person	You	You	Your
	Third person	He/she	Him/her	His/her
Plural	First person	We	Us	Our
	Second person	You	You	Your
	Third person	they	Them	Their

Across word classes, we can also differentiate between **lexical words**, which are open to new additions and derivations such as nouns, verbs, adjectives and adverbs, and **functional words** such as determiners, conjunctions, prepositions and pronouns, where new additions are rare and therefore might be called closed classes of words.

Exploring word classes

Nouns

You may have noticed that the word class of nouns has the potential to accommodate several types of lexical items. It is no surprise that nouns make up the largest word class in English. Text I below includes the following examples:

- Ferry – the name of an object with a physical existence.
- Calais – the name of a place.
- Silence – the name of a state with no physical existence.
- Their – a word that substitutes for a noun (in this case 'customs people').

Text I

My first sight of England was on a foggy March night in 1973 when I arrived on the midnight ferry from Calais. For twenty minutes, the terminal area was aswarm with activity as cars and lorries poured forth, customs people did their duties and everyone made for the London road. Then abruptly all was silence and I wandered through sleeping, low-lit streets threaded with fog, just like in a Bulldog Drummond movie. It was rather wonderful having an English town all to myself.

Bill Bryson, Notes From a Small Island, 1996

We are able to further classify nouns as indicated below (Table 6).

Table 6 *Further classification of nouns*

Type of noun	Example	Function
Proper	London, Paris	Refers to names of people or places
Abstract	pain, happiness	Refers to states, feelings and concepts that have no physical existence
Concrete	Countable, e.g. table Non-countable, e.g. furniture	Refers to objects that have a physical existence

Verbs

As previously noted, verbs are used to describe processes. It is important and useful to distinguish between verbs that describe actions and events and verbs that describe states of being, thinking and feeling. Broadly speaking, we can classify these as **material processes**, **relational processes** and **mental processes**. Another useful set of terms is **dynamic verbs** and **stative verbs**.

Table 7 *Classification of verbs*

Verb process	Type	Examples
Material	Describe actions or events	hit, run, eat, push, read, paint, remove, hold
Relational	Describe states of being or are used to identify	be, appear, seem, become
Mental	Describe perception, thought or speech	think, speak, believe, love
Dynamic verb processes	Processes where there is a change in state over time	paint, remove, eat
Stative verb processes	Processes where the situation remains constant	love, hold, believe

Key terms

Material processes: describing actions or events.

Relational processes: describing states of being, identification or attributes.

Mental processes: describing perception, thoughts or speech.

Dynamic verbs: verbs where the situation described by the verb process changes over time, for example 'he ate the cake' involves a dynamic process.

Stative verbs: verbs that describes a state of affairs rather than an action, e.g. 'know'.

Look at these two short extracts from novels (Texts J and K). Stylistically, each one relies on a predominant kind of verb process. Which is it and what effect is created in each?

Text J

The house fronts looked black enough, and the windows blacker, contrasting with the smooth white sheet of snow upon the roofs, and with the dirtier white upon the ground; which last deposit had been ploughed up in deep furrows by the heavy wheels of carts and wagons; furrows that crossed and re-crossed each other hundreds of times where the great streets branched off, and made intricate channels, hard to trace, in the thick yellow mud and icy water. The sky was gloomy, and the shortest streets were choked up with a dingy mist, half thawed, half frozen, whose heavier particles descended in a shower of sooty atoms, as if all the chimneys in Great Britain had, by one consent, caught fire, and were blazing away to their dear hearts' content. There was nothing very cheerful in the climate or the town, and yet there was an air of cheerfulness abroad that the clearest summer air and brightest summer sun might have endeavoured to diffuse in vain.

Charles Dickens, A Christmas Carol, *1846*

Text K

The Sith Lord leapt from the bridge on which they fought to the one above, strange face shining with the heat of the battle and his own peculiar joy. The Jedi followed, one coming in front of him, one behind, so that they had him pinned between them. Down the length of the catwalk they fought, lightsabers flashing, sparks flying from the metal railing of the walk as they flashed against it.

Then Darth Maul caught Obi-Wan off balance and with a powerful kick knocked the Jedi completely over the railing. Taking advantage of the Sith Lord's assault on Obi-Wan, Qui-Gon forced Darth Maul over the railing as well. Down the Sith Lord tumbled, landing hard on a catwalk several levels below Obi-Wan.

Terry Brooks, Star Wars: Episode 1 – The Phantom Menace, *2000*

Adjectives and adverbs

The role of an adjective is to add further description to, or to modify, a noun. An adjective typically occurs either before the noun it modifies, as in:

the small town
adj   noun

or modifies a noun following a verb such as 'to be', 'appear' or 'seem':

the town appears small
noun   adj

In addition, adjectives can be graded in order to show comparison. The base form of the adjective can be compared to the comparative and superlative forms through the addition of *-er/-est* as follows:

Base: small

Comparative: smaller

Superlative: smallest

Some longer adjectives use 'more' and 'most' for their comparative and superlative forms, for example 'beautiful' – 'more beautiful' – 'most beautiful'. The adjectives 'good' and 'bad' have the irregular forms 'good' – 'better' – 'best' and 'bad' – 'worse' – 'worst'.

Extension activity 5

The use of adjectives is a common ploy in brand advertising and in so-called 'price wars' between supermarkets and other retail businesses. Find examples of this practice, similar to the one below, and annotate them for your scrapbook.

Adverbs fulfil a variety of roles and words with a number of functions within a sentence are assigned to the class of adverb. These include those that add information about or modify verb processes, for example 'I ran *quickly*'; those that modify adjectives or other adverbs as in 'I ran *very* quickly' and 'the *very* small town'; those that modify whole sentences, often expressing an attitude, for example '*interestingly*, the town is small'. Adverbs also form comparative and superlative forms through the addition of 'more'/'most'.

Classroom activity 9

Identify all of the adjectives and adverbs used in Text L overleaf – an internet guide to the Australian city of Brisbane. How does their use help to convey an attractive image for potential holidaymakers? You could experiment with these choices by substituting alternative options including those that are less appealing to consider the importance of their inclusion. Explain the effect of each substitution that you make.

Text L

Australia's only tropical city, laid-back, self-assured and capital of its most beautiful state

For a former penal settlement established in 1863 Brisbane has come an awfully long way. From a troubled childhood – frequently bullied by big brothers Melbourne and Sydney – and a largely anonymous youth, 'Brizzie' has grown from strength to strength and now stands tall and self-assured in the nation's great city snapshot. Boasting an almost perfect climate and an enviable lifestyle exemplified by innumerable alfresco restaurants, cafés and outdoor activities, Australia's 'tropical city' has every right to revel in its reputation as home base and main focus for an impressive region.

www.expedia.co.uk

Extension activity 6

Find other examples of the conscious use of adjectives and adverbs for effect in travel brochures or travel writing. Explore why and how the text producer has used these lexical choices for a particular effect. Keep a record of these in your scrapbook.

Lexical cohesion

Lexical choices often help to create **cohesion** within a text. These may be in the form of lexical items that provide structure within the body of a text or those that provide cohesion across smaller stretches such as phrases and sentences.

Lexical connectors

These are words and phrases that provide cohesion within the body of a text (Table 8).

Table 8 *Lexical connectors*

Function	Example of lexical item
Addition	and, also, too, in addition, furthermore
Consequence	so, therefore, thus, as a result, consequently
Comparative	similarly, likewise, just as, as well, also, but, however, whereas, and yet, on the contrary, on the other hand
Temporal	later, next, now, soon, afterwards
Enumeration	firstly, then, finally
Summative	in conclusion, on the whole, with all things considered

Reference, substitution and ellipsis

Cohesion is also provided through the use of **referencing**. In the following examples, pronouns have replaced nouns yet the text still remains coherent.

Key terms

Cohesion: a measure of how well a text fits together as a whole, its internal logic and construction.

Referencing: when lexical items replace those already mentioned or about to be mentioned.

Example 1:
The Prime Minister spent his last day in office and at 3pm he left Downing Street for the last time.

Example 2:
I believe him. Tony would never lie.

You may have noticed that the two examples are different in terms of the order in which referencing occurs. In the first example, the pronoun 'he' refers back to a previously mentioned lexical item. We can call this type of cohesion **anaphoric referencing**. In the second example however, the pronoun 'him' anticipates the proper noun 'Tony', which occurs in the second sentence. This type of forward referencing is called **cataphoric referencing**.

Key terms

Anaphoric referencing: referencing back to an already stated lexical item.

Cataphoric referencing: referencing forwards to an as yet undisclosed lexical item.

Substitution: the replacing of one set of lexical items for another.

Ellipsis: the missing out of a word or words in a sentence.

Classroom activity 10

Pronoun referencing is common across a range of texts. As a quick indicator of what a text would feel like without it, rewrite Text M, replacing each pronoun with the noun to which it refers either **anaphorically** or **cataphorically**. What do you notice? What is the stylistic effect of this change?

Text M

Beryl was alone in the living room when Stanley appeared, wearing a blue serge suit, a stiff collar and a spotted tie. He looked almost uncannily clean and brushed; he was going out to town for the day. Dropping into his chair, he pulled out his watch and put it beside his plate.

Katherine Mansfield, At the Bay, *1922*

Two other types of lexical cohesion are **substitution** and **ellipsis**. Substitution involves replacing one set of lexical items for another. In the example below, the lexical items 'mobile phone' are replaced by another set 'newer model' to avoid awkward repetition and to place the emphasis on the need to acquire a more up-to-date version.

My *mobile phone* is so out of date, I must look into getting a *newer model*.

Ellipsis, on the other hand, involves omitting sets of elements. In this example, Speaker B's response, which omits the words 'I went to' is sufficient to be understood. In fact, in most contexts, reformulating Speaker A's initial words would appear not only uneconomical but also clumsy.

A: *Where did you go on holiday last year?*

B: *Portugal.*

Extension activity 7

As you might expect, certain text types will feature referencing, substitution and ellipsis much more than others. Spoken discourse for example, tends to be rich in elliptical structures, mostly due to their economical value in terms of word expenditure. Explore this in more detail by considering the texts you have collected in your scrapbook. Classify them according to which type of lexical cohesion they rely on.

Key terms

Denotation: a strict 'dictionary' meaning of a lexical item.

Connotation: an associated, symbolic meaning relying on culturally shared conventions.

Semantic or **lexical field:** lexical items that are similar in range of meaning and properties.

Lexical connotation

Some linguists distinguish between the strict semantic meaning of a word and the associative meanings that it may conjure up in a given context. This is a distinction between **denotation** and **connotation**. Lexical items are often used by text producers to draw upon a range of associated meanings.

Classroom activity 11

Look at the advertising extracts in Text N. What associated meanings would you draw from the words in italics? What do they suggest about the product being advertised?

See page 194 for feedback on this activity.

Text N

A – 'the new daily instant-smoothing serum proven to *boost radiance*' (skincare product)

B – '*Simply beautiful…beautifully simple*' (mobile phone)

C – 'The *sunny slopes* and *well drained soil* of Costa Rica' (instant coffee)

Extension activity 8

Find five more examples of strong connotative meanings from advertising texts, and annotate them carefully for your scrapbook.

Lexical fields

The examples in Classroom activity 11 demonstrate that texts rely on more than just the impact of individual words to engage a reader and generate meaning. Often, cohesive patterns are formed by clusters of words. For example, you might expect a car manual to contain references to parts of a car: engine; steering wheel; oil; seats; tools; etc. Lexical items that share certain semantic value are said to be from a defined **semantic** or **lexical field**. These are cohesive devices where the addition of unexpected or inappropriate members makes a text feel 'uncomfortable', though texts may use this for a certain effect.

Group membership

Page 10 introduced the idea of prototypes. Lexical fields also have prototypical members and, of course, can contain lexical items that are less obvious, although inclusion is generally controlled by cultural convention. As an example, ask 10 friends to name a mode of transport. Most people will answer 'car', 'train' or 'bus', a few may say 'motorbike' or 'plane', but not many will suggest 'llama'. If there is an underground or tram system in your area, these may feature high on your lists, but typically the first three will appear more than the others. Try this with other lexical categories such as furniture and fruit; it is remarkable how consistent people's responses will be.

Other semantic relationships

Classroom activity 12

1 Consider the semantic field of weather. List as many lexical items as you can that might be included in this field. Include as wide a range as you can.

2 Look carefully at your chosen words. What relationships can you see between them, for example are some opposites of others, do they share similar yet subtle meanings, do they have other relationships? Although this kind of exercise will never be exact, try to summarise your findings as distinctly as you can.

See page 194 for feedback on this activity.

The findings from this activity lead us to three important types of semantic relationship between lexical items: **synonymy**, **antonymy** and **hyponymy**.

Synonymy

Synonyms are lexical items that have generally equivalent meanings, for example:

1 cry, weep, howl, whimper
2 man, bloke, guy, dude, hunk, chap, gentleman, geezer
3 lavatory, toilet, water closet, john, bog.

There are, however, differences within synonymous groups of words that mean that we can never really say that two lexical items have exactly the same meaning. In the first example, you might say that 'howl' is a much stronger form of 'cry', whilst 'whimper' is less intense. Equally, the terms might be used to describe different reactions to emotions.

In the second group, the differences between synonyms is one both of formality and dialect and sociolect. You should see that context is all important in evaluating the use of a certain lexical item. Some are highly formal, for example 'gentleman', whilst 'geezer', as well as being much lower in formality, would originally have been used in certain parts of London.

The third group also relies on differences in formality between synonyms: 'lavatory' seems a great deal more polite than its counterpart 'bog', which is a blunt and even potentially offensive lexical choice. Words and phrases that are more acceptable substitutes for potentially distasteful language choices are known as **euphemisms**. The harsher alternatives are said to be **dysphemisms**. As with all synonyms, context and the intended impact of a text producer will govern language choice.

Key terms

Synonymy: words with very similar semantic value.

Antonymy: words with opposite semantic value.

Hyponymy: the term for the hierarchical structure that exists between lexical items.

Euphemism: a socially acceptable word or phrase used to avoid talking about something potentially distasteful.

Dysphemism: a harsh, 'to-the-point' and perhaps taboo term, sometimes used for a dark humorous effect.

Extension activity 9

Try this substitution exercise.

Take a copy of a daily newspaper and find an article of 150–200 words in length. Highlight the nouns within that article and then for each one, and using a thesaurus, find synonymous lexical items. Experiment with inserting these into your base text. What impact does this have? Explain why the writer of the article may have chosen one lexical item over another.

When you have completed this exercise, ensure that you add your texts and comments to your scrapbook.

■ Key terms

Complementary: truly opposite antonyms.

Gradable: antonyms that are not exact opposites but can be considered in terms of degree of quality.

Subordinate: a 'lower' word in the hyponymic chain; a more specific lexical item.

Superordinate: a 'higher' word in the hyponymic chain; a more general lexical item.

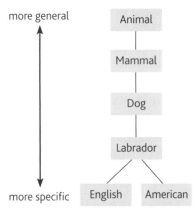

Fig. 6 *Hierarchical structure*

Antonymy

Antonyms are words with opposite meanings. In some cases, antonyms are **complementary**, that is, they represent true opposites such as:

    alive – dead   true – false   man – woman

In other cases, they are **gradable**, such as:

    narrow – wide   beautiful – ugly   long – short

The difference between the two is one of *absoluteness*. For example, a human being can only be either alive or dead, not somewhere between the two. On the other hand, someone might not be considered beautiful, but that does not necessarily mean that he or she is ugly. Gradable antonymy is of course subject to an individual's perception and value systems.

Hyponymy

Finally, a hierarchical structure exists between lexical items, known as hyponymy (see Figure 6).

Moving down the chain leads to a more specific lexical item, related to the item above it in a **subordinate** manner. The opposite movement leads to more general **superordinate** items. Hyponymy is an important cohesive device, for example:

    A: What kind of dog do you have?

    B: A labrador.

Interestingly, linguists have found that we tend to use one level of hyponomy much more than others. This is called the basic level and is a level such as 'dog' in Figure 6, where the lexical item is sufficiently detailed to be understood as a distinctive or specific category and therefore generally used. This explains why for example, we would tend to say 'I'm taking the dog for a walk' rather than 'I'm taking the labrador for a walk' (more specific) or 'I'm taking the mammal for a walk' (less specific).

■ Classroom activity 13

What seems wrong to you about these two (imaginary) examples?

Context: two friends talking about downloading some music.

A: *Did you download that track?*

B: *Yes, and I'm just in the process of putting it on to my electronic appliance.*

Context: two friends arranging a lift for the morning.

A: *Is there any way I can grab a lift in your Peugeot 205 1.9D?*

B: *Of course!*

See page 194 for feedback on this activity.

Extension activity 10

Under- and over-specificity can be used for stylistic and comic effect, often in a sarcastic manner or to state the obvious. You might like to find examples of this as you collect texts for your scrapbook.

Figurative language

Everyday language is rich in figurative expressions, often using metaphor to express something in a creative way. Often metaphors are expressed using the verb 'to be' as in 'He is a tiger on the football field'. Everyday language is also rich in **conceptual metaphors** that allow us to express abstract entities in physical terms and can be seen as a mapping of attributes from one entity to another, from a source to a target, for example:

'Colly Backs England To Battle On'

is an example of the conceptual metaphor 'Competition is war', where the attributes of war (seeing the other person as an opponent; attacking and defending positions and using battle strategies) help to structure our concept of the more abstract term of competition. This conceptual metaphor is commonplace in sports reports. Other common examples of conceptual metaphors are shown in Text O.

Text O

LIFE IS A GAMBLING GAME
I'll *take my chances*
The *odds are against me*
That's the *luck of the draw*
TIME IS MONEY
How do you *spend* your time these days?
Do you have *much* time *left*?
I've *invested* a lot of time in her
HAPPY IS UP; SAD IS DOWN
That *boosted* my spirits
I'm feeling *down*
He's really *low* these days

G. Lakoff and M. Johnson, Metaphors We Live By, *1980*

Extension activity 11

Find 10 linguistic expressions of conceptual metaphor (newspaper reports are particularly fertile ground for this). You might also find the following websites useful for further examples of conceptual metaphor. Add your examples, and your comments on them, to your scrapbook.

www.cs.bham.ac.uk/~jab/ATT-Meta/Databank/table.html

http://cogsci.berkeley.edu/lakoff

✓

Key terms

Under-specificity: the inappropriately vague, rather general answer to a question.

Over-specificity: the giving of an inappropriately too specific answer, sometimes with absurd effects.

Conceptual metaphor: the way in which abstract terms are mapped on to physical entities through an underlying conceptual structure.

Grammar and syntax

In this topic you will:

- understand the relationship between syntax elements and other units of language

- learn about the structure of different types of phrases, clauses and sentences

- explore the effects created through the use of different structures by text producers.

Key terms

Morphology: the area of language study that deals with the formation of words from smaller units called morphemes.

Morpheme: the smallest unit of grammatical meaning. Morphemes can be words in their own right or combine with other morphemes to form lexical units.

The linguistic rank scale: a system for showing the relationship between levels of language units. The movement from left to right indicates that a unit is structured from that which precedes it, for example clauses are structured from phrases.

Prescriptive approach/attitude: an approach that concentrates on how language ought to be structured (written or spoken) and sees alternative patterns or versions as deviant and inferior.

Descriptive approach/attitude: an approach to language study that focuses on actual language use.

Noun phrases: a group of words centred around a head noun.

What is syntax?

Strictly speaking, we can divide the framework of grammar into two sub-frameworks: **morphology** and **syntax**. Whereas morphology is concerned with how words or lexical items are formed from smaller units called **morphemes**, syntax looks at how lexical items are sequenced into larger units of language. The **linguistic rank scale** is a neat way of showing the relationship between these units. As we move along the scale from left to right in Figure 7, we can generally say that each unit is structured from those that precede it. So, for example, lexical items are formed from morphemes, phrases from lexical items and so on. Syntax is the level of descriptive analysis that deals with **phrases**, **clauses** and **sentences**.

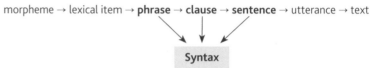

Fig. 7 *The linguistic rank scale*

Prescription or description?

Grammar is a complex and at times controversial area of language study. A **prescriptive attitude** to language often sees varieties of English other than Standard English as grammatically incorrect or bad, and is highly critical of uses of language that deviate from so-called established grammatical rules. A **descriptive approach** to language study and grammar, on the other hand, has no such attitude. The aim of a descriptive study is to comment on actual usage and describe not whether rules are being adhered to but how language operates in real examples and contexts. A descriptive approach to grammar may still use Standard English constructions as a benchmark, but prefers the terms *non-standard* and *variant* grammar to the more loaded *wrong*, *bad* or *deviant*.

Reviewing word classes

Before you proceed, it would be worth reminding yourself of the principal word classes from the topic on lexis and semantics (page 19). You should ensure that you are comfortable with this kind of exercise before you begin your work on syntax.

Phrases

Noun phrases

Noun phrases (NP) are centred round a noun (n), which serves as the head word or head noun (h) of the phrase. The following are examples of noun phrases (with the head word underlined).

> **A** <u>*Kerrang*</u>!
>
> **B** *The <u>Times</u>*
>
> **C** A small <u>island</u>
>
> **D** The noisy <u>party</u>
>
> **E** The pretty <u>cottage</u> by the sea

You will probably notice that all these noun phrases except **A** have additional elements. These form what is called the **constituent structure** of the noun phrase along with the obligatory head noun.

B contains a determiner (d) ('the'), whereas **C** and **D** contain not only a determiner but also an adjective, which comes before the head word. These represent what is called **pre-modification**, where an adjective is used as a **modifier (m)** *before* the head noun. **D** also contains a pre-modifying adjective 'pretty' and a head noun 'cottage', but also has a further constituent, in this case the **qualifier (q)** 'by the sea' This use of a qualifier *after* the head noun is known as **post-modification**.

We can now review the examples and annotate them as follows:

```
              NP
      A  Kerrang!
             h
              NP
      B  The Times
          d     h
                NP
      C  A small island
         d   m    h
                  NP
      D  The noisy party
          d   m    h
                    NP
      E  The pretty cottage by the sea
          d    m     h       q
```

Qualifiers as prepositional phrases

Sometimes post-modifying qualifiers are **prepositional phrases (Prep P)**. Prepositional phrases consist of a preposition (p) and an additional NP, which will contain a head noun of its own and any number of determiners, modifiers and qualifiers. Example **E** contains post-modification with a prepositional phrase and can now be re-labelled as:

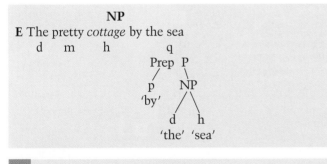

```
              NP
    E  The pretty cottage by the sea
       d    m     h        q
                        Prep  P
                       /    \
                      p      NP
                     'by'   /  \
                          d     h
                        'the'  'sea'
```

AQA Examiner's tip

Grammar is an important framework. You should ensure that you are able to undertake grammatical analysis clearly and accurately, but remember that such analyses should be *interpretative*, commenting on *effects* and in conjunction with *other frameworks* rather than merely 'feature-spotting'. You will gain little credit for just pointing out grammatical features.

Remember to use the term 'non-standard grammar', rather than 'wrong', 'bad', 'incorrect' or 'deviant grammar' when commenting on non-standard expressions and constructions.

Key terms

Constituent structure: the key components of a phrase.

Pre-modification: modifying that occurs before the head noun.

Modifier: a word, usually an adjective or a noun used attributively, that qualifies the sense of a noun. Adverbs of comment also act as modifiers, e.g. obviously.

Qualifier: further information to complete the phrase.

Post-modification: a modifying phrase or lexical item that occurs after the head noun in a noun phrase.

Prepositional phrase: a phrase consisting of a preposition and an added noun phrase.

Classroom activity 14

Look at the following examples of noun phrases, all taken from newspaper headlines. Identify the constituent structure of each using the terms **NP, Prep P, p, d, m, h** and **q**.

1. Violent robbers in rubber masks.
2. 'Wild west' town.
3. Loyal fans of pop music.
4. Three record hot years predicted before end of decade.
5. Superb collection of coloured prints.

See page 194 for feedback on this activity.

Text P

on test football boots

kick off

The football season is about to start, but which of these boots should be your new signing?

1 Puma v1.06, £99.99
Puma's lightest boot yet is made with ultra-thin fabric so you can zip speedily across the park. The smooth, moulded upper is good for quick touches around the box but less suitable for long passes.
Stockists: puma.com

2 Reebok Sprintfit, £125
Reebok has toned down the technology, choosing instead to focus on comfort. The seamless upper on this pared-down boot means you can ping the ball about with greater accuracy.
Stockists: rbk.com

3 Nike Total 90 Laser, £120
With its twin aims of improving power and accuracy, this wasp-coloured boot puts a sting in your shots. The Air Zoom heel gives you added comfort and the sweet spot is forgiving when you play long-range passes.
Stockists: 0800 056 1640

4 Adidas +Predator Absolute, £120
These boots feel bespoke and the snug fit gives you confidence that the ball will reach its target. The grip on the instep means they're great for playing swerving, defence-splitting passes.
Stockists: 0870 240 4204

5 Diadora Maximus RTX 14, £99.99
These feel natural to wear and the tucked-away laces mean you get a true contact. If they were a player they'd be industrious and reliable but ultimately not quite world-class.
Stockists: prodirectsoccer.com

6 Umbro X Boot III, £99.99
The instep is rippled with material crafted in conjunction with the tyre maker Michelin. The result is a boot that gives you a good touch and precise distribution.
Stockists: umbro.com

Verb phrases

The topic on lexis and semantics identified verbs as processes indicating actions, events or states of being, thinking and feeling. Verb phrases are larger structures built around a **main verb (mv)**. The newspaper headlines below contain examples of verb phrases (in italics).

> **A** Prime Minister *takes* big lead
>
> **B** Internet scam *nets* millions
>
> **C** Cement *tipped into* lake by vandals
>
> **D** GCSE coursework *to become* history
>
> **E** Banks *have not signed* required customer code

In a similar way to our work on noun phrases, we can also label the constitutent structure of verb phrase as follows

Examples A and B contain a single verb in the present tense. This acts as a main verb (mv). Example C contains a further constituent 'into' following the main verb in the **past tense**. This additional constituent is known as an **extension (e)**. Example D features the **infinitive** form 'to become', whilst example E contains both a main verb 'signed' together with an **auxiliary verb (aux)** 'has' and a **negating particle (neg)** 'not'. We might therefore annotate the examples to show the constituent structure of the verb phrase as follows, with the **mv** as the **obligatory component** and the others as **optional** ones.

>   **VP**
>
> **A** Prime Minister *takes* big lead
>   **mv**
>
>   **VP**
>
> **B** Internet scam *nets* millions
>   **mv**
>
>   **VP**
>
> **C** Cement *tipped into* lake by vandals
>   **mv**   **e**
>
>   **VP**
>
> **D** GCSE coursework *to become* history
>   **mv (inf)**
>
>   **VP**
>
> **E** Banks *have not signed* required customer code
>   **aux neg mv**

Types of auxiliary verb

Auxiliary verbs 'help out' main verbs in a verb phrase, to signal a shift in tense or to express modality. The **primary auxiliaries** 'be', 'do' and 'have' often help to distinguish tense, for example 'he was running', 'he has run', whilst **modal auxiliaries** cover a number of verbs that show *possibility* or *necessity*, such as 'may', 'could', 'will', 'should', 'can' and 'ought'.

Text Q

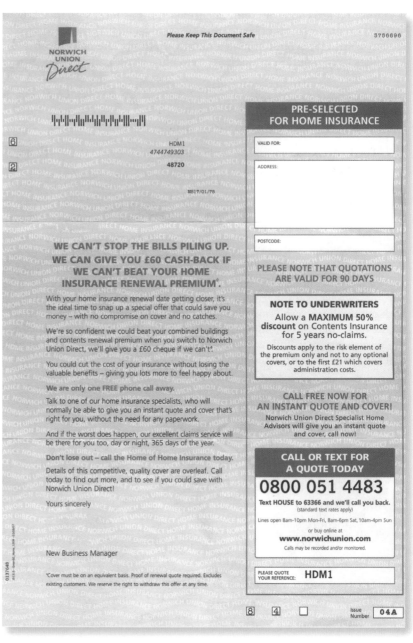

Key terms

Semi-auxiliary: a combination of a primary auxiliary and another verb part.

Catenative: a verb that can attach to another to form a chain.

Semi-auxiliaries and catenatives

These combine with other verbs to form verb phrase chains. **Semi-auxiliaries** follow the formula:

primary auxiliary + another word + 'to'

e.g 'be supposed to', as in 'You *were supposed to* do the washing up!'

Equally, **catenative** verbs such as 'appear', 'get' and 'seem' form similar chains but without the use of a primary auxiliary as in:

'She *appeared* to run away.'

'He *got* to play for the first XI.'

'You *seemed* to like it here.'

Active and passive voice

Look at the examples below. What difference do you notice and what is its effect?

A MoD *issues* gag order on armed forces.

B Gag order *is issued* on armed forces.

In **A**, the person (or in this case the organisation) issuing the order is identified: the MoD (Ministry of Defence). In **B**, however, no **actor** is identified. Passive constructions like **B** subtly avoid specifying **agency** and are often used to avoid drawing attention to the person or body responsible for the action. Sometimes a prepositional phrase can indicate agency as in **C**, although there remains a difference in stylistic effect. In **C**, although we are told who carried out the act of issuing, placing the actor at the end of the clause has arguably less impact than placing it at the beginning.

Prep P

C Gag order *is issued* on armed forces *by MoD*.

Structurally passive constructions use a primary auxiliary verb and a participle, formed by adding an *-en/-ed* bound morpheme to a verb stem. The difference between the active and passive voice is summarised in Table 9 below.

Table 9 *Difference between the active and passive voice*

Voice	Features
Active	Includes an *actor* or *agent*; verb phrase includes a finite *present* or *past tense* verb
Passive	Omits an *actor* or *agent* or includes the agent as part of a *prepositional phrase* after the verb

> **Key terms**
>
> **Actor:** the individual or entity responsible for the action.
>
> **Agency:** the responsibility for, or cause of, an action.
>
> **Adjectival phrase:** a phrase with an adjective as its head, for example 'very big'.
>
> **Adverbial phrase:** a phrase with an adverb as its head, for example 'very quickly'.

> **Extension activity 13**
>
> Find different newspaper headlines on the same story that use active and passive forms. What is the effect of this different use of voice? Is it related to a political ideology or other vested interest that the text producer might have? Think about whether agency is made explicit and foregrounded in an active construction or made less explicit or omitted in a passive one.
>
> Keep a record of your observations in your scrapbook.

Adjectival and adverbial phrases

These perform similar roles to those of the word classes adjective and adverb. **Adjectival phrases (Adj P)** generally appear after the verb 'to be', whilst **adverbial phrases (Adv P)** modify verb phrases or other adverbial phrases.

NP VP   Adj P

He is very intelligent

NP   VP   Adv P

He fought bravely

🔍 From phrases to clauses

In labelling phrases we have considered the form or class, for example noun phrases, verb phrases and prepositional phrases. We can also describe them in terms of function as follows:

```
        NP     VP   NP    Prep P
The man drank beer in the pub
        S      V    O      A
```

```
        NP       VP     Adj P
The man became drunk
        S        V       C
```

Clause element functions

A **clause** may be defined as a group of words clustered around a verb phrase, containing the elements listed in Table 10 below.

Table 10 *Clause element functions*

Element	Function
Subject (S)	Usually indicates the element responsible for carrying out the verb process
Verb (V)	The verb phrase
Object (O)	That affected by the action of the verb phrase, for example 'I kicked *the ball*'
Complement (C)	An attribute that provides more information about a subject or object, for example 'She is *ill*'; or 'We painted the room blue'
Adverbial (A)	The circumstances of the action or event (the where, when, how), for example 'I saw him *at the concert*'

Variations in clause patterns

There are seven basic clause types, summarised below.

```
S    V
I yawned

S    V      O
I opened the door

S V   C
I am ready

S V      A
I went to London

S V   O   O
I gave him a pen

S V    O      C
I got my shoes wet

S V    O        A
I put the box on the floor
```

David Crystal, The Cambridge Encyclopedia of the English Language, *p221*

Key terms

Clause: a group of lexical items centred round a verb phrase.

Clause patterns: patterns produced by writers using certain types of clause for impact and effect.

Double-object construction: a clause with a verb that has two objects: one direct and the other indirect.

Direct object: an object directly affected by a verb process, for example in 'I gave him the pen', 'pen' is directly affected by the giving and is the direct object.

Indirect object: an object indirectly affected by a verb process, for example in 'I gave him the pen', 'him' is the indirect object.

Ditransitive verb: a verb that requires two objects to form a double-object construction.

Monotransitive verb: a verb that only requires one object.

Intransitive verb: a verb process such as 'yawned' or 'slept' that has no object.

Sentence structures: the kind of sentence(s) used by a writer for impact and effect.

Simple sentence: a sentence consisting of a single main clause.

Compound sentence: a sentence containing two or more main clauses, connected by coordinating conjunctions, or sometimes just separated by punctuation (semi-colon).

The SVOO clause is a **double-object construction** where there are two **objects**: a **direct object** 'pen' and an **indirect object** 'him'. Verbs such as *give* are **ditransitive** in that they require two objects (one *direct* and one *indirect*), as opposed to **monotransitive** verbs such as 'put' that take only one. An **intransitive** verb such as 'yawn' requires no object.

Although these represent basic patterns, additional elements may also be present. For example, the clause 'I went to London yesterday' has an SVAA structure (an additional adverbial element), yet 'Yesterday I went to London' has an ASVA structure. As this example shows, adverbials can commonly occur at the front of clauses. In addition, variations in the order of clause elements within these basic patterns can produce striking effects.

Sentences

In the same way that phrases make up the larger structure of a clause, clauses are the components of the larger grammatical **structure** of the **sentence**. A sentence contains one or more clauses and may be of one of the following types:

Simple – contains one clause.

S   V   O

One clause —— He kicked the ball

Compound – contains two or more clauses joined by **coordinating conjunctions**.

S V O conj V O

He kicked the ball and scored a goal

Two clauses – note here that the subject of the second remains the same as the first. These clauses can both stand independently.

Complex – contains two or more clauses, where one is the **main clause** and the other(s) a **subordinate clause(s)**. Linking is through **subordinating conjunctions**. A main clause can stand independently as a unit of meaning and will be a simple sentence in its own right.

conj S V C S V O

Although he was tired, he kicked the ball

Two clauses – the first is dependent on the second to complete a full sense of meaning; the second is a simple sentence in its own right

Compound–complex – contains both coordination and subordination.

S V O conj V O conj S V C

Three clauses with both coordination and subordination present —— He kicked the ball and celebrated his goal even though he was tired

Classroom activity 18

Which of the sentences opposite are examples of simple, compound and complex sentences?

See page 195 for feedback on this activity.

A He laughed softly to himself as he wrote.

B Isabelle leaned forward on to the table and covered her face with her hands.

C Up in his room Stephen listened to the noises of the night.

D She opened her eyes again and smiled at him.

E On the first-floor landing he hesitated.

F At the edge of the skirmish the police officers began to swing their batons in a threatening way as they moved into the crowd.

G Stephen watched their hard exchange but felt dissociated from it, as though they only spoke in slogans.

Sebastian Faulks, Birdsong, 1994

Classroom activity 19

Stylistic patterns created by the use and variation of sentence types are often manipulated for their effect on the reader. Read through Text R, highlighting the *sentence types*. Now consider the *effect* of this particular patterning. How does the use of different sentence types and clause patterns lead to the effect that the writer is trying to achieve?

Text R

There was a man beside him missing part of his face, but walking in the same dreamlike state, his rifle pressing forward. His nose dangled and Stephen could see his teeth through the missing cheek. The noise was unlike anything he had heard before. It lay against his skin, shaking his bones. Remembering his order not to stop for those behind him, he pressed slowly on, and as the smoke lifted in front of him he saw the German wire.

It had not been cut. Men were running up and down it in turmoil, looking for a way through. They were caught in the coils where they brought down torrents of machine-gun fire. Their bodies jerked up and down, twisting and jumping. Still they tried. Two men were climbing vainly with their cutters among the corpses, their movement bringing the sharp disdainful fire of a sniper. They lay still.

Thirty yards to his right there was a gap. He ran towards it, knowing it would be the focus of machine gun fire from several directions. He breathed in as he reached it, clenching for his death.

His body passed through clean air and he began to laugh as he ran and ran and then rolled down into a trench, bumping his heavy pack on top of him. There was no one there.

Alive, he thought, dear God, I am alive. The war lifted from him.

Sebastian Faulks, Birdsong, 1994

Sentence mood and function

Consider the following **utterances**:

A Before Easter, she had driven over to a development in Fife.

B Is it done yet?

C Look at the evidence.

D That was not an excuse!

Key terms

Utterance: a group of spoken words, roughly equivalent to the sentence in written terms.

All are simple sentences containing one clause. **A** states a *fact*. **B** asks a *question* while **C** *invites* or *demands* that the receiver of the utterance do something. These are the three main sentence moods. Each has a distinguishable grammatical form: sentences telling facts have a basic subject + verb clause structure, whilst those asking questions tend to include a primary auxiliary verb before the subject and another verb following it; those inviting or demanding usually begin with a verb followed by a complement or an adverbial element. These are basic patterns and there are many exceptions, but generally, sentence mood may be summarised as seen in Table 11.

Table 11 *Sentence mood*

Sentence mood	Feature	Structure	Example
Declarative	Telling	S + V	Before Easter, she had driven over to a development in Fife
Interrogative	Asking	V + S	Is it done yet?
Imperative	Inviting, demand	V + C	Look at the evidence

In addition, **D** is often labelled an exclamatory sentence, although this is a question of function more than mood. Exclamatory sentences are mostly declarative ones with emphasis added by an exclamation mark. Again, its use is one of *stylistic effect*.

Form v. function

Often, the function of an utterance can differ radically from its grammatical form. Classroom activity 20 should help you to consider how the form of a sentence or utterance is not necessarily equivalent to its function.

Classroom activity 20

Consider a situation where you are asking someone to shut a door that has been left open, and the various contexts in which this utterance might occur. Write down as many ways of performing the same speech act as you can think of. Then consider their likely impact and the contexts in which you might use them. Does one have a particular force or subtlety that the others don't? What might each tell you about the relationship between the speakers?

See page 195 for feedback on this activity.

Extension activity 14

Find examples of different texts that use varying sentence types for effect. Can you categorise these by genre or intended readership?

Rewrite the text in Classroom activity 19 as:

- an advertisement (you decide what it will advertise)
- a pop lyric.

Think about your choice of sentence types, your *context* and *audience/implied readership* and your work on genre to help you.

Further reading

Crystal, D. *The Cambridge Encyclopedia of the English Language*, Cambridge University Press, 1995

Freeborn, D. (2nd edn) *A Course Book in English Grammar: Standard English and the Dialects*, Palgrave, 1995 (a more advanced text)

Phonetics and phonology

What are phonetics and phonology?

Phonetics and phonology are the frameworks that look at the sounds of English. Phonology is the conceptual study of the sound system, whereas phonetics deals with the actual sounds of speech, considering how sounds are physically articulated and language phenomena such as accents. For the purposes of study at AS Level, we can say that these frameworks are a way of exploring *sound patterns* and their *effects* in texts.

The phoneme

Phonemes are the basic units of sound from which language is constructed. They can be represented using a variety of transcription systems, but symbols representing sounds are usually written between slashes like this: /c/, /a/, /t/, /cat/.

The main consonant groups

Consonant sounds are often used by a text producer for a particular effect. For example, plosive sounds such as /p/, /b/, /t/, /d/, /k/ and /g/ tend to have a harsh or abrupt feel when they are foregrounded in a text. The main consonant groups are listed in Table 12.

Table 12 *The main consonant groups*

Consonant group	Examples
Plosives	b, p, t, d, k, g
Fricatives	f, v, s, z, sh
Africates	ch (church), dj (judge)
Nasals	m, n, ng
Approximants	r, j, w

Extension activity 15

Find some newspaper headlines that use consonant groups for effect. Which consonant group is prominent and what is the effect of its use in the context of the headline and story?

Sound patterns and effects

Sound symbolism is the term used to describe how sounds are used to represent actual events and to mirror the actions they describe. It covers both the features of sound patterning and the way the sound patterning is structured.

Onomatopoeia

Onomatopoeia is an alternative term that strictly covers the feature of sound patterning with which you may well be familiar. Onomatopoeia can occur in both lexical and non-lexical forms. Common examples of **lexical onomatopoeia** such as 'crash' and 'bang' work on our ability to draw similarities between the sounds of the words and the real-world actions. **Non-lexical onomatopoeia** equally draws a similarity between a sound and the real world, although this relies on a sound or cluster of sounds that are not lexical items, as such 'vroom' or 'grrr'.

Foregrounding sounds

Some other common phonological patterns can be achieved by structurally foregrounding particular groups of sounds. This is often done using the techniques of **alliteration**, **assonance** and **consonance**.

Key terms

Lexical onomatopoeia: actual lexical items that rely on a similarity between sound and meaning.

Non-lexical onomatopoeia: 'non-words' that work in the same way as lexical onomatopoeia.

Alliteration: a sequence of words beginning with the same sound.

Assonance: the repetition of vowel sounds for effect.

Consonance: the repetition of consonant sounds for effect.

Classroom activity 21

Texts S–V use sound symbolism for effect. For each one, consider the effect of phonological patterning.

See page 195 for feedback on this activity.

Text S

The silence surged softly backward,
When the plunging hoofs were gone

Walter de la Mare's 'The Listeners', *describing the sound of a horse retreating*

Text T

And shells came calmly through the drizzling air
To burst with hollow bang below the hill

Siegfried Sassoon's 'The Working Party', *describing an attack on a trench*

Text U

All shod with steel,
We hissed upon the polished ice

William Wordsworth's The Prelude, *describing skating*

Text V

This darksome burn, horseback brown,
His rollrock highroad roaring down

Gerard Manley Hopkins's 'Inversnaid', *describing a stream in the Scottish Highlands*

Extension activity 16

First World War poetry is a good place to start when exploring sound symbolism in literary texts. The poems of Siegfried Sassoon and Wilfred Owen in particular rely heavily on phonological patternings for some of their effects. Find a good anthology such as Jon Silkin's *The Penguin Book of First World War Poetry* and explore this.

Equally, non-literary texts such as product brand names rely on phonological features: think about the sound symbolism in snacks such as 'Monster Munch' or 'Crunchie' and in hair products such as 'Herbal Essences', 'Supersoft' and 'Silvikrin'. Collect examples for your scrapbook and explore phonological patterning in them. How do phonological features combine with lexical and grammatical ones to produce a particular effect?

Phonology and humour

One of the most novel uses of sound is to create humour. Often, language can be manipulated to create a comic effect, sometimes with only the smallest of changes. The (terrible) jokes that can be found inside Christmas crackers use **phonological manipulation**, for example:

Q: What did the grape say when the elephant stepped on it?

A: Nothing, it just gave out a little wine.

Key terms

Phonological manipulation: the ways in which text producers play with sounds and their effects.

This relies on the **homophones** 'whine' and 'wine', with the same pronunciation but different spellings.

> Q: When do astronauts eat?
>
> A: At launch time.

This relies on **phonemic substitution**, with /au/ replacing /u/ for comic effect.

Sometimes homophones are used in conjunction with a stress on two lexical items rather than one and rely on the reader's understanding that they will produce a coherent semantic field, for example:

> Books and their authors:
>
> *The Laser* by Ray Gunn
>
> *Bricks and Mortar* by Bill Ding

■ **Extension activity 17**

Find further examples of jokes that rely on phonological manipulation for your scrapbook. Television situation comedies provide particularly fertile ground for this kind of work. Can you explain, using your learning from this topic area, how humour is created in your examples?

☑ Pragmatics

In this topic you will:

■ understand the difference between semantic and pragmatic meaning

■ explore the concepts of context, implication and inference

■ explore how language works to determine shared context through the use of deixis.

■ What is pragmatics?

Consider Text W, an advertisement found in a broadsheet Sunday newspaper.

Initially and at a strictly semantic level, there is something odd about a text welcoming would-be air travellers to a zoo, and those who know that Heathrow is an airport might struggle to understand the meaning that the text producer is trying to convey. However, if we consider that at the time of release, Heathrow airport was receiving a great deal of bad press regarding delays and lost luggage, and also had to deal with protests over the proposed building of another runway, then the message becomes clearer. The text producer is relying on shared knowledge between text producer and receiver regarding these problems to communicate and generate a coherent message. The implication is that Heathrow is zoo-like and chaotic, and we are expected to infer that using it would not be a good idea if we would like a stress-free journey.

Text W

WELCOME TO
Heathrow Zoo

Private terminal at Luton. New York £999. flySILVERJET.com

In contrast, 'Silverjet', as the advertisement informs us, flies from a private terminal at Luton airport, which we might assume will be a more pleasant experience than flying from Heathrow. This way that language and meaning rely on contextual information, shared knowledge and implication and inference can be studied as the language framework of pragmatics.

Context, implication and inference

Much of what is understood arises less from the literal semantic value of words than from the contexts in which they are produced and understood. As we have seen, implied meanings where an intended meaning beyond the literal one is conveyed rely on implication on the part of the writer or speaker and on the ability of the reader or listener to infer. The relationship between implication and inference however is not always straightforward and obviously not all implied meanings are understood as intended. Most readers and listeners will, however, choose the most relevant meaning for them in the context of what is being said and other background knowledge.

Classroom activity 22

To explore the relationship between context and implied meaning, take the question 'What have you done?' Imagine that this is said in the following contexts. What might be implied in each case?

1. You haven't completed the independent study that was set for you last night and you ask a friend to show you theirs.

2. You arrive home to find that your younger brother/sister has moved some of your CDs.

3. A friend shows you some very impressive changes that he/she has made to a room in their house.

4. A friend shows you some not so impressive changes that he/she has made to a room in their house.

Grice's Maxims

Another way of explaining how implied meanings work is to consider what is known as the **cooperative principle**, following the work of the linguist and philosopher Paul Grice. Grice determined that speakers adhere to four maxims in maintaining cooperation:

1 Quantity: use an appropriate amount of detail.
2 Quality: speak the truth and do not knowingly mislead.
3 Relevance: keep what is being discussed relevant to the topic.
4 Manner: avoid vagueness and ambiguity.

Generally it is assumed that conversation is a cooperative enterprise and that speakers tend to keep to these maxims. When they are broken or flouted, they can also give rise to an implied meaning, which Grice called an *implicature*. Look at the two examples below, where a father is asking his daughter about her homework.

> Example 1:
> *A*: *Have you finished your homework?*
> *B*: *Yes, I have finished my homework.*
>
> Example 2:
> *A*: *Have you finished your homework?*
> *B*: *What time are we going out?*

Key terms

Cooperative principle: the principle that suggests that all communication is essentially a cooperative act.

In Example 1, B seems to flout the maxim of quantity by including the clause 'I have finished my homework' when a simple elliptical 'yes' would have sufficed. The implied meaning here could be that the daughter is not happy with her father checking on her!

In Example 2, however, B flouts the maxim of relevance by changing the subject completely. We might assume here that she has not completed her homework, or wants to check how much time she has left to complete it.

■ Deixis – the importance of shared context

Deixis is the name given to words that point towards something or someone and are used by speakers to refer to things within a shared context. For example the utterance 'I am here now' means little when it is taken from its context of production. Its meaning relies not on the semantic properties of the individual lexical items but the centre from which they come. The words 'I', 'here' and 'now' are deictic because they point towards a person, a time or a place relative to the immediate context. If you read these words aloud today, they will have a very different meaning from someone else's reading of them tomorrow or the day after, or in 10 years' time.

Deictic words can be divided into three types: **person deixis**, which includes words such as 'I', 'me' and 'you', **spatial deixis**, including words such as 'here', 'there', 'left' and 'right' and **temporal deixis**, including words such as 'now', 'then', 'today' and 'tomorrow'. We can also distinguish between **proximal** and **distal** deictic terms in relation to what is known as the **deictic centre**, as Figure 8 demonstrates.

DISTAL	that	those	there	then	
PROXIMAL	this	these	here	now	↑
		Deictic centre of speaker			**Distance**

Fig. 8 *Proximal and distal deixis*

Text X

La rive gauche or the left bank of the Seine that's left if you're floating down the stream (.) still has many of the twisting lanes and narrow buildings from medieval times (.) the right bank is more modern and business oriented with wide boulevards and stressed-out Parisiennes in suits (.) here along the river bank on the left side the big business is second-hand books displayed in little green stalls along the river (.) these literary entrepreneurs pride themselves on their easy-going business style (.) with flexible hours and virtually no overheads (.) they run their businesses as they have since the medieval times.

www.ricksteves.com

Graphology

In this topic you will:

- understand the role of graphology features in shaping and determining meaning

- explore the use of signs, typography and space in texts.

Key terms

Typography: font type, size, colour, emboldening, italicising, underlining and any other modifications to font types.

Cultural model: an organisational structure based on shared and agreed criteria by groups of people within a society.

Graphology is concerned with the *visual elements* of a text, both verbal and non-verbal, for example shape, image, colour, space and **typography**. Some texts, for example media texts, may rely heavily on graphological features to help generate their intended effect. Others may rely on more subtle features as a way of contributing to meaning. Graphology is sometimes neglected by students as being an insignificant framework. Whilst it is true that examiners are more likely to reward candidates who have a clear grasp of more complex frameworks such as grammar and pragmatics, many successful answers to examination texts show a precise and perceptive ability to consider and analyse the graphological features of a text in conjunction with other language-based analyses. That is to say, that you should always consider how a text's use of graphology sits with other language-based features such as those of a lexical or grammatical nature.

Shape

The shape of a text often gives an indication of its genre and text producers may rely on a reader's knowledge of genre convention to help them identify the purpose and meaning of a text.

Classroom activity 24

1. Look back at Texts A–F on pages 5–8. Without using any words, draw the shape of each one, using lines, bullet points and symbols to represent text, images and photographs. How typical of their genres are these six texts in terms of shape?

2. Now search for texts in each genre that are not shaped so conventionally and perhaps are closer to a completely different type of writing. Consider the impact of each of these and the importance of the shape of a text as a whole.

Images

We can refer to language as a system in which individual elements or signs take their meaning from how they are combined with other elements. Broadly speaking we can then differentiate between two types of sign: those that are iconic and those that are symbolic.

Iconic signs

An iconic sign is a direct picture of the thing it represents, although this is often simplified to provide a basic reference for the reader. Iconic signs tend to be simple ones offering a straightforward representation of what they stand for.

Symbolic signs

These draw on association or *connotation* and are usually defined by cultural convention, based on existing **cultural models**. Symbolic signs therefore provide meaning because society has placed certain values

Convention: an agreed or shared feature.

or qualities on them. For example, the rose has no likeness or causal association with the signified meaning of love or passion. The symbolic relationship that exists in our culture is based on a culturally agreed and socially acceptable method of meaningful exchange. That is, the symbolic meaning is one of **convention**.

Classroom activity 25

1   Which of the road signs below are iconic and which are symbolic?

2   For the symbolic signs, what *connotations* are called up in the reader's mind? How do these rely on *cultural models* and *conventions* in terms of image and colour?

See page 196 for feedback on this activity.

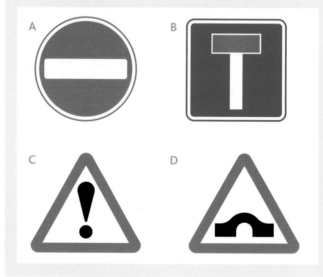

Extension activity 19

Find further examples of iconic and symbolic signs, explaining their use and the contexts in which they occur.

■ Photographs and artwork

Photographs and artwork can also provide strong associative meanings and work in the same way as logos to produce meanings for a reader.

Classroom activity 26

1   Look at Text Y opposite. Initially ignoring any writing, what does the image alone suggest and why do you think it has been chosen by the text producer? What does the image tell and not tell us?

2   Now look at the writing. How does the image *support*, *enhance* or *contradict* lexical and grammatical choices? How might you summarise the *relationship* between these formal textual properties?

Text Y

THICK & CREAMY
PURE & NATURAL
TOTALLY DELICIOUS
(AND IT REALLY IS MADE IN GREECE)

Made in Athens, traditional straining methods are used to remove the watery whey and give Total its thick, creamy texture. Total uses only natural ingredients and no artificial additives. It is pure, healthy and totally delicious. No wonder Total is the No.1 best-selling Greek yoghurt in the world. We think you'll find it irresistible too.

Don't compromise. Don't settle for anything less than real Greek yoghurt.

www.totalgreekyoghurt.com

Total ΘΑΓΕ

Totally delicious, Totally Greek

Typography

Typographical features such as font sizes and styles are key graphological features and their use is clearly informed by a text's purpose and implied readership.

Classroom activity 27

For each of the messages below. For each one, explain how the choice of font (indicated in brackets) might indicate a certain context for the writing and receiving of the message. What might it tell you about the relationship between text producer and receiver?

See page 196 for feedback on this activity.

1. You are invited to a meeting (TIMES NEW ROMAN)
2. YOU ARE INVITED TO A MEETING (JOKEWOOD)
3. YOU ARE INVITED TO A MEETING (COPPERPLATE GOTHIC)
4. **You are invited to a meeting (PORKEY'S)**
5. You are invited to a meeting (EMILY'S HAND)

Extension activity 20

Find three texts that rely on font to create a certain effect or tone. Rewrite them, using a variety of different fonts, varying between subtle and more outlandish choices. How does this alter your base text? What other changes to a font might you utilise and what is their impact?

Space

So far, in considering the graphological features of texts, we have looked at:

- layout and shape
- iconic and symbolic signs
- connotations drawn from images and logos
- typographical features such as fonts.

It is important to consider space as well as the verbal and non-verbal features listed above. The layout of a text in terms of the positioning of images and text is all important in maximising its impact on a reader, as is the amount of detail that a text contains. Cluttered and unhelpfully laid-out texts or those that contain insufficient detail are poor examples of writing.

Empty spaces

We can also consider the use of empty spaces, which as Goddard (1998) suggests: '…are as meaningful as filled ones. Where we expect language to occur, its non-occurrence is in itself an attention-seeking device.'

Classroom activity 28

How does Text Z make use of empty space? How is this related to explicit lexical and grammatical choices and to the intended impact and effect of the text?

Text Z

Archives

```
generation upon
generation upon
generation upon
generation upon
generation upon
generation upon
generation upon
generation upon
generation upon
generation upon
generation upon
generation upon
generation upon
generation upon
generation upon
generation upon
generation upon
generation upon
g  neration upon
g  neration up  n
g  nerat on up  n
g  nerat  n up  n
g  nerat  n   p  n
g   erat  n   p  n
g   era   n   p  n
g   era   n      n
g   er    n      n
g   r     n      n
g         n      n
g         n
g
```

Edwin Morgan, Archives, 2000

Discourse

In this topic you will:

- understand how written texts are organised to ensure cohesion
- explore the structure and features of spoken discourse
- analyse how in conversation, speakers cooperate to construct dialogue and meaning.

This topic covers two further short sub-topics: **discourse structure** and **discourse analysis**.

☑ What is discourse structure?

Throughout this unit we have used the word 'text' to refer to a stretch of written or spoken data. This word derives from the Latin verb *texere*, 'to weave', and was first used to describe something as 'being woven'. We still tend to metaphorically think of writing as a kind of fabric, having a *pattern* and being *crafted* by a text producer, for example when we speak of a *well-crafted* novel, or some well-written *material*.

The important points made in the Examiner's tip on page 4 about foregrounding and pattern forming should have made you focus on distinct linguistic patterns that have emerged as you have worked through this unit and collected and explored your own texts. **Discourse structure** then, is the way in which texts are organised into coherent wholes in addition to these internal cohesive patterns. Essentially it is the framework that explains how texts are put together, and this topic will concentrate solely on written texts. Throughout this topic, you should revisit your scrapbook to look at the examples you have collected so far and reconsider them in the light of the new learning that you will encounter.

Classroom activity 29

Text AA below has been re-arranged so that it is not in its original written structure. Re-organise it, considering the various strategies and textual clues that you use to help you to. How much do you rely on genre conventions?

See page 196 for feedback on this activity.

Text AA

Repulsive and Riveting!

Mr Kobayashi wetted each burger before stuffing it into his mouth. After two minutes, he had consumed 23, leading Joey Chestnut, America's great hope by one.

In Chattanooga, Tenessee, last November I watched Takeru Kobayashi devour a record 97 hamburgers with buns, onions and mustard in eight minutes flat – one every five seconds. It was a repulsive, riveting and astounding feat.

Participants in the annual World Hamburger Eating Championships had sought to persuade me that competitive eating was a sport requiring extraordinary physical ability and mental toughness.

Finally the buzzer sounded. Mr Chestnut had devoured 91 – 21 more than the world record but six fewer than Mr Kobayashi. 'Awesome', muttered my neighbour.

I felt sure that they would vomit, but they kept going – each bun a triumph of mind over rebellious body.

I was deeply sceptical until I watched the baby-faced wisp from Japan in action. The 13 'gurgitators' lined up, the MC counted down, and they were off – a blur of flying hands, bobbing heads and gaping gullets.

Within five minutes both had smashed the previous record of 69, and the 3000 spectators were roaring.

The Times, *27 June 2007*

Types of structures in written texts

The list-type structure that you saw in the above extract is just one of the discourse structures that written texts might follow. Table 13 lists others that commonly feature in written texts.

Table 13 *Common discourse structures in written texts*

Discourse structure	Key features	Examples
List/instructions	Logical progression through stages, use of imperative verbs to instruct, guide	Recipes, instructions, guides
Problem-solution	Identifies a problem	Product advertisements
Analysis	Breaks down key ideas into constituent parts Evaluates and explores	Academic articles, newspaper editorials
Narrative	Details a series of events, can be chronological or non-chronological	Novels, witness accounts

Extension activity 21

Find examples of texts that fit the structures listed in Table 13 and annotate them for your scrapbook. You may want to revisit the section on lexical connectors on pages 24–25 to look at how these texts use lexical items in order to be coherent.

Discourse analysis

Another key element of the discourse framework looks at how texts present information in order to create identities for particular individuals or institutions, and the ideologies that are often inherent in these. You may like to look again at Text D on page 7 or any of the media texts you have encountered in this section or in the course of your own data collection to consider ways in which this happens. This topic will be dealt with in greater detail in Section B: Language and social contexts.

🔍 ☑ Spoken discourse

This topic deals with the analysis of spoken language in more detail. Section A of Unit 1 will always contain two spoken texts and it is important that you are confident in using accurate linguistic terminology when discussing these and their place within any groupings that you have made. In this topic we will cover both one-speaker (narrative) and multi-speaker (conversational) discourse. Before you read on, it would be a good idea to refer back to some of the ideas discussed on speech and writing at the beginning of this unit (pages 9–16).

One-speaker discourse: analysing oral narratives

Labov's narrative categories

When a speaker talks for an extended period, we can say that he or she is narrating. Most of us would expect a written narrative to have a clear discourse structure. In the same way, we can apply a framework to spoken narratives, which may involve quite detailed storytelling. The sociolinguist William Labov put forward a six-part structure for oral narrative, based on his extensive fieldwork in New York, analysing oral accounts of narrative events. The **narrative categories** below are listed in the order they would be expected to appear in a narrative.

■ **Abstract (A)** – the indication that a narrative is about to start and the speaker wants a listener's attention.

Key terms

Narrative categories: six key categories developed by Labov which appear in a narrative – generally in a set order.

■ **Orientation (O)** – the 'who', 'where', 'what' and 'why' of the narrative. This sets the scene and provides further contextual information for the listener.

■ **Complicating action (CA)** – the main body providing a range of narrative detail.

■ **Resolution (R)** – the final events, the 'rounding off' to give the narrative closure.

■ **Evaluation (EV)** – additions to the basic story, to highlight attitudes or to command the listener's attention at important moments.

■ **Coda (C)** – a sign that the narrative is complete. This might include a return to the initial time frame before the narrative.

A narrative may not contain all of the above. Also, **evaluation** may occur at any point, as shown in Figure 9.

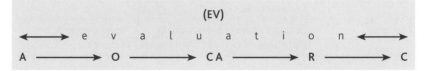

Fig. 9 *Labov's narrative categories*

> ### Classroom activity 30
>
> Text BB is a short narrative and is a speaker's recollection of a childhood holiday. Try to annotate it using Labov's categories. What other language features are present?
>
> See page 196 for feedback on this activity.

Text BB

> From the age of two every single year we used to travel down (.) in my dad's Ford Popular (.) with myself and my sister and my brother in the back to go and stay at my nan and grandad's they used to have a (.) cottage (.) in Cornwall (1) near Redruth that was two miles from another house (.) we used to have sheep and cows and chicken and geese (.) and the whole (.) six weeks that we used to spend there we used to play on the fields (.) and on the farm and just er have so much fun that was about four miles from the nearest beach so er (.) we used to go down and play on the beach and er play with the sand and the cliffs and in the er (1) in the caves that they used to have down there (1) we used to have about twenty cows on the farm and we used to try to name every single one (.) and we would try to ride them like horses er and try and jump on their backs and see how fast we could go on them which wasn't very fast at all (2) every morning we used to have to go down and fetch fresh water from the stream because they had no water (.) that you could drink in the cottage (.) they just about had electricity where we used to go (.) we used to take big urns down the road down to where the stream was and just (.) collect the fresh water and bring it all the way back (3) My grandad used to work on the railway so he used to go into Camborne or Redruth where he was stationed and then work on the railways in the daytime my nan run the farm (1) my dad used to sometimes leave us there it seemed like it took us all day to get there cos it was I suppose in a Ford Popular (.) it used to be about twenty (.) twenty five miles an hour with no motorways and just stopping every now and again for a cup of tea and letting us out for a break (2) it (1) it was just a different world.

More on evaluations

It is possible to divide evaluations into two types: **external evaluations**, which are often added by the narrator at the time of recounting and are not usually part of the sequence of events, for example:

- 'This is an incredible story.'
- 'Now I'm getting to the good part.'
- 'It makes me laugh when I think of it now.'

and **internal evaluations**, which have occurred at the same time as those detailed in the complicating action. Internal evaluations can be divided into a number of different types, including:

- **intensifying evaluation** – contributing vividness via gestures, repetitions or dramatic sounds:

  Fred ran into a wall, *ouch!*

- **explicative evaluation** – providing reasons for narrative events:

  Fred annoyed his mum, because he was always noisy.

Extension activity 22

Oral narratives will often not neatly fit into Labov's pattern. Collect some data by recording speakers reminiscing about their childhood, as in Classroom activity 30.

- Can you discover any patterns based on their age or gender?
- Are there differences depending on what is being discussed?

These would be good items for your scrapbook and to discuss in pairs or groups to see if wider patterns are emerging. You should also record and transcribe television and radio talk shows to see what narrative patterns emerge. Again, add these annotated examples to your scrapbook.

Labov's categories can also be applied to written texts in a similar way, for example Text BB in Classroom activity 30. You might like to apply this framework explicitly to that text and to other texts that you have collected and annotated in your scrapbook.

The analysis of conversation

Conversational analysis (CA) provides a framework for looking at multi-speaker discourse. This is largely based on the concept of the conversational turn and the basic consequence of that turn, the **adjacency pair**, which forms an **exchange structure**.

The exchange structure below is a simple example of an adjacency pair integrating an example of **turn-taking**. This question–answer structure is one of the most common examples of an adjacency pair.

> Context: A and C are walking together and A notices B.
>
> **A**: *Good morning, how are you?*
>
> **B**: *Fine thank you!*

Conversations, as you will know, are rarely this straightforward. Often speakers will insert information at various points to create a larger exchange structure. This can be in the form of a triadic structure known

Key terms

External evaluation: an evaluative comment outside the narrative sequence.

Internal evaluation: an evaluative comment occurring at the same time as events in the narrative sequence.

Intensifying evaluation: adding detail and vividness.

Explicative evaluation: explaining reasons for narrative events.

Conversational analysis: the analysis of the structure and features of conversation.

Adjacency pair: two utterances by different speakers which have a natural and logical link, and complete an idea together; a simple structure of two turns.

Exchange structure: a series of turns between speakers.

Turn-taking: the sharing of speaking roles, usually cooperatively.

Initiation–response–feedback (IRF): a triadic structure in speech that allows the first speaker to feed back on the response of a second speaker.

Insertion sequence: an additional sequence in the body of an exchange structure.

Transition relevance point: a point at which it is natural for another speaker to take a turn.

Topic management: the control of the conversation in terms of speaking and topic.

Powerful participants: those who hold some degree of status in a conversation and can to some extent control its direction and the potential of speakers to contribute.

■ **Link**

The topic Language and power in Section B Language and social contexts will deal more fully with this important aspect of conversational analysis.

as **initiation–response–feedback (IRF)**, for example if A responded to B by saying 'Good, I'm pleased that everything is OK!' or as in the example below, which contains another element called an **insertion sequence**.

> **A**: [to B] *Good morning, how are you?*
>
> **A**: [to C who has begun to walk off] *See you later tonight.*
>
> **C**: *OK.*
>
> **B**: *Fine, thank you! You?*
>
> **A**: *Yeah pretty good.*

In this example, A inserts an additional sequence (to C) into the dialogue before B has a chance to complete the original turn before initiating another sequence with the question 'You?', which A completes to formulate the adjacency pair.

Taking turns and keeping control

Knowing when to take a turn is crucial and natural in conversation. There are often points when a speaker will know that he or she is expected to speak, for example when being asked a question. Other **transition relevance points** can occur as a consequence of natural pauses or a complete break on the part of a speaker to allow another to speak. The decision as to what gets talked about is termed **topic management** and is often a result of **powerful participants** applying constraints on what gets said and who says it, including the use of interruptions. On the other hand, speakers cooperate through a range of structural and linguistic features and as we saw in the topic Pragmatics, cooperation is normally considered as a prerequisite for effective communication.

■ **Extension activity 23**

Interviews are a good place to start looking at conversational analysis. You could collect data from television and radio interviews (chat shows, current-affairs programmes, political interviews) and consider their structure in the light of your learning.

You could also begin to explore some of the ways in which topic management is secured and maintained and speakers cooperate with each other.

All the data you collect should be annotated and added to your scrapbook.

Other features of spoken discourse

Table 14 lists other common features of spoken discourse.

■ **Classroom activity 31**

Using all of your learning from this topic, identify as many features of spoken discourse as you can from Text CC on page 56. To what extent are these features influenced by contextual factors?

AQA **Examiner's tip**

When we speak of grammar, we often think solely of written discourse. Spoken language also has a grammatical structure that can be described using the terminology covered in this topic. Remember that we are using the term 'grammar' in a descriptive, not prescriptive sense. It would be wrong to label any spoken language as ungrammatical.

Table 14 *Common features of spoken discourse*

Discourse feature	Description	Examples
Back-channelling	A feature of speaker support: non-verbal utterances to show attention or agreement	*Mmm, yeah, OK*
Discourse marker	Signal a shift in conversation and topic areas. Can also announce a counter-argument	*OK, right then, so, but*
Fillers	Non-verbal sounds that can act as pauses in speech, either naturally or to give a speaker thinking time. May signal speaker uncertainty	*Er, um*
Hedging	A strategy used to avoid directness or to minimise a potentially face-threatening act. Also commonly undertaken using a range of epistemic modal forms	*Kind of, sort of, maybe, perhaps, possibly* and modal verbs such as *will, could, might*
False starts/repairs	False starts are when a speaker begins to speak, pauses then recommences A repair returns to correct a previously stated phrase or sentence	*It began er Arsenal kicked off the second half* (false start *it began*) *He sorry she broke the vase* (repair *she* from *he*)
Skip connectors	A return to a previous topic of conversation, essentially a type of discourse marker	*Anyway, coming back to our original discussion*
Fixed expressions	A conventional and routine expression in colloquial communication, sometimes metaphorical. Listen to any football interview and you'll hear a range of these!	*As a matter of fact, basically, at the end of the day*
Vague expressions	Similar to hedging, deliberately non-committal expressions in informal contexts	*Anything, something, thing*
Ellipsis	Omission of words for economical purposes, as appropriate to informal contexts or to avoid awkward repetition. Spoken discourse may contain many different types of elliptical structures	*Just seen Jack* (ellipsis *I've*). *Return to Paddock Wood please* (ellipsis *I'd like to buy*). *Tonight, 8pm* (ellipsis *I'll meet you… at…*)
Tag questions	These consist of an auxiliary verb, a negating particle and a pronoun, and can be a sign of speaker support, uncertainty (similar to hedging) or a request for clarification	*You did really well* **didn't you?** *It was tomorrow* **wasn't it?** *I've missed that train* **haven't I?**
Deixis	Pointing words in a perceptual, temporal or spatial dimension. Deictic referencing is common in spoken discourse	*I, you, me, they.* *Now, yesterday, today.* *Here, there, this, that, these, those*
Non-fluency features	Non-verbal occurrences	Pauses, hesitations and repetitions that occur in spontaneous speech

Text CC

Context: this is the opening of a phone call between two friends, Juliane and Maureen.

> Key
> (.) Indicates a brief pause.
> Numbers within brackets indicate length of pause in seconds.
> Underlining indicates emphasis in speech.
> Words between vertical lines are spoken simultaneously
> Relevant contextual information is given within square brackets.
>
> ***Maureen***: hi Juliane
> ***Juliane***: Maureen (.) hold on a mo (1) I'm just er finishing this er work off
> ***Maureen***: okay [laughs] do you want me to call you back
> ***Juliane***: no it's fine, you know how it is (.) got to get it done (.) did you manage to get the tickets
> ***Maureen***: well (.) there's a problem (1) he couldn't ‖ get them ‖
> ***Juliane***:   ‖ you're <u>joking</u> ‖
> ***Maureen***: afraid not
> ***Juliane***: well he said that (.) it wouldn't be difficult (.) would it
> ***Maureen***: I think there's been a mix up somewhere (.) you know (.) with that email he sent (.) it's not the date they told him (.) they actually went on sale <u>yesterday</u> and they haven't got (.) they've sold out
> ***Juliane***: so now we can't go
> ***Maureen***: we can't go (.) unless you can ask that guy you know (.) do you (.) can you
> ***Juliane***: I don't know (.) he's like really busy I could ask but (.) you know it's gonna be difficult now (.) so late and all that (.) I'll see what I can do (.) but (.) it's very short notice you know
> ***Maureen***: sorry ‖ I didn't ‖
> ***Juliane***:   ‖ nothing ‖ you could have done (.) not to worry (.) <u>basically</u> can't see it happening now though

---

💡 **Extension activity 24**

If you have access to a small recorder or have a mobile phone with a recording device, you can begin to collect spoken data of your own as well as looking to television and radio for examples. This is an excellent way of developing your data-collecting skills in anticipation of further work in Section B Language and social contexts and your A2 units (particularly your A2 language investigation). There are some important things to remember when collecting spoken data:

▪ Think about your choice of subjects carefully. It may be tempting to record hours of talk from the sixth-form common room, but will it yield interesting results?

▪ To avoid the observer's paradox (the fact that telling someone that s/he is being recorded will inevitably affect and influence what that person says), do not announce that a recording is taking place. However, you must ask for permission to use your data from those on the recording afterwards. When openly interviewing people, remember that some speakers may be a little nervous!

▪ Include notes and references on who is speaking so that you can identify speakers as you transcribe afterwards.

When you transcribe data, you also need to bear in mind contextual features such as movements and actions, and mark pauses and hesitations. Generally, the following notation will suffice:

- (.) to indicate a brief pause.
- (2) indicates a longer pause with the number of seconds in brackets.
- [*demonstrates*] place actions and movements in italics and in square brackets.
- || mark overlaps in conversation with a set of vertical lines.

For a more detailed set of guidelines on recording and transcription, see Wray, et al. *Projects in Linguistics: A Practical Guide to Researching Language*, Chapters 12, 15 and 18.

Grouping texts: using the frameworks

You should remember that the frameworks are there to support your interpretative comments and ensure that your ideas can be clearly followed by another reader, teacher or examiner. It is also important to remember that language frameworks do not exist in isolation; rather a text's impact relies on a number of different linguistic features interacting with you as a reader to give a sense of meaning. Many texts that you encounter will be multi-modal ones, that is, they rely on a number of different communicative systems (the visual, the verbal, the aural) to express their meaning.

■ Further reading

General

Carter, R., Goddard, A., Reah, D., Sanger, K. and Bowring, M. *Working with Texts: A Core Book for Language Analysis*, Routledge, 2001

Crystal, D. *The Cambridge Encyclopedia of the English Language*, Cambridge University Press, 1995

Simpson, P. *Stylistics: A resource book for students*, Routledge, 2004

Wray, A., Trott, K. and Bloomer, A. *Projects in Linguistics: A Practical Guide to Researching Language*, Arnold, 2004 (a range of topics with some excellent ideas for further research and data collection)

Discourse

Carter, R. 'Language at full stretch – analysing spoken English', *emagazine* 22, 2003 (an excellent and very accessible article on the grammar of spoken language)

Carter, R. *Language and Creativity, The Art of Common Talk*, Routledge, 2004

Goddard, A. *The Language of Advertising*, Routledge, 1998

Textual analysis

The following articles are good recent examples of analyses of a range of texts using the language frameworks:

Bleiman, B. 'Cold Mountain – exploring the language of prose', *emagazine* 30, 2005

Clayton, D. 'The real cost – analysing a charity ad', *emagazine* 36, 2007

Farndon, B. 'Stoprevivesurvive – Australian road signs', *emagazine* 27, 2005

Giovanelli, M. 'Small packet, big eat: tearing open a bag of crisps', *emagazine* 24, 2004

Examination preparation and practice

☑

In this topic you will:

- learn about the requirements of the assessed task on Section A

- develop your ability to think about the grouping of texts using interactive tools

- explore applying your learning from this section and have opportunities to assess your work against assessment criteria.

💡 🔍 ↻ The examination question

The question below is like the one that you will face in the examination on Section A of Unit 1. Read it carefully and look at the tips given to you to explain what the examiner will be looking for.

1 Study Texts A–F on pages 58–62. These texts illustrate **different** varieties of language use.

> 'different varieties' informs you that you will be expected to consider a whole range of texts in a similar way to those you have encountered in this book

Discuss **various** ways in which these texts can be grouped, giving **linguistic** reasons for your choices.

> 'various ways' means that you will need to consider a number of possible ways of grouping these texts and consider some of the problems inherent in attempting to classify texts

> 'linguistic reasons' means that you will need to use an appropriate and correct linguistic terminology and explain your ideas through reference to the language frameworks

Text A

This is a page from user guide to Hewlett Packard printer (PSC1510)

Print from a software application

Most print settings are automatically handled by the software application you are printing from or by HP ColorSmart technology. You need to change the settings manually only when you change print quality, print on specific types of paper or transparency film, or use special features.

To print from the software application you used to create your document (Windows)
1. Make sure you have paper loaded in the paper tray.
2. On the **File** menu in your software application, click **Print**.
3. Select the HP All-in-One as the printer.
4. If you need to change settings, click the button that opens the **Properties** dialog box.
   Depending on your software application, this button might be called **Properties**, **Options**, **Printer Setup**, **Printer**, or **Preferences**.
5. Select the appropriate options for your print job by using the features available in the **Paper/Quality**, **Finishing**, **Effects**, **Basics**, and **Color** tabs.

> 💡 **Tip** You can easily select the appropriate options for your print job by choosing one of the predefined print tasks on the **Printing Shortcuts** tab. Click a type of print task in the **What do you want to do?** list. The default settings for that type of print task are set, and summarized on the **Printing Shortcuts** tab. If necessary, you can adjust the settings here, or you can make your changes on the other tabs in the **Properties** dialog box.

6. Click **OK** to close the **Properties** dialog box.
7. Click **Print** or **OK** to begin printing.

To print from the software application you used to create your document (Mac)
1. Make sure you have paper loaded in the paper tray.

Print from your computer

Text B

This is an extract from a Further Education prospectus for Hadlow College.

10 REASONS TO CHOOSE HADLOW COLLEGE

1. Practical experience in an outdoor classroom – hands on training from day one! The College comprise of a 256 hectare estate encompassing a range of habitats, farms, woods, plant collections, gardens, paddocks and pastures. All these facilities enable students to learn a wide range of land-based subjects.

2. Supportive people – our staff are dedicated, enthusiastic and passionate about their students and their subjects which makes Hadlow College a friendly place to study!

3. High quality education with an international reputation – Hadlow College is one of the UK's top 3 specialist colleges and welcomes students from across the world.

4. Location – Hadlow College lies in tranquil rural countryside, just 40 minutes from central London and the south coast.

5. Students – our student population is very diverse, attracting people from 7 to 70 years of age and different backgrounds, Hadlow College has something for everyone.

6. Courses – our expertise and experience of over 40 years working with land-based industries has enabled us to develop innovative courses to meet the needs of tomorrow's industry.

7. Gain the skills employers need – all of our courses are tailored to careers in the land-based industries and involve a high degree of work experience. We actively engage with a range of employers to ensure our courses offer what they need for their future workforce.

8. Flexible study – we recognise the importance form many people of being about to work and study in parallel so the majority of our courses can be studies on a part time basis.

9. Value for money – we believe our courses represent excellent value for money in the competitive education market.

10. Enjoyment – above all, studying should be fun and our students tell us they enjoy their time at Hadow College with many recommending us to their friends!

Text C

This is a Seat car advertisement entitled 'Different rituals, same spirit'.

Text D

This is a poem from a collection written for teenagers.

BIRTHRIGHTS

☆ **Baby** *is* a SUPERSTAR
She really **luvs** de stage
She's **HOT**
She's *cool*
Yu **cannot** guess her age,
Baby *is* a SUPERSTAR
Don't tell *her* wot to do
She's **safe**
She's **GREAT**
She's very much *like you*.
Baby *is* a SUPERSTAR
So tek a picture *quick*
She *shines*
She's fine
So very *poetic*,
Baby *is* a SUPERSTAR
She **sings**, she **plays**, she *writes*
Let's **listen** to her freedom songs
She's in *concert* tonight.

25

Benjamin Zephaniah, 'Birthrights', Funky Chickens, 1997, p25

Text E

This is an extract from a weather bulletin on BBC Radio 4.

Key
(.) Indicates a brief pause.
Numbers within brackets indicate length of pause in seconds.

Well Peter we're all holding our breath (.) will it rain or will it shine and the answer to that question will come after the end of this forecast for the short term and we have some big contrasts across (.) the country today most areas are seeing in fact some (1) warm sunshine however the exception is in the south east of England here it's cloudy damp very unpleasant quite frankly with er some rain as well so it really is er (1) parts of Kent Essex into East Anglia as well where it'll stay like that for most of the day cloudy and drizzly that is and only sixteen degrees on the Kent coast (.) as far as the Midlands and the South West of the country are concerned that is across England (.) er here lovely weather temperatures up to twenty-four degrees Celsius it really does feel like summer (.) for Wales apart from the western fringes of Wales (.) er where it's a little bit on the hazy side on the whole we're looking at clear blue skies for the rest of the day across the bulk of Wales and temperatures in Cardiff could get up to twenty-four degrees.

Text F

This is a transcript between two boys (A and B) and a girl (C) who are playing a game building a tower out of spaghetti.

Key
(.) Indicates a brief pause.
Numbers within brackets indicate length of pause in seconds.
Words between vertical lines are spoken simultaneously.
Other contextual information is in italics in square brackets.

A: right let's get some spaghetti
B: yeah
C: spaghetti! [*laughs*]
B: we won't need (1) get rid of that
A: right we need a base first ‖ so it's   ‖
B: ‖ so do a triangle base ‖
A: yeah so ‖ that's there ‖ so we need another one there
B: ‖ that's there ‖
B: twoooo then
C: what are you doing?
A: right do a triangle base
B: then that ‖ needs   ‖
A: ‖ you need to go like that don't you? ‖
C: right then we'll have another one here (.) er (2) oops [*laughs*]
A: get 'nother bit of spaghetti
B: spaghettiiiiii
A: spaghetti (1) ah go for it go for it (.) argh and it's a triumph [*waves arms*]

Student's response

My first grouping is between Texts B, C and D, as all make extensive use of graphological features. However, while C consists of a large image which dominates the page (to grab the audience's attention), B and D's use of image is relatively minor – although multi-modal, these texts rely mainly on writing.

Text C also features a four-part list consisting of four imperative verbs, 'check… check… check… operate'. The homonym 'operate' is used meaning that its implication is ambiguous, as it belongs both to the lexical field of surgery, and the lexical field of action – however, as the writing underneath, 'Michael… Assistant Surgeon' suggests that 'operate' is meant to be understood in medical terms, this gives the car a sense of precision.

Through its rigidly structured layout and use of specialist register such as '17 alloys' and 'impressive 1.8 20V T 150PS engine', Text C has a greater degree of formality than B and D; this is arguably because both B and D were meant to appeal to a mainly teenage audience.

Indeed, this is reflected in the graphological features of Text D, which uses informal pop-art style illustration. This is appealing to its implied audience as it makes the poem look less daunting to read. This purpose of using image is in contrast to Text B, which uses a small picture of teenagers at the college being described, in order to convey how the college is a friendly, multi-age and -background environment, and shows that the people there are enjoying themselves; this helps B to fulfil its purpose of persuading the audience to join the college. Text B also fulfils its purpose by using the inclusive first-person plural pronoun 'we', which further helps to suggest that the college is a friendly place; like a big happy family. Text D, however, uses typographical variation within the poem to further fulfil its purpose of being entertaining and appealing to its audience; the variation in fonts emphasises certain words, and also gives them connotations, for example 'age' is in an archaic font.

I have decided to group Texts D, E and F, as they all share elements of spoken discourse. E and F can further be linked by the fact that they are obviously of the spoken mode – however, E is monologic, whereas F is dialogic. This difference between E and F means that crucial differences are evident between them: E demonstrates use of fillers such as 'er', which conventionally occur in monologues as a way of the speaker allowing him/herself time to think what to say, without leaving a conscious silence. In contrast, F does not feature any fillers; instead it makes use of traditional conversational techniques, for example the overlapping that occurs between person A and B; 'so it's' and 'so do a triangle base'. This is an expected feature in a text where the emphasis of the task is on collaboration.

Here Nicola introduces her first group but immediately draws attention to the fact that there are differences within the group, which she points out.

These comments show a more developed discussion of the properties of Text C using accurate and controlled expression and terminology (AO1).

Nicola continues her discussion on her first grouping by drawing attention to further differences between the texts with a clear linguistic approach (AO2) in conjunction with an understanding of the likely context of reception and readership (AO3).

There is more sustained discussion here using the graphology framework (AO1), which moves beyond merely feature-spotting to consider the effect of use of image and font. There is more clear engagement with contextual factors such as audience and purpose (AO3).

Nicola's next grouping recognises that typical aspects of spoken discourse may vary according to the type and context of speech (AO2 and AO3). Again, she shows secure linguistic terminology and maintains a strong comparative focus within her grouping.

Nicola's points here are sound, even if she generalises on written texts being more formal than spoken ones. Again, she is continually drawing attention to differences within her grouping (AO2).

There are some insightful points here about standard and non-standard forms, in particular the comments related to technology and audience (AO2). In addition, Nicola shows that she understands the contextual factors governing the register of Texts D and E (AO3).

Nicola's grouping here switches to purpose and, again, she immediately draws attention to crucial differences within the group. She shows accurate and perceptive linguistic knowledge (AO1) in her analyses of the use of noun phrases and carefully considers the inclusion and impact of lexical items in the light of the context of production (AO3).

Although this section is weaker and undeveloped in places, there are still some valid comments on lexis here and Nicola maintains a secure use of precise linguistic terminology (AO1).

Texts E and F are different to D, in that D is a poem that initially appears as a written text, although its strong emphasis on features of spoken discourse mean that it is likely to be read aloud (it is a performance poem). Such features include the fact that elliptical constructions such as 'she's' are used, which are conventionally associated with speech, as written discourse tends to have a greater degree of formality.

Text D also uses non-standard spelling, for instance 'luvs', 'tek' and 'wot'. 'Wot' and 'luvs' are words that would usually be used by teenagers in such modes as texting, as a time- and space-saving device. It is significant for the poem to make use of this, as its intended audience is teenagers: therefore using their type of language would further increase the likelihood of teenagers being attracted to the piece and enjoying it. The word 'tek', however, is more likely to have been used as a sign of dialect or accent, thus making the text authentic due to the phonetic spelling of the word 'take': it is also colloquial. This use of dialect or accent in Text D is different to E; because of E's context as a radio broadcast, dialect would not feature: as Radio 4 is broadcast worldwide, it needs to be understood universally – therefore, presenters would normally use Standard English, as the presenter does in Text E.

My next grouping is Texts B and C, as both have a purpose to persuade. However, their methods in addressing their purposes are different, as the genres of the texts differ: C is an advertisement, whereas B was extracted from a prospectus. Text B makes extensive use of pre-modified noun phrases, such as ' high quality education' and 'international reputation' and prepositional phrases, for instance 'in tranquil rural countryside' giving the impression that the college is a renowned place with many positive attributes; thus persuading the reader to join the college. Adjectives such as 'dedicated', 'enthusiastic' and 'passionate' ensure that the reader understands the value of learning, and makes it seem as if the teachers at the college are the best. In fact the prospectus acts as an advertising tool for the college and so this kind of persuasive technique is important to attract new students.

Text C also makes use of adjectives, although not as extensively – 'the sporty Ibiza FR' is an example. However, C mainly relies on the four-part list, as already mentioned, and the idea that driving is like surgery: that to drive this car requires meticulousness and precision – indeed the last sentence, '…you may feel inclined… before releasing the clutch' implies that this car is like nothing else, that it is special and superior to any other car, that the experience you would get by driving it is incomparable to any other driving experience; it implies that there is something special about the car, and that it needs special handling.

The collaborative pronoun 'we' is used throughout Text B, creating the impression that the college is a friendly environment in which the tutors and students will work together to get the end result – however, Text C instead makes use of the personal pronoun 'you', which is emphasised by the use of modal verbs such as 'may', and imperative verbs such as 'check', which work together to create the experience you would have if you bought the car.

My final grouping is Texts C, A and E, as they all use specialist lexis. It is evident that A makes the greatest use of specialist lexis (such as 'ColorSmart technology' and 'File menu'), which can be explained by the fact that the text is context bound: it would only be read if the person had bought the printer and was reading the manual; it is not something that could potentially occur almost anywhere, as C and E are. Text C is an advertisement, and would usually be found in a variety of sources, including magazines, newspapers and even billboards. In order to address a wider audience, the text uses a minimal amount of specialist lexis; concentrating on using specialist lexis would restrict its audience.

For instance, Text C was found in *Cosmopolitan* magazine, a magazine for women, and so specialist lexis would be kept to a minimum, as women are stereotypically thought to not understand terminology to do with cars. However, C does still use specialist lexis, such as, 'the impressive 1.8 20V T 150PS engine' – but this specialist lexis being modified by the adjective 'impressive' means that women automatically understand this to be a positive feature of the car. By contrast, A assumes that the reader knows what is being referred to by the use of specialist lexis; for instance '...summarized on the Printing Shortcuts tab', as people would generally be using the manual whilst attempting to fulfil the task; they would be able to see the 'Printing Shortcuts tab' on their computer.

Text E is different to both C and A as it is a spoken discourse that would be heard on the radio. Text E uses specialist language such as 'twenty-four degrees Celsius' in order to convey information to the audience, which is comparable to Text A. However, it is also comparable to Text C in that it assumes the audience knows what is meant by '...degrees Celsius', and does not explain; of course, it is a generic term that most people are familiar with.

> Nicola's comments here, again, show insight into the influence of contextual factors (AO3).

> Although some of the first comments are a little clumsy, Nicola is evaluating and engaging with contextual factors (AO3) and understands the reasons for the more specialised lexis in Texts C and E.

Examiner's overall comments

Nicola offers a number of valid and interesting groupings with the use of accurate and perceptive linguistic knowledge and accurate and controlled expression (AO1). She develops her ideas on her groups in some detail (AO2), although at times she could focus more on some of the more complex differences between texts in her groups. Nicola shows a clear understanding of a range of contextual factors and supports her comments and interpretations well (AO3). These qualities would place her work within the 15–16 band for AO1 and high in the 11–14 band for AO2 and AO3.

Introduction

In this section you will:

- understand the demands of Section B and the kinds of focuses you will be exploring in your studies

- develop your expertise in analysing data and commenting on language using linguistic terminology

- explore the ways in which written and spoken texts can be explored in conjunction with theoretical ideas about power, gender and technology

- have the opportunity to work on the kinds of texts that might appear in an examination question on this unit.

Section B gives you an opportunity to study three topic areas in depth: language and gender; language and power; and language and technology, using and building on the skills you have acquired from Section A. In Section A you explored how your own language use has been influenced by the various *discourse communities* to which you belong and considered some of the ways in which you might adapt your language according to *contextual demands*. You also looked at how we might make *assumptions* about language use, for example in the way we perceive differences between speakers of different social classes, age, race and gender, and considered how assumptions can easily turn into *attitudes* that we hold. These attitudes were explored in conjunction with how groups of people are *represented*.

These focuses on influence, assumptions, attitudes and representation remain a concern in this section. In addition, we will look at how writers and speakers engage in communication with an eye to establishing and/or maintaining *social relationships* and *hierarchies* and will investigate varieties of language that are seen as markers of *cooperation* and *difference* amongst users of different *social status* and *gender*, considering to what extent these are conditioned and shaped by external social factors. Finally, we will look at another powerful influence on the ways in which humans use language either individually or as members of discourse communities: new and rapidly growing technologies.

It is also worth highlighting some important points to remember as you begin your learning in this section. Firstly, the emphasis on language as a social phenomenon is demonstrated in the importance attached in this section to AO3:

- AO3: Analyse and evaluate the influence of contextual factors on the production and reception of spoken and written language.

Secondly, although there is only one question on this section, you are strongly advised to study all the topics in detail. For not only is there a significant degree of overlap in content and skills, but in studying all of the topics, you will ensure that you have a thorough basis for the more advanced study that you will undertake at A2 Level.

Lastly, you should maintain the collecting of your own data in your scrapbook. Indeed, whilst you will be presented with a great deal of published research and theoretical ideas, it is your own ability to investigate and analyse that will illuminate your study and help you develop a good understanding of these topics.

AQA Examiner's tip

As you work through this section, remember to focus on analysing and evaluating the influence of contextual factors. As you maintain your scrapbook, you should make a note of the contexts surrounding your data to help you practise this.

Language and power

In this topic you will:

- understand how we might classify different types of power and how these impact on linguistic choices and behaviours

- consider and explore how written texts are representative of power relations and the exercising of powerful ideological stances

- explore how powerful speakers exert power and authority over less powerful ones in spoken discourse

- analyse how texts aim to influence and persuade.

Key terms

Political power: power held by those with the backing of the law.

Personal power: power held by individuals as a result of their roles in organisations.

Social group power: power held as a result of being a member of a dominant social group.

Instrumental power: power used to maintain and enforce authority.

Influential power: power used to influence or persuade others.

Power in discourse: the ways in which power is manifested in situations through language.

Power behind discourse: the focus on the social and ideological reasons behind the enactment of power.

Ideology: a set of belief systems, attitudes or a world view held by an individual or groups.

Classroom activity 1

What does it mean to be powerful? Think of the speech or discourse communities to which you belong, and identify the most powerful participants of each one. What is it that gives them certain degrees of power, authority and influence over others? How might this be evident in their language?

See page 196 for feedback on this activity.

One way of classifying types of power, according to Wareing (1999) is in terms of whether they represent **political**, **personal** or **social group power**. These may be summarised as shown in Table 1.

Table 1 *Types of power*

Type of power	Example
Political	That held by politicians, the police and those working in the law courts
Personal	Those who hold power as a result of their occupation or role, such as teachers and employers
Social group	Those who hold power as a result of social variables such as class, gender and age. Typically (though not exclusively) white, middle-class men hold positions of power

In addition, power may be either **instrumental**, when it is used by individuals or groups to maintain and enforce authority, or **influential**, when it is used to influence and persuade others.

Another useful set of terms is that described by Fairclough (2001), who distinguishes between **power in discourse** and **power behind discourse**. The former is concerned with situations where power relationships are set up and enacted, whilst the latter is concerned with the organisation of institutions and the *effects* of those power relations on various uses of language. These distinctions provide different but complementary ways of approaching sets of data. Whilst an approach that focuses on power in discourse might look at actual language use and how power is exercised linguistically, considering power behind discourse provides a way of contextualising linguistic features according to wider ideologies, hierarchical structures and power relationships that shape language use.

Ideology refers to the belief systems, attitudes and world views that an individual or collective might hold, which are displayed through the use of language. A text producer may attempt to project a certain series of beliefs on to a text receiver who is positioned as an implied or ideal reader so that they are invited to share these ways of thinking about the world. These are often in the form of specific lexical choices that express a point of view, for example the choice of *terrorist* over *freedom fighter*, but they can be found through graphological and grammatical constructions. 'Ideology' is sometimes only used in a political sense; it should be remembered that although many ideological stances are political ones, the true definition of the term is much broader.

Some linguists such as Norman Fairclough place a key focus on the inextricable link between language and society and see all texts as being underpinned by strong ideological perspectives. This branch of study, called critical linguistics or critical discourse analysis, contends that no example of language use is ever completely neutral, but always contains elements of some ideological and often controlling viewpoint.

Classroom activity 2

Re-read the theoretical section above and consider whether each of your examples from Classroom activity 1 is an example of *political*, *personal* or *social group* power and whether that power is *instrumental* or *influential*.

Power in written texts

Written texts contain many examples of language that is used to exert power and authority. The following examples will allow you to explore a variety of written texts where text producers exert power to apply restrictions on and to persuade their readers.

Text A is an example of a standard set of legal disclaimers that appeared on the reverse side of a loyalty coupon offered by a leading supermarket chain.

Text A

TESCO   TESCO   TESCO

• Tesco Clubcard coupons are and shall remain the property of Tesco Stores Limited, have no cash redemption value, are not for resale or publication and are valid in the UK and IOM only. • Copied, damaged or defaced coupons will not be accepted. • Hand this coupon to the checkout operator along with your Tesco Clubcard to receive the benefits overleaf. • Coupons can only be redeemed once and must be redeemed by the person to whom they were issued. • eCoupons can only be redeemed online and only one eCoupon starting XX, CC, TDX or TFX valid per transaction. • See online for eCoupon terms and conditions. • Points from extra points coupons will be added to your next Statement. • Purchases of tobacco products, Esso fuels, Café, lottery products, E top-up, prescription medicines, infant formulae milk and gift cards are excluded. • Age restrictions may apply. • Customers must be 18 years or over to purchase alcohol.

Given that customers would receive this as part of a loyalty promotion in which they are being rewarded for shopping at a particular store, the text contains a number of constraints. All but two of the sentences are in the declarative mood, signalling authority and a lack of ambiguity. The two imperative sentences detail exactly what the customer needs to do to benefit from this promotion. Equally important is the choice of verb processes, which are summarised below.

■ Extensive use of *modal auxiliary verbs*, which detail the conditions of use. These range from **epistemic modality** such as *shall* and *will*, which strongly clarify any elements of possibility, the coupons 'shall remain' and 'defaced coupons *will* not be accepted' to examples of **deontic modality** which express elements of permission, obligation and at the strongest level, requirement. These examples include 'Age restrictions *may* apply' and '(coupons)…*must* be redeemed by the person to whom they were issued'.

Key terms

Epistemic modality: constructions that express degrees of possibility, probability or certainty.

Deontic modality: constructions that express degrees of necessity and obligation.

■ Use of the verb *to be* to add clarity to other forms of control and obligation, for example 'Tesco Clubcard coupons *are* the property of Tesco stores' and 'purchases of tobacco products, Esso fuels... *are* excluded'. Notice here that the complements of the verb processes are the lexical items *property* and *excluded*, which have strong associative meanings related to control and prohibition.

As we saw in Section A (page 33), modal verbal forms often project situations into which the reader is invited. This example of power in action projects a series of situations where the reader/consumer is constrained by the series of restrictions imposed by the text producer/ organisation. These restrictions are in turn the result of legal obligations.

We can also establish a checklist for the kinds of language features that we might draw upon to aid us in our analyses of texts. Table 2 is based on the example above; no doubt you will want to add to this as you progress through this topic and explore data that you have collected for your scrapbook.

Table 2 *Language features checklist*

Language framework	Questions
Discourse	How is the text organised?
	What structural devices are used to assist meaning?
Lexis and semantics	What kinds of vocabulary choices are made?
	What associative meanings exist?
	Which lexical fields dominate?
	What are the relationships between words in terms of synonymy, antonymy and hyponymy?
	What might you say about the formality of the lexical choices?
	How does the text producer use pronouns to establish a relationship with the reader?
Grammar	What kinds of verb processes dominate?
	To what extent are examples of epistemic and deontic modality used?
	Are sentences mainly declarative/imperative?
Pragmatics	What can we say about the relationship between producer and receiver? Implied author and reader?
	What conversational strategies are in operation?
	What implied or shared meanings exist beyond the literal? What ideological assumptions are present?

Classroom activity 3

Using the above analysis as a guide, consider the ways in which power is demonstrated in Text B on page 70, the reverse of a gift voucher. How does the text producer project legal constraints through the language features that are used?

Text B

Gift Card Instructions

How to purchase this card – Simply take this card to any till and tell the staff member how much you want to add to the card. You can pay for the card in the normal way.

How to use this card – You can use this card as full or part payment of any goods at HMV stores in the UK, Isle of Man and Jersey (excluding Selfridges, Harrods and Guernsey). The amount of your purchase will be deducted from the balance on the card.

How to top-up this card – You may want to top-up this card for your own use or for passing on to your family or friends as a gift. Simply present this card at any till point and pay in the normal way.

Balance enquiry – The remaining card balance will be displayed on receipts issued when you use the card to make a purchase or to top it up. You can check your card balance at any time by presenting your card to a staff member at any till.

If you would like help using your card, please ask in-store or contact us on 020 7467 1109 (Mon - Fri 09.00 - 18.00 and Sat 09.00 - 17.15).

Gift Card Terms and Conditions
1. Validly activated cards can be used as full or part payment of any goods at HMV stores throughout the UK, Isle of Man and Jersey (excluding Selfridges, Harrods and Guernsey). No change or refunds will be given but the balance may be applied to future purchases. **2.** The card cannot be used to purchase gift vouchers/additional gift cards and the card (and any card balance) cannot be exchanged for cash, used as a deposit on a credit agreement or to settle an HMV Card Account. **3.** The card is for personal use only and it may not be used for commercial purposes (including but not limited to resale) without HMV's prior written consent. The card is exempt from HMV's Standard Returns Policy. **4.** The minimum amount required to activate or top-up this card is £1 and the maximum card limit is £500. **5.** Only card holders who can prove that they are of the appropriate age can use this card for purchasing any goods which are subject to age restriction. **6.** This card is not a cheque guarantee, credit or debit card. **7.** If the card is not used for a consecutive period of 24 months (whether to make a purchase, top-up or to make a balance enquiry), the card will automatically expire and any remaining balance will be deducted. If the card shows a zero balance and no transaction(s) for a continuous period of 180 days, it will automatically expire at the end of that period. **8.** HMV cannot be held liable for lost, stolen, damaged cards or any credit amounts on such cards. HMV reserves the right to issue another card for the balance of the original card at its discretion on production of your original receipt, but HMV is not responsible for funds used without your knowledge. **9.** HMV reserves the right to add to or waive these terms and conditions on reasonable notice for legal, security or regulatory reasons or to discontinue the gift card scheme at any time in the event of circumstances beyond its reasonable control. Customers will be notified in advance via in-store displays and the HMV website in the event of any such change. **10.** The card may be used as payment for goods of a higher price than the current card balance, on payment of the difference. Over payments, where goods are subsequently exchanged for goods of a lower price, will be added to the balance on the card.

Cards issued by HMV UK Limited, Film House, 142 Wardour Street, London, W1F 8LN.

© HMV UK Limited 2007

KGD13068/V1

Power in advertising

Advertising is one of the most pervasive and powerful phenomena in the 21st century, constantly drawing our attention to products that (so we are told) will add a certain something to our lives. In this way, advertising often works as a projected world that the reader/consumer is invited to become part of. As a by-product of a capitalist economy, advertising is often seen on the one hand as encouraging the private acquisition of goods at the expense of all else and, on the other, as being an essential part of economic prosperity for countries, companies and individuals (Dyer 1982).

According to Fairclough (2001), advertising exists as a prime example of ideology at work through building a relationship between text producer and receiver by constructing a 'product image' that, in turn, helps to position the receiver as a potential 'consumer'. Fairclough's framework for analysing power in advertising texts is applied to Text C overleaf.

Text C

The first stage of Fairclough's model focuses on what he terms 'building relations through personalisation'. In this instance, the text producer's direct imperative address to the reader ('imagine flipping from your music') sets up a relationship in which the text producer is seen as a single human addresser rather than the faceless representative of a corporate organisation. This is maintained through lexical choices such as the second-person pronouns 'your' and 'you' and the implied familiarity with the reader: 'both sides of your personality'. Other lexical items such as 'flipping' and 'special' serve to present the relationship between producer and receiver as both close and complimentary. All these examples represent what Fairclough calls **synthetic personalisation**, a 'trick' to ensure that despite the fact that advertising is received en masse, readers feel that they are being addressed individually by a warm and personable addresser.

The second stage concerns itself with how advertising works in conjunction with a reader's ideological background knowledge in the form of *cognitive* and *cultural models* (what Fairclough calls **members' resources**) to create an *image* of the product being advertised. In our example, the visual elements of the text (using a famous pop star to help) evoke a mental picture or frame of the young and image-conscious individual whose dynamic lifestyle demands the best in new technology. This is supported by the language or verbal cues used, the idea of 'flipping' from music to life suggests a modern, busy lifestyle, where ease of access to music and video are paramount and having a technological appliance to suit that busy lifestyle and changing needs is essential.

Finally, all of this can be seen as *building the consumer*, placing the text receiver in a desired position in relation to the advertiser and advertised product. This means that the receiver is seen as an ideal consumer of the product and in agreement with the ideologies that it presents, in this case, lifestyle. The *implied reader* of this advertisement and, by consequence, the implied consumer of this product is of course the one for whom this particular construction of image and product represents a closeness to their own values and lifestyle. As this advertisement appeared almost exclusively in women's lifestyle magazines, we might assume that this also reaches out predominantly to females. You might want to consider whether this last sentence can be justified by considering graphological, lexical, grammatical and pragmatic features of the text!

This model can be therefore summarised as:

- synthetic personalisation: the construction of a relationship between producer and receiver
- creating an image of a text: using visual and verbal cues to evoke knowledge, behaviour and lifestyle frames
- building the consumer: positioning the receiver as an ideal reader and therefore consumer of this text and product, in line with the text's ideological viewpoint.

■ Classroom activity 4

In order to explore ideology and power in advertising texts and Fairclough's model in more detail, analyse Text D using the suggested framework. This text is an advertisement for Nelson Thornes. You can also collect and explore texts of your own using this model, particularly those that aim to sell a particular 'lifestyle'. Good examples of these would include advertisements for electronic goods, holiday/travel companies and cosmetics.

Text D

Extension activity 1

Undertake a small research project looking at power in written texts in one of the following areas:

- Charity advertisements (you could use Fairclough's model for this and compare the kinds of strategies used in comparison to other types of advertising).

- Newspaper articles or editorials or television/radio reports that are evidence of editors' and journalists' power over the ways in which news is presented to the public. You might like to focus on the assigning of agency or the ways in which implied readers are assumed by the text producers.

- Legal documents/correspondence and/or correspondence from financial institutions and insurance companies where legal restrictions are presented to customers and readers.

- Instructional texts such as product manuals that contain a range of modal constructions. Can you account for the ways in which these are examples of power in action?

Power in spoken discourse

Before you begin to work through this topic, it would be useful to revisit the topics on Pragmatics and Discourse (spoken) in Section A (pages 42–44 and 50–57).

Powerful and less powerful participants

In many instances of spoken discourse, there is a degree of **power asymmetry** between speakers. This is most obvious where one speaker has a higher status or role, for example a judge talking to a defendant or a manager talking to an employee. These power relationships give rise to what may be termed **unequal encounters** (Fairclough 2001), with one speaker seen as the **powerful participant** and others as **less powerful participants** (note that the term *less powerful* rather than *non-powerful* suggests that there may be degrees of power and therefore influence relative to the powerful speaker). In unequal encounters, the normal conventions of turn-taking, such as an individual's ability to select turns and change the topic of conversation, do not operate. Instead, it may be said that powerful participants place **constraints** upon less powerful ones and that these are a direct result of the power relationship between speakers.

A straightforward example may be found in the language of the classroom. Conventionally, the role and status of a teacher set up an established and secure amount of personal and instrumental power in relation to that of the student. This affects the kinds of accepted discourse that can take place in the classroom with the teacher in the role of powerful participant, able to apply constraints upon those less powerful participants, the students. Text E is from the beginning of a lesson on Shakespeare's *Richard III*.

Text E

T: ok in our last lesson we looked at the ways in which Shakespeare presents Richard in his opening soliloquy (.) can anyone summarise what we discovered from our reading

S1: that Richard doesn't like peace and would prefer to be at war

T: good and what does that suggest about how Shakespeare might be presenting him

S1: that he is violent and uncivilised

T: yes and of course in comparison to his brother Edward Richard is unable to function without war and that presents him as an outsider (1) even to his own family(.) right (.) what else did we look at

S2: that Richard is deformed and ugly to look at

T: can you remember that line James

S2: that dogs bark at me

T: and Sarah why might Shakespeare have wanted to present Richard in this way

S3: I don't know

T: who was on the throne when he was writing it

S3: Elizabeth

T: and Elizabeth was

S3: related to Henry VII

T: she was his granddaughter yes so

S3: so Shakespeare would want to show her in a good way or he might be in trouble

T: well done

In this example, there are a number of easy questions in which the teacher presents herself as a powerful participant. First, she establishes an agenda for the lesson by referring back to previous learning and maintains a set discourse structure that is common in classroom interaction, that of an initiation–response–feedback (IRF) model (Coulthard and Sinclair 1975, 1992).

> Initiation: Can anyone summarise what we discovered from our reading
>
> Response: that Richard doesn't like peace…
>
> Feedback: Good and what does that suggest…

The teacher also *selects* the individuals who contribute to the discussion, in two cases by using their names: students cannot contribute unless they are selected by the teacher. Equally, she applies constraints in terms of *content*: students can only comment on *Richard III* and more specifically on their reading of the opening scene during the previous lesson. This control of topic is important in ensuring that the discussion remains *relevant* to the lesson and to the teacher's intended learning objectives. In one instance, the teacher **formulates** S2's response: 'Yes and of course in comparison to his brother Edward…' to provide a more acceptable and developed answer, which may also serve to check or clarify others' understanding. In addition, when S3 is unable to provide a clear answer to the final question, the teacher uses further questioning to *enforce an answer* that is both *explicit* in terms of detail and acceptable to the teacher.

Key terms

Formulation: the rewording of another's contribution by a powerful participant to impose a certain meaning or understanding.

Extension activity 2

1. Explore the language of the classroom by collecting similar data to that above and analysing to what extent the teacher remains a powerful participant in teacher–student interaction.

You may find other examples of teachers applying constraints, for example through interrupting, silencing or reminding students of accepted ways of speaking and behaving. The IRF model has been shown to be structurally more complex than the simple example above suggests.

2. Can you find any variations on this model in your own data, for example in the kinds of questioning that the teacher uses or more detailed responses to students' answers? Explain them in the context of what is happening in the classroom and include your data and comments in your scrapbook.

Classroom activity 5

Other examples of unequal encounters are those involving the legal and medical professions and the police.

Text F on page 76 is an extract from a cross-examination in a Scottish court. The barrister is questioning a witness (Mr Neill) about his involvement with the man on trial (Mr Peterson). Analyse how the barrister places constraints on Mr Neill as an effect of his personal and instrumental power.

Text F

> Key
> (.) Indicates a brief pause.
> Numbers within brackets indicate length of pause in seconds.
> Underlining indicates emphasis in speech.
> Words between vertical lines are spoken simultaneously.
> Relevant contextual information is given within square brackets.
> Bar = barrister.
> Mr N = Mr Neill.
>
> ***Bar***: according to you Mr Neill (.) this ill-feeling (.) this grudge on Mr Peterson's part towards you stemmed from an incident (.) months previously (.) when er you had er (.) done something to to a gate he wanted you to repair a gate
> ***Mr N***: yes
> ***Bar***: is that right what happened to this gate
> ***Mr N***: er I accidentally (.) bumped it slightly with er the rear of my car
> ***Bar***: the rear of your car (.) now (.) did anything happen to you (.) as a result of driving your car that day
> ***Mr N***: (2.5) no
> ***Bar***: did the police come to see you
> ***Mr N***: no I can't remember 'em s-seeing me no
> ***Bar***: you can't remember whether they came to see you or not
> ***Mr N***: I don't think they did no
> ***Bar***: is that because the police have been to see you so many times Mr Neill that you can't remember when they were up to see you about one incident (.) as compared to another incident
> ***Mr N***: [*laughing quietly*] that's not true no
> ***Bar***: and you know very well that the reason why there is ill feeling (.) between you and Mr Peterson is that you believe Mr Peterson shopped you to the police (.) at the time you ran into his garden gate and the police claimed that you were driving with no insurance at the time (.) isn't that right
> ***Mr N***: (1.0) no it's not right
> ***Bar***: so nothing like that happened at all
> ***Mr N***: I was prosecuted (0.5) possibly a week or so later I believe
> ***Bar***: what for
> ***Mr N***: for having no insurance on the car
> ***Bar***: you put two and two together Mr Neill and made five and suspected Mr Peterson of having shopped you to the police for driving a car without insurance
> ***Mr N***: that's not true it's not what I thought no
> ***Bar***: that didn't cross your mind at all
> ***Mr N***: no

Key terms

Face: a person's self-esteem or emotional needs.

Positive face: the need to feel wanted, liked and appreciated.

Negative face: the need to have freedom of thought and action and not feel imposed on.

💡 Politeness in conversation

The idea of **face**, similar to an individual's self-esteem, was first used by Erving Goffman and expanded by the linguists Brown and Levinson to complement their own ideas on politeness theory.

In politeness theory, face can be categorised as either **positive face** or **negative face**. Positive face is an individual's need to feel valued, liked and appreciated, whilst negative face represents an individual's need to not feel imposed on or have their freedom of action threatened.

In everyday communication, there is the potential to *threaten face*, for example in asking someone to carry out a task or in speaking about a sensitive issue that may offend. These situations represent potential **face-threatening acts (FTA)** and a speaker has the choice of a number of different strategies to either minimise the loss of face or save face completely.

As an example, consider a situation where a friend has just bought a copy of the latest album by your favourite band and you (not having managed to obtain a copy due to financial difficulties) desperately want to listen to it.

This is a potentially face-threatening act, since (depending on your view) your friend's positive- and negative-face needs are under threat. You could simply and directly say, 'Give me that CD so that I can listen to it,' which clearly threatens negative face and, except in extreme cases, would be considered rude and inappropriate. Or you could use a **positive politeness strategy** such as, 'I really appreciate all the music you've lent me recently, can I borrow that some time?' which would ensure that your friend feels valued and respected as an individual. Your third option would be to use a **negative politeness strategy** such as, 'I'm really sorry to ask you again, but is there any chance I could make a copy of that new CD?' In this instance, your aim is to not make your friend feel threatened or obliged to part with the new album. Finally, you could avoid being direct and say something that hints without being explicit, such as, 'It's a shame I won't be able to listen to that.' Although this last example is likely to be understood by your friend as a request to borrow the album, technically it stands as an observation rather than a direct request.

Your choices, following Levinson and Brown's model, can be summarised as in Figure 2.

In addition to these, there is a fifth option that completely avoids any potential face-threatening act: do not say anything at all.

Fig. 1 *Positive and negative face needs*

'I want to listen to my friend's new CD but can't get a copy of my own!'

Fig. 2 *Politeness options*

Politeness theory and power

A speaker's choice of communicative acts including possible politeness strategies is not random. Rather, Brown and Levinson suggest that it is the consideration of three important variables:

$$\begin{array}{ccccc} \text{social} & & \text{power} & \text{degree of} & \text{weight of face threat} \\ \text{distance} & + & \text{distance} & + \text{imposition} = & \text{to be compensated by} \\ & & & & \text{appropriate linguistic} \\ & & & & \text{strategy} \end{array}$$

One of the strengths of this formula is that it has a degree of *predictive power* in suggesting that the greater the distance of power between speaker and hearer, the greater the likelihood that the less powerful participant will use appropriate politeness strategies in the light of a potentially greater face-threatening act. You can test this by considering further variations of the 'asking-for-a-CD' example involving someone other than a close friend, and thinking about the communicative act that might be used in each case.

Although this formula makes an explicit link between politeness and power, much of Brown and Levinson's work centred on informal contexts and made little mention of contexts where there are embedded power hierarchies such as organisations and the workplace. More recent research on power in these contexts has focused on the notion of power not as a fixed or necessarily personal attribute, but more as a part of a role or set of behaviours that individuals carry out as part of their organisational position. Janet Holmes and Maria Stubbe (2003) term this 'doing power', to recognise the ways in which power is demonstrated by superiors (those higher up in organisational hierarchies) as a way of carrying out their occupational role.

Text G

Context: Ginette, a production team manager, giving her team instructions at the early morning meeting.

> *Ginette*: the very last twenty-five cases that you take off that line I want them put aside the very last twenty-five cases put them on a pallet get them stretch wrapped they're going to be a memento for everybody so make sure you er remember that

J. Holmes and M. Stubbe, Power and Politeness in the Workplace, *2003, p33*

In Text G, as Holmes and Stubbe note, a whole string of imperative utterances act as bald on-record acts given Ginette's status as a superior in the organisation, where due to her powerful position, there is little danger of an FTA.

Politeness and power in organisations

Whereas the example above shows power being wielded by a more powerful participant in the workplace, it should be clear that many organisations would not prosper, let alone survive, without a sense of team spirit, mutual respect and collaborative support. Powerful participants may therefore use politeness strategies to ensure a productive workplace atmosphere and motivate others to perform at their best. On the other hand, less powerful participants need to adopt an appropriate linguistic register when speaking to a superior colleague.

■ Small talk

One of the most fascinating aspects of power and politeness in the workplace is **small talk**: language that is primarily concerned with establishing and maintaining interpersonal relationships. Whereas some researchers argue that small talk is relatively unimportant, others have

■ Key terms

Small talk: talk that is primarily interactional in orientation and is geared towards establishing relationships.

stressed its importance not only in its interpersonal function but also in the way it may be used in work contexts in terms of 'doing power'. In Text H, a manager controls the amount of small talk that is allowed in a discussion with her PA.

Text H

Context: Beth, Hana's PA, has just returned from holiday.

> **Beth**: so no it was good I didn't have to worry about meals I didn't have to worry about bills or kids or um work or anything just me
> **Hana**: just a holiday for you
> **Beth**: yeah [*tut*] it was unreal [*laughs*]
> **Hana**: now listen are you going to be wanting to take some time off during the school holidays

J. Holmes and *M. Stubbe*, 2003, p102

As Holmes and Stubbe point out, Hana applies a constraint on Beth by controlling the degree of small talk that is allowed, in this case by directing the conversation towards any time off that Beth might want in the future, which is primarily a work concern. This is a **repressive discourse strategy**, a more indirect method of maintaining power relations, which although it serves to strengthen social ties and avoid face threats by using small talk as a positive politeness strategy, still represents the doing of power by the dominant participant. This contrasts with a more direct or **oppressive discourse strategy**, which openly exercises power and control.

■ Key terms

Repressive discourse strategy: a more indirect way of exercising power and control through conversational constraints.

Oppressive discourse strategy: linguistic behaviour that is open in its exercising of power and control.

■ Extension activity 3

If you have a job, you may be able to collect useful data from your workplace and consider how oppressive and repressive strategies are used by superiors acting as powerful participants in conversational encounters. You may wish to ask the following questions of your data:

- Is there evidence of direct exercising of power?
- Is power 'done' in more subtle ways? How?
- Are staff addressed individually or in groups? Are there differences in the strategies used?
- What role does small talk play? How is it used by those in powerful roles?

You could also consider the following research findings in the light of your own data:

- Morreall (1991) who suggested that *humour* was used in the workplace to maintain good working relations; and Winnick (1976) who demonstrated that humour can be used to criticise authority.
- Bernsten's (1998) claim that *imperatives* are used frequently when power relationships are clear and stable in an organisation.

■ Classroom activity 6

To check your understanding of the coverage of this topic, read Text I, a transcript of a radio interview between a journalist with a reputation for unsettling his interviewees and a local politician. They have been talking about the need to reform local services for residents.

See page 197 for feedback on this activity.

Text I

Key
(.) indicates a brief pause.
numbers within brackets indicate length of pause in seconds.
underlining indicates emphasis in speech.
words between vertical lines are spoken simultaneously.
relevant contextual information is given within square brackets.

I: you can decide on any of those you like which is it
P: well well let me say first of all something about the facilities available (.) erm the sheer range that we offer here is something that er (.) we we really value (.) it's something we've done for the last five years it's something we will continue to achi ‖eve‖
I: ‖can‖
I talk about that later on (.) for now
P: whateve ‖r   ‖
I: ‖I will‖ come back to that later
P: whatever people er (.) pay in council tax (.) the one thing that I am absolutely certain about is that we will continue to provide top quality services for the general public (.) and that will mean some tough decisions are needed because we want to make sure that people receive the very best there is
I: right but is it (.) we'll come back to that later if we may (.) but do you (.) still think (.) that people are paying too much for services that they do not really need
P: well (1)
I: by that I mean let's talk about flower displays (.) street decorations and still some people are living in streets where rubbish is not being collected
P: well I (.) I (.) think that people will know by the way we've erm tried to do the job that what's been on my mind er doing the job well we had to deal with a financial shortfall from the previous year (1) we then had the er problems of the storms (.) we dealt with that in a way which I think people will recognise as being successful in a way it didn't happen in (.) in the past (1) we're dealing with all sorts of issues and we are ‖trying to   ‖
I: ‖ right so there‖ is no difficulty in admitting that some services are not good enough
P: ‖I, I ‖
I: ‖you‖ will admit that to listeners of this show (.) you can accept that people will not be happy with what you are providing

🔍 Power and politics: rhetoric and persuasion

One of the final ways in which we can explore language and power is by considering speeches that aim to exert considerable influence and in doing so become examples of power in action. Politicians often use what are called rhetorical strategies in attempting to persuade and influence their listeners.

■ Classroom activity 7

Text J is from a speech by Tony Blair to the Labour Party conference in Blackpool in 1994, his first speech as Labour leader. In it he signals his vision for modernising the Labour Party and returning it to government.

As you read Text J, consider how language features are used to persuade and influence the audience (not only those at the conference but the public watching a televised version and subsequent reports in the media). How do these features contribute to making this extract an example of powerful language?

See page 197 for feedback on this activity.

Text J

A belief in society. Working together. Solidarity. Cooperation. Partnership. These are our words.

This is my socialism. And we should stop apologising for using the word.

It is not the socialism of Marx or state control. It is rooted in a straightforward view of society. In the understanding that the individual does best in a strong and decent community of people with principles and standards and common values and aims.

We are the party of the individual because we are the party of community.

It is social-ism.

Our task is to apply those values to the modern world. It will change the traditional dividing lines between right and left. And it calls for a new politics. Without dogma and without swapping our prejudices for theirs.

It is time to break out of the past and break through with a clear and radical and modern vision for Britain.

Today's politics is about the search for security in a changing world. We must build the strong and active society that can provide it. That is our project for Britain.

Market forces cannot educate us or equip us for this world of rapid technological and economic change.

We must do it together.

We cannot buy our way to a safe society. We must work for it together.

We cannot purchase an option on whether we grow old. We must plan for it together.

We can't protect the ordinary against the abuse of power by leaving them to it; we must protect each other.

That is our insight.

B. MacArthur (ed.), The Penguin Book of Twentieth-Century Speeches, 1999

Extension activity 4

Political speeches provide fertile ground for exploring the various techniques that are used to exert influence, persuasion and power.

The following websites present a range of examples of speeches that you can annotate and explore. As always, your data and comments should be added to your scrapbook.

www.bbc.co.uk

Radio 4 provides interviews in full from a variety of news and current affairs programmes. You will need to transcribe these – good practice for your transcription skills!

www.number-10.gov.uk/output/Page12035.asp

A collection of the Prime Minister's speeches.

www.wfu.edu

An American site with a wide range of speeches in written and audio form and extensive further links. Use the search engine to look for speeches.

Further reading

Dyer, G. *Advertising as Communication*, Routledge, 1992 (the final chapters contain some very good analyses of advertisements)

Fairclough, N. (2nd edn) *Language and Power*, Longman, 2001

Holmes, J. and Stubbe, M. *Power and Politeness in the Workplace*, Longman, 2003 (contains extensive research details with a range of data examples)

Thomas, L. and Wareing, S. *Language, Society and Power: An Introduction*, Routledge, 1999

Wray, A., Trott, K. and Bloomer, A. *Projects in Linguistics: A Practical Guide to Researching Language*, Arnold, 1998 (a range of topics with some excellent ideas for further research and data collection)

Language and gender

Key terms

Sex: biological differences between males and females.

Gender: the differences in behaviour and roles that are a result of societal expectations.

Socialisation process: a process by which individuals' behaviours are conditioned and shaped.

Some initial questions

Classroom activity 8

As a way of considering your initial thoughts on some of the issues covered in this topic, look at the statements below. Of course, they are generalisations, and as such not to be taken on trust, but think about how far you believe them to be true. What evidence are you using to support your opinion, and where does that evidence come from?

■ Boys and girls are brought up and expected to behave in different ways

■ English is an inherently sexist language

■ Women are conventionally represented in negative ways by the media

■ Women talk more than men

What do we mean by *gender*?

An important distinction to make in your study of this topic is between **sex** and **gender**. Whereas *sex* refers to biological differences between males and females, *gender* refers to behavioural characteristics that are a result of social and cultural influences. In other words, *masculine* and *feminine* behaviour are not necessarily a result of a person's sex, but part of a **socialisation process** that begins when we are children.

Examples of this can be seen in texts that are aimed at young childen and their parents. To look at the ways in which socialisation processes are apparent, collect some examples of pages from toy catalogues (or from internet sites) that advertise toys for boys and girls, considering the ways in which the toys are clearly marked as either for 'girls' or 'boys'. What might you say about the ways that boys and girls are represented? How are *lexical, grammatical* and *graphological* features used to help *construct gender*?

Extension activity 5

You could explore to what extent advertisements aimed at older children and adults continue to represent gender in similar ways to those aimed at young children. Search for data across a number of magazines aimed at either men or women, and consider how behavioural expectations and gender norms are portrayed. If you have access to some older magazines, an interesting task would be to complete a diachronic study: that is to compare the construction of gendered behaviour across time.

Include your texts and your comments on them in your scrapbook.

The construction and representation of gender in fiction

Before you read Text K, it would be useful to re-read the topic on Grammar in Section A (page 30).

Text K

He leaned forward to where his jacket lay and took something from one of the inner pockets. There was a click as he opened a jewel case, a shimmer of gems, a waterfall of blue across the skirt of her dress as he reached for her right wrist and gripped it so she couldn't pull away. In a kind of fascination she watched him, his smoking cigar clenched in his teeth, lean fingers locking about her wrist a bracelet of chain-linked sapphires that glowed against her skin like chinks of dazzling blue sky.

Violet Winspear, Love in a Stranger's Arms, *1977*

One of the ways in which events in a narrative are presented is through the use of different verb processes, which help in the construction of characterisation. In Section A we distinguished between material, relational and mental processes. We will now develop some of those ideas in looking at the way in which female characters are portrayed in a text.

The three types of process provide a way of highlighting how actions in a text are represented and identifying those responsible and those affected by the actions. A character whose behaviour is mostly represented through material processes as an **actor** might be said to have more control over his or her actions and ability to make decisions than one who is represented largely through relational or mental processes. Equally those characters who are **affected** by verb processes, that is who act as *objects* rather than *subjects*, can be said to be less powerful in their ability to make decisions and therefore remain less powerful characters or participants in the narrative.

Looking at these choices of representation in fiction can help us to identify how male and female characters are represented and consequently identify aspects of stereotyping around gender roles. In the extract above, Arabel, the main female character, having lost her memory in an accident, wakes up in a hospital bed to be told that she is the wife of a stranger: Don Cortez Ildefonso de la Dura. Looking at this short extract we can see that the majority of material processes are assigned to Don Cortez:

- 'He leaned forward…'
- '[He] took something…'
- 'He opened…'
- 'He reached for her right wrist…'

> **Key terms**
>
> **Actor:** the individual or entity responsible for the action of a verb process.
>
> **Affected:** the person or entity affected by a material action process.

In comparison to this Arabel is represented by the mental process 'she watched him' (which in turn is preceded by the prepositional phrase 'in a kind of fascination' suggesting that she is undoubtedly under the power of Don Cortez) and the negated material process 'she couldn't pull away'. In addition, her right wrist is the affected in the process 'he reached', portraying her as less powerful and in the control of the powerful male character.

This kind of analysis is useful in exploring how gender is represented in both fiction and non-fiction. The text is typical of the ways Mills and Boon romantic fiction of the 1970s and 1980s represented female characters.

Classroom activity 9

Read through Text L, an extract from another Mills and Boon novel. Analyse how the male and female characters are represented through transitivity choices in terms of the number of material, mental and relational processes used to describe them and whether the characters are placed as the affected in any of the processes you have identified. What patterns do you see emerging?

Text L

She drew back nervously. Gabriel felt the withdrawal and his eyes darkened.
'I hate it when you shrink away from me!'
'I can't help it. I don't mean to do it.'
'What are you afraid I'll do to you? Do you think that I want to hurt you?' The gentle caressing hand had become harsh, closing round her chin and biting into her soft flesh.
She froze, feeling the violence inside him. Gabriel looked at her, his grey eyes probing her face, an icy anger in them.
He dragged her to her feet, his face closed in that cold rage, and his mouth came down in a fierce, searching movement, closing over her lips and parting them. Marissa was too startled to resist in the first moment. Her mouth quivered weakly under the attack of his kiss. Gabriel's hands released her shoulders and began to move over her in a sensuous exploration. A strange melting heat began inside her.

Charlotte Lamb, Seduction, *1981*

Extension activity 6

Analyse a more modern piece of fiction, or one in which male and female roles are not as sharply stereotyped and defined as in the Mills and Boon extracts. As you investigate, consider whether more powerful participants are always represented through material processes. Can you find examples where this is not the case?

A sexist language?

Marked expressions

One of the features of English is that lexical items used to describe females are often **marked** to distinguish them from those used to describe males. The act of marking suggests deviation or difference from a norm, the **unmarked** item. A straightforward example of marking can be seen in *antonyms*. Here, a form of **covert marking** takes place, where one item in a pair is seen as the norm and another as somehow deviant. One of the most obvious (and frequently cited) examples of this is in the use of the antonyms 'young' and 'old'. It is usual to ask 'How old are you?' rather than 'How young are you?' which would strike us as unusual. In this way, a pair of antonyms such as 'young'/'old', which sit at opposite ends of a continuum, has one marked and one unmarked item. Of course in some contexts, there is a shift in *markedness*. For example, it might be natural to ask 'How young are you?' in some situations and for some antonyms, for example 'hot' and 'cold', markedness depends very much on context: compare asking the same question about the temperature in England in summer and in winter.

In English, a more obvious form of marking called **overt marking** often occurs through the addition of the suffix *-ess*. So for unmarked items such as 'manager' and 'actor', we have the marked terms 'manageress' and 'actress'.

Classroom activity 10

Below are pairs of marked and unmarked terms. For each pair, decide what difference, if any, is suggested between them.

- master – mistress
- waiter – waitress
- instructor – instructress
- lion – lioness
- priest – priestess

Another way in which overt marking often draws attention to some suggested sense of difference is through modification. Look at the noun phrases below. How do they suggest difference from a norm?

- female doctor
- woman writer
- career woman
- male nurse
- male prostitute

Generic terms

The use of masculine pronouns ('he'/'him'/'his') as generic pronouns when the gender of the referent is unspecified is generally no longer considered acceptable, as for many people these terms are examples of *exclusive language* in that they represent a male-centred world. Replacing these exclusive terms with *inclusive language*, however, is not as straightforward as it might appear.

Classroom activity 11

Read Text M, an extract from the Police Regulations 2003. Rewrite the part of this extract containing the masculine pronoun *he* so as to make the text more neutral. What choices do you have? Which do you think might be the most appropriate?

See page 197 for feedback on this activity.

Text M

> ## Police Regulations 2003, Schedule 1, Regulation 6 states:
>
> A member of a Police Force shall at all times abstain from any activity which is likely to interfere with the impartial discharge of his duties or which is likely to give rise to the impression amongst members of the public that it may so interfere; and in particular a member of a Police Force shall not take any active part in politics.

www.cumbria.police.uk

Stereotyping

Stereotyping involves assigning a basic set of characteristics to represent a group as a whole. These may be positive or negative, and depending on how they are used to make judgements on or maintain ways in which we expect groups of individuals to behave, can lead to prejudice. Stereotyping can also lead us to believe that certain roles are normal and that group members ought to conform to these roles and behavioural expectations.

> ### ■ Key terms
>
> **Stereotyping:** assigning a general set of characteristics to a group as a whole, often with negative connotations.

> ### ■ Classroom activity 12
>
> Look at Texts N and O. To what extent do you feel that Text N presents a stereotypical view of women (and excludes men)? What do you make of the alternative Text O?

Text N

> The Mothers and Toddlers Group is a very welcoming and friendly meeting place for mums to chat while their children can play safely and in a fun environment. We welcome mums with children of all ages and would love to see you whenever you can make it.
>
> Whilst the children play, the mums can relax and chat and enjoy tea or coffee and biscuits. Many of our members enjoy this time to talk about their families and share experiences of their children.

Text O

> The Mother/Father/Grandparent/Nanny and Toddler Group
>
> Please come and join us for a cup of tea or coffee whilst your children enjoy some play time, refreshment and a craft activity
>
> Only £1.00 for your Toddler (Babies 50p)
>
> We meet in the Pavilion every Tuesday from 9.45am - 11.45am
>
> Everybody is welcome.
>
> If you would like to borrow the tables and chairs for a private party at home, they are available.
>
> To help raise funds a small donation (£2 to £5) would be appreciated.

Semantic derogation

It has been claimed that some terms in English that are reserved for use when referring to women, have a strong negative connotation attached to them when compared to the corresponding term used to refer to men. Sara Mills (1995), following previous research by Deborah Cameron (1990) and Muriel Schultz (1975), highlights the following examples (Table 3) of lexical pairs where the male term suggests a positive attribute while the female term suggests a negative one.

Table 3 *Male and female terms*

Male	Female
courtier	courtesan
master	mistress
host	hostess
governor	governess
adventurer	adventuress
sir	madam
bachelor	spinster
lord	lady
king	queen
priest	priestess
god	goddess

Mills, *1995, p110–111*

Mills points out that many of the female equivalents are marked as indicative of sexual promiscuity ('courtesan' and 'adventuress'). In addition (and as often noted) whilst 'bachelor' retains positive connotations of a free-spirited, independent lifestyle, as in 'bachelor party' and 'bachelor pad', 'spinster' has more negative connotations. Other pairs such as 'lord' and 'lady' have experienced dramatic shifts in meaning across time: whilst 'lord' still suggests high status, 'lady' is more widely used and according to Mills has undergone **semantic deterioration**, shown in its use in terms such as 'dinner lady' and 'cleaning lady' (contrast here with the rather absurd-sounding 'cleaning lord').

Key terms

Semantic derogation: the sense of negative meaning or connotation that some lexical items have attached to them.

Semantic deterioration: the process by which negative connotations become attached to lexical items.

Classroom activity 13

Schultz, Cameron and Mills were all writing some time ago. To what extent do you think that their observations about semantic derogation and deterioration are still valid today? Discuss these ideas in the light of your own use of language and observations of those around you and in the speech communities that you belong to.

You could set up an investigation using the 11 pairs of lexical items to gauge whether these words still have negative connotations and explore their use in different media. Are there other pairs that you could add to this list?

■ **Extension activity 7**

You could continue your work on Classroom activity 13 by considering the following research findings and testing them through your own investigations.

■ Julia Stanley (1973) claimed that there was a marked inequality in the number of words for a sexually promiscuous female (200) compared to those used to describe males (20) and that most of the female-oriented words had negative connotations.

■ Stanley (1977) also suggested that women occupy negative semantic space because of the number of marked forms that exist to describe female equivalents of male roles. She quotes examples such as 'female surgeon' and 'lady doctor' as well as more conventional marked forms through affixation to claim that women are unable to move into the positive space occupied by men because they will always carry a mark of femaleness and therefore inequality with them. You might want to think about other examples here: the world of sport would be a good place to start.

Avoiding sexist language

■ **Classroom activity 14**

Text P below is from Margaret Doyle's *The A–Z of Non-Sexist Language*, which offers alternatives to what the author considers to be sexist words, including examples of linguistic marking, generic terms, stereotyping and semantic derogation. Read the entries shown and consider the following questions:

1 To what extent do you feel that there is value in making some of the changes that Doyle suggests? Are some of the problems with terminology valid ones?

2 Doyle's book was published in 1995. Are some of the items listed still in use? If so, what does that suggest about the process of meaning change in a language?

3 Does your work in this topic lead you to believe that English is a sexist language and therefore *produces* a sexist society, or is it merely *reflecting* sexism in society as a whole?

Text P

schoolmaster/schoolmistress *Schoolmaster* is one of the few '–master' words that is used in a gender-specific way, so it is not in itself a sexist term. Nevertheless, its feminine 'counterpart', *schoolmistress*, suffers from the illicit and often derogatory connotations of MISTRESS as used today. Better to replace both with less loaded gender-neutral terms, as is increasingly being done in the educational community. See MASTER.
OPTIONS: head teacher, schoolteacher, teacher, educator, lecturer, instructor, principal.

scold (verb) Avoid using in a way that reinforces negative stereotypes of women. In such contexts, replace with a less loaded term that can be applied equally to women and men. See also BITCH; DOMINATE; NAG; PUSSY-WHIPPED; SHREW.
OPTIONS: gripe, reprimand, berate, chastise, bully, lecture, upbraid, lambaste, rail, abuse.

scold (noun) OPTIONS: pest, abuser, bully.

Scotsman This usage demonstrates that compounds with '–man' are not gender-neutral – consider the absurd sound of 'She's a Scotsman'. Replacing such terms can require reconstructing the sentence – such as by changing 'She's/He's a Scotsman' to She's/He's Scottish'. In this case, 'Scots' is also an acceptable alternative. For plural usage, 'the Scots' or 'the Scottish' is better than 'Scotsmen'. See topic note on pag 63.

Secretary Avoid the assumption that these are exclusively women; do not, for example, use 'make secretary'. This is an example of how stereotypes perpetuated by language can actually lead to discrimination: A recent poll of businesses found that 63 percent thought their workers would be amused to see a male secretary; 21 percent would be downright critical (*Independent*, 26 May 1993). Presumably, these companies would not hire a man for the job. One alternative would be to reserve *secretary* for Cabinet ministers and use *assistant* as a gender-neutral term free of drogatory connotations.

seductress This and similar terms (SIREN, TEMPTRESS) perpetuate an offensive stereotype of women. They blame women for men's behaviour, and excuse men by suggesting that they are not responsible for their sexual actions. If you must use, avoid the –ess ending and use *seducer* equally for men and women. See topic note on page 26.
OPTIONS: seducer, tempter, heartbreaker.

seminal Some object to this term's relation to 'seed/semen' as the source of creativity or value.
OPTIONS: original, germinal, originative, pivotal, influential, innovative. *Ovular* has been suggested as an alternative; see topic note on page 41.

serviceman/servicewomen 1. OPTIONS: service personnel (plural), member of armed services, recruit, officer, soldiers, serviceman/servicewoman.

Male and female speech styles

Assumptions about and attitudes to male and female talk

Text Q

One tongue is enough for a woman

English proverb

Text R

You got a beautiful chin, you got beautiful skin, you've got a
  beautiful face, you've got taste.
You've got beautiful eyes, you've got beautiful thighs,
You've got a lot without a doubt, but I'm thinking 'bout blowing you
  out, cos
You won't stop talking, why don't you give it a rest?
You got more rabbit than Sainsbury's, it's time you got it off ya
  chest.
Now you was just the type of girl to break my heart in two,
I knew right off when I first clapped my eyes on you,
But how was I to know you'd bend my earholes too with your
  incessant talking?
You're becoming a pest.
Rabbit, Rabbit, Rabbit, Rabbit

Charles Hodges and *David Peacock*, Rabbit

So far this topic has concentrated on how language is used to refer
to males and females and on some of the differences that have been
highlighted, for example in the use of lexical items, stereotyping and
representation in the media and in fiction. One of the most widely
researched areas in sociolinguistics focuses on a different use: that of
language by male and female speakers in terms of speech style, both in
same-sex and mixed-sex interaction.

A great deal of ground has been made since the 1970s when researchers
began to explore assumptions about female language. Many of these
existed to reinforce stereotypes about female speech as deviant from
and subordinate to a male norm. Much of this is what we now call
folklinguistics, a term used to describe attitudes and assumptions that
have no evidence behind them, yet are accepted and appear in the form of
the proverb and song extracts above.

> **Key terms**
>
> **Folklinguistics:** attitudes and
> assumptions about language
> that have no real evidence to
> support them, for example in
> the assumption that women are
> generally more 'chatty' or prone to
> gossip than men.

> **Extension activity 8**
>
> What other folklinguistic expressions regarding female speech can you think
> of or find? What do they reveal about attitudes to male and female language
> styles?

Some important early research into speech styles

Two important pieces of research were undertaken by Peter Trudgill
(1974) and Jenny Cheshire (1982), who both used large samples of data
in the form of recorded talk, which were analysed to show differences in
male and female use of language.

Trudgill's work was undertaken in Norwich and involved the study of how male and female speakers pronounced the suffix -ing as in 'walking', 'laughing'. Trudgill discovered that across social classes, men tended to use a more non-standard pronunciation. He also found, through a self-evaluation test that asked informants to choose between a standard and non-standard pronunciation of a word, that men tended to under-report, that is they marked themselves as using non-standard forms even when they did not. Women, Trudgill discovered, did the opposite: they over-reported. All of this led Trudgill to conclude that male speakers attached a **covert prestige** to non-standard forms.

Trudgill's work is supported by that of Jenny Cheshire, who in analysing the talk of teenagers in Reading, found that in nearly all cases boys used non-standard forms more than girls did. She seeks to explain this by drawing on the type of social network to which the boys and girls belonged. Boys were found to be members of much denser networks where their language converged towards the vernacular as a shared show of linguistic and social solidarity.

Key terms

Covert prestige: a form of high status given to non-standard forms.

AQA Examiner's tip

Much early work on language and gender was conducted using small datasets from a limited range of participants. You should be open to some of the potential problems that research findings pose, and conduct your own investigations to test them. References to your own studies can be used where relevant to support your interpretations in an examination answer.

Extension activity 9

You could test these findings by investigating non-standard usage amongst female and male speakers in your own speech communities and testing Trudgill's findings that males tend to under-report when asked about their linguistic behaviour.

Add your findings to your scrapbook.

■ Models of describing approaches to language and gender

Research such as Trudgill's and Cheshire's, which focused on phonological and grammatical variation, is just one way of exploring the language styles of males and females. Other researchers have explored language use and styles as part of more general focuses on communication and discourse and the linguistic behaviour of males and females. These focuses or approaches have been labelled the deficit, dominance and difference approaches. Whilst some of the elements within these approaches differ greatly, there is also considerable overlap between them. The dominance and difference models in particular have been usefully seen as complementary approaches.

The deficit approach

Robin Lakoff's *Language and Woman's Place* (1975) is often viewed as characteristic of a deficit approach to the study of language and gender in which female language is seen as deficient in some way to the established male norm. Lakoff claimed that much of the women's language lacked real authority when compared to that used by men, and proposed a set of features that characterised women's language as deficient when compared to men's. These included:

■ the use of a specialised vocabulary centred around domestic chores

■ precise colour terms, e.g. 'mauve', 'magenta'

■ weak expletive terms, e.g. 'oh dear'

- 'empty' adjectives, e.g. 'charming', 'sweet'
- tag questions to show uncertainty, e.g. 'isn't it?' 'doesn't she?'
- more polite forms than men use, e.g. euphemisms such as 'spend a penny', 'powder my nose'
- the use of hedges, e.g. 'sort of', 'you know'
- intensifiers, e.g. 'so'.

Lakoff suggested that socialisation played an important role in ensuring that female language remained less assertive and more insecure when compared to that of men and so the differences were more socially constructed than biologically based. In an academic climate that was still dominated by men, much of what Lakoff proposed was glossed over and what remained was the unfortunate conclusion that Lakoff considered her observations as representative of women's innate linguistic behaviour. Consequent research aimed to support some of these features of 'women's language' without taking into account other variables that could have accounted for unconfident speech styles amongst women.

Some alternative explanations of Lakoff's findings

Tag questions as politeness and boosting devices

Janet Holmes (1992) suggests that **tag questions**, rather than being simply a sign of uncertainty in a speaker, may also function as a device to help maintain discussion or to be polite. Holmes suggests that rather than being mere signs of weakness, tag questions are multi-functional and gives the following examples of tag questions being used in different ways.

> **Key term**
>
> **Tag question:** a group of words that turn a declarative into an interrogative, for example 'It's cold' becomes 'It's cold, isn't it?'

> **Classroom activity 15**
>
> Read Text S, which consists of two examples from Holmes' work. How are tag questions used by Claire and the Superintendent? What function do they play in the interaction between the speakers?
>
> See page 197 for feedback on this activity.

Text S

Context: Zoe and her mother Claire have just come home from the supermarket. Zoe empties the shopping basket all over the kitchen floor.

Claire: That was a bit of a daft thing to do wasn't it?

Context: a police superintendent is interviewing a detective constable and is criticising the constable's performance.

Superintendent: You'll probably find yourself um before the chief constable, okay?

Constable: Yes sir understood

Superintendent: Now you fully understand that don't you?

Constable: Yes sir indeed yeah

J. Holmes, An Introduction to Sociolinguistics, *1992, p319*

■ Key terms

Hedging device: a linguistic device used to express uncertainty.

Boosting device: a linguistic device used to intensify the force of an expression for added emphasis or power.

Holmes also suggests that many other features of so-called 'women's language', for example lexical **hedges** and fillers, are used for a variety of functions and that to suggest that they are simply markers of indecision is grossly misleading.

In another interesting set of observations, Betty Dubois and Isobel Crouch (1975) found that in their data men used more tag questions than women, although it was not suggested that they were less confident speakers as a consequence of these findings!

William O'Barr and Bowman Atkins (1980), following their research into the language of the courtroom, discovered that many of Lakoff's suggested features did actually occur in women's speech, although their findings that a number of men from lower-class backgrounds tended to use similar features led them to believe that features of uncertain speech were more dependent on power relations rather than gender. Consequently, they suggested that the term 'powerless language' was a more useful one than 'women's language'. Although this represents a move away from a deficit model, it pays more attention to social status than gender as a key variable in establishing dominance.

■ Extension activity 10

You can develop your thoughts on Lakoff's work by collecting data from both male and female speakers in different contexts and annotating them for your scrapbook. Do you agree that the term 'powerless language' is a more accurate and useful label for the phenomena that Lakoff discovered in her data?

In addition, you could test Janet Holmes' claims that tag questions and hedges are often used as politeness and **boosting devices**. You might also like to consider the following:

■ Holmes also suggested that women in all-female groups used far more compliments as further acts of politeness and solidarity than men did.

■ Jennifer Coates (1989) showed that in many cases, women used epistemic modal forms such as 'perhaps', 'sort of' and 'probably' to avoid face-threatening acts when talking to other females. This too was seen as a sign of female cooperation and speaker support.

■ The dominance approach

The second approach to male and female talk focused on the ways in which men were seen as controlling and dominating mixed-sex interactions. One of the most-quoted pieces of research is by Zimmerman and West (1975), who found in their (albeit small) set of data that 96 per cent of all interruptions in mixed-sex conversation were made by men. They saw this as a sign both that women had restricted linguistic freedom and that men sought to impose their dominant status through applying explicit constraints in conversational practice.

Much subsequent research into mixed talk concluded that women and men do not hold equal conversational rights. In fact, Zimmerman and West later carried out a study of the interactions between parents and children, and concluded that parents interrupted and assumed power in those interactions in the same way that men had done in mixed talk.

■ The difference approach

The difference approach to language and gender takes an alternative stance. Variation in the ways males and females use language can be examined using a difference model as being evidence of men and women belonging to different sub-cultures with different attitudes to, and preferences for, types of talk as a result of cultural differences and pressures. Much research from this particular angle focuses on same-sex talk as a way of exploring the different conversational strategies that women and men use in these contexts. In a similar way to some of the reactions to Lakoff's 'women's language', many studies have highlighted positive features of female speech linked to the need to establish and maintain strong social relationships. In this way, one of the strengths of the difference model has been that it has focused on the linguistic achievements of women and, at the same time, avoided blaming men for simply being too dominant. Some of the most important studies using this approach are summarised below.

■ Jennifer Coates (1989) suggested that all-female talk is essentially cooperative in the way that speakers help to *negotiate* discussions and *support* each other's rights as speakers. She argues that as these patterns are not found in mixed talk, they are evidence of differing socio-cultural expectations and a key insight into differences in sub-cultures.

■ Jane Pilkington (1992) also found that women in same-sex talk were more collaborative than men were in all-male talk. She concluded that whereas women aimed for more *positive politeness strategies* in conversation with other women, men tended to be less complimentary and supportive in all-male talk (see Language and power, page 67).

■ Equally, Koenraad Kuiper (1991) found that in all-male talk amongst members of a rugby team, men were likely to pay less attention to the need to save face and instead used insults as a way of expressing solidarity. Similar findings on all-male talk have also highlighted this difference in cooperation amongst all-male groups.

More controversially, this approach has also been adopted to consider mixed-sex talk, for example in Deborah Tannen's (1990) *You Just Don't Understand: Men and Women in Conversation*. Tannen was reacting to a dominance-based approach to male and female speech styles and attempted to explain 'male–female miscommunication' by claiming that male–female speech was 'cross-cultural communication' (Tannen 1990:43–44). Tannen's work influenced a whole range of both academic and more populist works on male–female differences in speech behaviour. However, Tannen's book and others that have followed it have been criticised both for ignoring the important issue of power and in some cases making assertions and generalisations based on minimal research evidence.

■ Gender or power?

More recent work on gender has led researchers to consider talk in a wider social context and in particular the ways in which speakers 'do gender' in the same way as they 'do power'. This approach even throws doubt on the whole polarisation of male and female talk and on the status of male and female as static fixed identities. Instead, it emphasises how the notion of gender is very much a *social construct*. Indeed, some of the most interesting questions about how gender is constructed have centred on how gender is performed in communication that is not face-to-face, such as that afforded by the technologies of email and instant messaging.

💡 🔲 Using these approaches in your work on language and gender

There has been a great deal of work on trying to explain the differences between male and female speech, and it is important for you to understand some of the advances that have been made over the last 30 years or so. As with any research findings, however, there comes a warning! You should remember that published theories are there to be challenged, not accepted as the final word. After all, it is in challenging existing theories that researchers gain new insights and ideas!

In addition, although much of the work on speech styles in this topic has concentrated on providing you with some theoretical work, you should remember that ideas from the study of language (AO2) are not limited to the work of professional academics. To this end, you should use the areas for investigation suggested in the Extension activities to test some of these ideas for yourself. As well as giving you an opportunity to develop your data-collecting, handling and interpretative skills, they will also give you fresh insights into some of the issues and concepts that you have read about.

Extension activity 11

Your final work on this topic could involve setting-up a mini-project to investigate one of the following areas.

- How males and females represent themselves, for example in the writing of 'lonely hearts' advertisements and declarations of love in St Valentine's Day announcements.
- Lexical items used by male and female speakers in different contexts.
- The use of politeness strategies and compliments (see topic 1) used in same-sex and mixed talk.
- The use of interruptions and overlaps (see Language and power, page 67).
- The representation of male and female speech on television, for example in soap operas or dramas.
- The speech styles of participants on internet chat rooms and message boards where it is not clear whether speakers are male or female. Are there signs of *gendered language* in action?

Compare your findings with the research mentioned here, any other background reading that you have undertaken and other students on your course. How can you explain the findings from your data?

Further reading

Cameron, D. *The Myth of Mars and Venus: Do Men and Women really speak Different Languages*, Oxford University Press, 2007 (an accessible and clearly written book that is critical of supposed language differences between men and women)

Coates, J., (ed.) *Language and Gender: A Reader*, Blackwell, 1998 (a wealth of research papers including those by Trudgill, Cheshire, Coates, Pilkington and Kuiper)

Goddard, A. and Patterson, L. *Language and Gender*, Routledge, 2000 (a good summary which covers a range of issues)

Holmes, J. *An Introduction to Sociolinguistics*, Longman, 1992 (contains two very good chapters on women's language)

Mills, S. *Feminist Stylistics*, Routledge, 1995 (a wide-ranging book that has more extensive examples of the representation of gender in media and fiction texts)

Spender, D. (2nd edn) *Man Made Language*, Routledge and Kegan Paul, 1987

Wray, A., Trott, K. and Bloomer, A. *Projects in Linguistics: A Practical Guide to Researching Language*, Arnold, 1998 (a range of topics with some excellent ideas for further research and data collection)

The following articles are also particularly useful for A Level students:

Bleiman, B. 'Language and gender' *emagazine*, 23, 2004

Reah, D. 'Gender, language and crime fiction' *emagazine*, 18, 2002

Language and technology

In this topic you will:

■ understand how technology has affected the ways in which language is produced and received

■ explore the impact of technology on face-to-face and group communication

■ consider to what extent various technological media can be said to display distinct varieties of language use.

Key terms

Summons/answer: a sequence that opens the channel of communication on the telephone.

Identification/recognition: a sequence in which speakers identify themselves to each other.

Greetings sequence: a series of turns designed to initiate a shared social space.

'How are you' sequences: examples of phatic talk that maintain the social relationship before the main business of the telephone call commences.

Language and technology: what is it?

This topic will explore the ways in which technology has affected the ways that we produce, receive and use language. Technology, however, does not only refer to new inventions; some of the technologies that are covered, for example the telephone, were invented many years ago. Instead, the term is used to refer to how a particular medium shapes, influences and applies constraints on linguistic choices and behaviours. Our main objective is to discover whether we can identify distinctive language features that are indicative of different channels of electronic communication.

The discourse structure of telephone conversation

Following work by early researchers in conversational analysis, the linguist Emanuel A. Schegloff (1986) attempted to discover a set of patterns or discourse structure that speakers used when communicating via the telephone. His work suggested a *canonical sequence* or *pattern* for the beginning of telephone conversations, as shown in Figure 3.

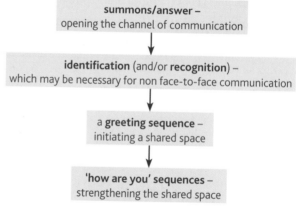

Fig. 3 *The pattern of a telephone conversation*

In his analyses, Schegloff argued that although the sequence constituted what he called a *routine*, this was anything but mundane and formulaic and could be seen as a remarkable collaborative venture on the part of speakers. His analyses of opening sequences are detailed and emphasise the creative nature of discourse depending on the crucial variables of speaker relationship and context and purpose of dialogue.

Classroom activity 16

Read Text T, which is an extract from a telephone conversation between two friends.

1 To what extent can you apply Schegloff's model to this text? What issues does this raise?

2 Using your work from earlier in this unit, can you say what other features of language use are evident?

See page 198 for feedback on this activity.

Text T

> *John*: hello
> *Steve*: John, it's Steve
> *John*: oh, hi, hi how are you doing?
> *Steve*: good thanks, you?
> *John*: yeah not bad just recovering from this cold thing you know
> *Steve*: it's all around
> *John*: yeah we're all sniffing at the mo
> *Steve*: [laughs] yeah?
> *John*: so what's happening next week?

Extension activity 12

Although telephone conversations are not as easy to record as other examples of spoken discourse, you may be able to collect some data of your own (make sure you have the speakers' permission to use anything that you record). Analyse the opening sequences, using Schegloff's model, paying attention to any variation that you find. In particular, you could look for any differences that occur according to:

- the *relative power* and *intimacy* status of the speakers. The example in Text V was between two close friends. What patterns emerge when looking at data between speakers who do not know each other well? You could look for the various *politeness strategies* that speakers use in these situations
- the *gender* of speakers. Are there differences between same- and mixed-sex talk? Between all-female and all-male conversation?
- *cultural expectations and differences*. Many researchers have found that Schegloff's model does not hold for all communities and cultures. You could investigate this and produce some cross-cultural comparative analyses
- the possibilities afforded by *new technologies* such as the videophone. Are identification/recognition and to some extent greetings sequences no longer evident when speakers can see each other? What discourse patterns might be present in these contexts?

AQA Examiner's tip

Don't be afraid to challenge Schegloff's model. Technology and communication practices have changed dramatically over the last 20 years, and your observations may contradict his research.

Telephone pre-closings and closings

It is also useful to consider and analyse some of the ways in which speakers signal that they are to stop talking and hang up the telephone. Again, this can be viewed as primarily a collaborative venture between speakers, consisting of a series of pre-closing and closing sequences. **Pre-closing sequences** act as signals that one speaker wishes to discontinue the conversation, for example through the use of **metatalk** such as 'well I'd better stop talking and go and do some work!'; **phatic speech acts** such as 'well it's been great talking to you'; *discourse markers* such as 'well' or 'anyway'; or lines anticipating further conversation, for example 'speak to you next week' or 'I'll ring you tomorrow'. Often pre-closing sequences are carefully managed by speakers so as not to threaten the *face* of their co-speakers, often using positive and/or negative politeness strategies such as 'it's been really good talking to you' or 'I won't keep you from watching your favourite TV programme'. Closings consist of the final end of the conversation and may be represented by a number of different **valedictions** such as 'see you', 'goodbye', depending on the intimacy of speakers and the context of the conversation.

Key terms

Pre-closing sequences: signals that one (or both) speaker wishes to end the conversation.

Metatalk: talk that draws attention to the act of talking itself.

Phatic speech acts: turns designed to maintain a sense of cooperation or respect for the other speaker.

Valediction: an item that acts as a farewell.

Answerphone messages

Answerphone messages (either landline or mobile) are an easier way of collecting data to analyse. One of their most obvious features is that they are *monologic*, with a speaker engaged in talking to a machine rather than a human. In the same way as telephone conversations, language choices, particularly with regard to formality, are likely to vary depending on the relationship between the speakers, the degree of shared knowledge and the purpose of the message that is being left.

💡 Texting

The impact and influence of mobile phones has led to the rise of what is sometimes called **textspeak**. With the number of text messages being sent in Britain reaching a record high and growing from month to month, text messaging has become a quick and easy way to communicate.

Key terms

Textspeak: the language (in terms of both lexis and grammar) used by those sending text messages on a mobile phone.

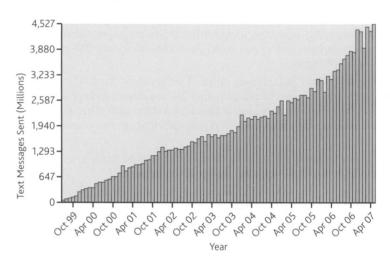

Fig. 4 *Text messages sent in the UK, 1999–2007*
www.text.it/home

Lexical features of 'textspeak'

David Crystal's *A Glossary of Netspeak and Textspeak* (2004) provides a guide to some of the abbreviations found in textspeak, although as he acknowledges, his list is more representative than definitive. Text users' constant creativity and experimentation also means that many of his examples may be outdated. New abbreviations as a result of group membership or idiosyncrasies are likely to appear all the time as speakers search for economy of expression.

It would be useful, however, to look at some common ways in which textspeak is created. All the examples in Table 4 overleaf are from Crystal (2004).

Hybrid items

In addition to those listed in Table 4, many abbreviations are hybrids of vowel omission, homophones, phonetic and variant spelling, initialism and acronymy. For example the abbreviation *ttul8r* (talk to you later) is a blend of an initialism and homophonic representation, and *pls4givme* (please forgive me) is a blend of vowel omission, homophonic representation and phonetic spelling!

Table 4 *Common ways in which textspeak is created*

Type	Examples
Vowel omission	pls (please), ppl (people), hv (have)
Homophonic representation	2L8 (too late), M8 (mate), 2Day (today), CR8 (create), qt (cutie)
Phonetic spelling	omigod (oh my god), iluvu (I love you), cos (because)
Initialism	lmk (let me know), ptmm (please tell me more), dwb (don't write back)
Acronymy	lol (laughs out loud), sal (such a laugh),
Variant spelling	wot (what), wen (when), cuz (because)

Some other key points regarding textspeak

The following are offered as opportunities to develop further discussion and could be used as part of any investigative work that you might carry out.

■ As with any communication, register will depend on context: the situation and purpose of the message and the relationship between the speakers or writers. Whereas some examples of textspeak are more generally used, some are highly idiosyncratic and may exist only among certain discourse communities. They are part of a *sociolect* just as much as other forms of language.

■ Technological advances (such as videophones) that allow multi-modal expression and communication, as well as the need for economy in time, cost and any constraint on the number of characters that a message may contain, mean that change in construction and use of textspeak abbreviations is rapid.

■ The variation and creativity in such language means that there can never be a standard form (some analysts have compared textspeak to English spelling before it was standardised in the 18th century). Instead there is a range of varieties and sub-varieties.

■ Attitudes to textspeak vary considerably. Whilst some critics have bemoaned slipping standards and the destruction of English, others have welcomed creativity and even suggested that knowledge about how texting operates might improve literacy standards. Some articles that might stimulate discussion can be found in the following websites:

  – www.guardian.co.uk/comment/story/0,,1681004,00.html

  – www.guardian.co.uk/technology/2004/dec/23/schools.mobilephones

  – http://itpro.co.uk/news/111518/txting-may-spell-bad-news-for-standards.html

Key terms

Vowel omission: leaving out vowel sounds in textspeak and other electronic communication.

Homophonic representation: the use of single letters and numbers to represent words based on a similarity in sound.

Phonetic spelling: a spelling that represents the sound of a word as opposed to its conventional spelling.

Initialism: an abbreviation that uses the first letter of a group of words and is pronounced as individual letters.

Acronymy: the process of abbreviating that uses the first letter of a group of words but, unlike an initialism, an acronym is pronounced as a single word.

Variant spelling: deliberately non-standard spelling for effect.

Classroom activity 17

Read Text U, a selection of text messages sent by Vanessa, a 15-year-old girl, over the course of two days. What types of constructions does she use? What can you tell about her relationship with each of the recipients of her messages?

Text U

1. Hi have u gt footie 2nite coz Mandy want to meet me at bluewater & thought u could do cinema? txt b quickly coz shes waitin x

2. Wat doz:-p mean? and lol dw im really confused anyway now lol okay wuu2 this wknd cumin? tb x

3. Yer i cn understand that bt i am alot busyer than i usd 2 b so its nt i dnt wana txt u its smetimes i cnt txt u x x x

---

Extension activity 13

Collect and analyse your own examples of textspeak using your learning from this section. A suggested framework for analysis is provided in the table below.

Features	Example 1	Example 2 (etc.)
Examples of lexical/grammatical/ phonological features and construction of abbreviations		
Register		
Purpose		
Relationship between speakers		
Other contextual factors		

Radio and television

Although both radio and television rely predominantly on the spoken word, the absence of visual codes in radio make its reliance on speech more marked. Your learning and investigations on the language of television and radio will centre on factual rather than dramatic programming through focuses on radio phone-ins and television sports commentaries. As you explore this topic, you will also consider how the absence of images impacts on the linguistic features of, and behaviours in, radio discourse.

Radio phone-ins

Radio phone-ins are opportunities for members of the public to give their opinions on a topic set by the programme producers, from current affairs to the latest sporting results. Although they are often set up to allow the public to 'have their say', these programmes are hosted by a presenter, an authority figure who can manage the conversation, select and deselect speakers and in many cases provide the final word in the discussion. Contributions to phone-ins are also made via text-messaging and email.

Although phone-ins often appear to be live and spontaneous, production teams undertake a range of practices to eliminate unwanted problems. The following, taken from editorial guidelines posted on the BBC website, will give you some idea of how phone-ins are managed.

Editorial guidelines for phone-ins

- Contributors to phone-ins should normally be called back and if necessary briefed before they go on air.
- Content producers should read emails and texts before they are broadcast.
- Presenters should be adequately briefed on BBC Editorial Guidelines and the law and be able to extricate the programme from tricky situations with speed and courtesy.
- When producing a phone-in on a difficult or controversial subject such as child abuse, the production team should be briefed on how to deal sensitively with contributors and support systems should be in place.
- When a programme is contacted unexpectedly by someone wishing to share their difficult story, we should consider the implications and refer if necessary.

www.bbc.co.uk

Analysing conversation in the radio phone-in

Table 5 shows a framework for analysing conversation.

Table 5 *A framework for analysing conversation*

Framework	Questions
Lexis/ semantics	What kind of register is adopted?
	Are particular lexical fields present according to the topic of conversation?
	Are there examples of technical or inclusive language?
Grammar	What kinds of sentence constructions are used?
	Are there instances of elliptical structures, deictic expressions, discourse markers (including skip connectors and false starts)?
Discourse structure	What is the overall discourse structure?
	How are openings and closings managed?
	How are turns and larger exchange structures managed and controlled?
	Can longer contributions be explained using models such as the narrative categories proposed by Labov?
Pragmatics	To what degree are aspects of shared knowledge present between speakers?
	Do contributions adhere to conversational maxims and ideas about speaker support and cooperation?
	Are politeness strategies used to preserve face needs?
	To what extent are linguistic constraints applied by the presenter and/or the nature of the phone-in?
Phonology	Are there any **prosodic features** present such as tone, intonation and stresses? (Note that these may not be easily recognised from a printed transcript.)

Classroom activity 18

Discuss some of the implications of the radio phone-in guidelines. To what extent might some of these guidelines affect the ways in which discourse situations are set up and managed on radio phone-ins?

Key terms

Prosodic features: paralinguistic vocal elements of spoken language used to provide emphasis or other effects.

AQA Examiner's tip

You should ensure that you are comfortable with analysing features of spoken discourse in order to analyse radio phone-ins successfully. Refer back to Section A (page 51) if necessary.

Classroom activity 19

Using Table 5 to guide you, read Text V, an extract from a live phone-in focusing on claims that A Level examinations are becoming easier when compared to previous years. The presenter (P) has just introduced a speaker Dennis (D), who is a teacher. Identify the features of spoken discourse in the text, and describe what they tell you about the speakers.

See page 198 for feedback on this activity.

Text V

Key

(.) Indicates a brief pause.

Numbers within brackets indicate length of pause in seconds.

Underlining indicates emphasis in speech.

Words between vertical lines are spoken simultaneously.

Relevant contextual information is given within square brackets.

P: Dennis morning to you

D: good morning

P: you are a teacher are (.) do you agree with the comments made this morning?

D: not at all (.) I'm very angry it is like every year you know we're told that examinations are becoming easier and that students aren't being challenged but the bottom line is that both students and teachers are are working very hard and (.) I never understand why we automatically dismiss their work (.) it's like we're trying to find excuses for what students are now achieving (.) er we should be praising instead of ‖ constantly crit‖

P: ‖ Denis (.) let's ‖ look at what those critics are saying then (1) questions that aren't testing enough (.) coursework that sometimes isn't the students' own ‖ and ‖

D: ‖ but ‖ that's a different issue (.)

P: okay but in your years of teaching (.) how long have you been teaching

D: twenty years

P: you must have seen a change in the way that exams are being set and administered

D: well I'm not convinced that the questions are easier (.) for example in my subject (.) English (.) students are now having to deal with more mod (.) modern ways of reading and accessing texts (1) if anything the questions are more demanding (.) I just feel very angry about it all (.) teachers like the police and nurses seem to get the blame for all of this and at the same time the government is you know employing more and more unqualified teachers and not paying the qualified ones enough

P: well okay then (.) let's return to the issue of coursework

Extension activity 14

You can investigate the language of phone-ins in more detail by recording, transcribing and analysing examples on a range of issues for your scrapbook. BBC Radio 5 Live (www.bbc.co.uk/fivelive), which offers downloads of recent phone-ins in MP3 format, is a good place to start, but you could also compare radio phone-ins with those on television, for example on daytime shows or sports programmes.

Television commentaries

Classroom activity 20

Text W is a series of extracts from a television commentary on a one-day cricket international between England and Sri Lanka in 2006. Read these and identify examples of distinctive language features. To what extent can these be explained by the fact that television is the medium of communication?

See page 198 for feedback on this activity.

Text W

1 Ooh that's an unbelievable ball (.) in fact that's a magnificent first over from Chaminder Vass (4) superb example of controlled swing and seam

2 Cor dear me this is terrific stuff from (1) Chaminder Vass who's got the ball to go nice and late that's the key he bowls that sort of tempting length that just draws you forward

3 Terrific start from Chaminder Vass he's got the ball to go away from Marcus Trescothick very late drawing him into the strokes and er beating the strokes it's er one for none after three overs good start by the Sri Lankans

4 First run off the bat and it gets (.) an ironic cheer from the crowd here at Headingley (.) England have won the toss they've chosen to bat first and it's not been anything like the smooth passage they hoped it might be

5 Shot (2) well that's helped hasn't it Marcus Trescothick four on the off side (.) a pull on the leg side (.) just got the scoreboard rolling along

6 Oh that's (1) well it's a good stroke but really shouldn't have been four really poor misfield there (.) it was a decent ball from Chaminder Vass (7) England thirty nine for none after the first ten overs and Sri Lanka have taken their second power play

7 No no there's a problem here (.) he's got stranded (1) ooow that was a missed call by Cook (1) and he really had Trescothick in trouble there (3) if Darranga had hit (.) I think that he was gone there

8 Dilhara Fernando from the football stand end (3) short and wide and that will be (.) welcome relief to (2) fifty up for England thirteen overs

9 Ooh well bowled (.) Is that out? (.) there's some sort of noise (.) but no the umpire's not interested it went between bat and pad (.) they're all shouting it (1) there was a noise but what (.) what did it hit? (2) [action replay shows] Fernando bowling round the wicket (.) Trescothick gets beaten on the inside (.) well (.) it didn't look to be anybody or (1) in the way (.) it looked as if it might have been the inside of the bat

Extension activity 15

1. To explore the differences between sports commentary on radio and on television, rewrite Text Y for a radio audience. You will need to consider to what extent the absence of images will dictate what the commentator should say to ensure that viewers can follow the action. Write a commentary to accompany your rewriting, explaining what changes you have made and why you have made them.
2. An additional task would be to record and transcribe a television and radio commentary on the same sporting event and compare their discourse structure and lexical and grammatical choices.

The language of emails

The first question that we should ask is: is there a language of emails? After all, electronic communication may appear in many different forms and genres, ranging from quick messages to friends, mailings we have requested from companies, mailings we have not requested (junk mail) and bank correspondence. Many companies are now encouraging job applications by email. Are there nonetheless general linguistic properties that we can say are representative of 'email language'?

As we saw in Section A, we can speak of writing and speech as two different modes of communication and claim that each has generally distinguishing features. We also saw that many texts appear to sit somewhere on a continuum between the two (mixed-mode texts), sharing conventional features of both.

David Crystal (2006) suggests that the sheer diversity of purposes of email makes it difficult to generalise about the language features it uses. He does, however, suggest that it is relatively straightforward to identify and summarise a set of *structural elements* that typify emails.

Extension activity 16

Collect some examples of emails and consider what properties of spoken and written texts they contain.

Headers

Date: automatically inserted by software

From: the sender, an obligatory element

Subject: the topic of the message, not obligatory

To: the recipient either entered manually or through a prompt that recognises a name from an address book

Optional elements

Cc: a carbon or courtesy copy sent to another person

Bcc: a blind carbon copy sent without the main recipient's knowledge

 Signalling that there is a text, picture or sound attachment

Fig. 5 *Structural elements in email headers (adapted from Crystal, 2006, p95–96)*

Key terms

Framing: cutting and pasting parts of an original message into a new message.

Some other issues when discussing and analysing emails

What is also distinctive about emails is that once sent, they may be forwarded and even modified by any number of other users. Modification of a message can take place through **framing**, where parts of an original message are cut and pasted into a new message to identify and respond to them. This saves time and space, but could cause problems if words are placed outside their original context. Equally, the possibility afforded by email for any message to be forwarded to anyone else (or even sent as a bcc) could be worrying for some senders.

Extension activity 17

The best way to develop your understanding of the language of emails is to undertake some research of your own. Collect a small corpus to investigate the following:

- Variations in subject lines, greetings and farewells.
- Use of informal lexical items, non-standard spellings and grammatical constructions and graphological features.
- Obvious dialogic strategies such as exchange structures that are set up and maintained electronically.

As you analyse you should consider the purpose and context of each of your emails and the relationship between e-participants. Finally, remember that you need to consider carefully the effect that this medium has on linguistic features and behaviours.

Message boards and chat rooms

The main distinction between message boards and chat rooms is that while message boards are, like emails, examples of **asynchronous discourse**, chat room conversations occurring in real time are **synchronous**.

Common features of message boards

- These are populated by **users** with an interest in a topic. Users create their own **username**, which may be linked to the nature of the board, and in many cases gives little indication of the speaker's age, gender or geographical location (though these may be obligatory). Some boards show the number of posts a user has made and assign seniority to high-posting users.

- Users post contributions to a main site which may be moderated by those running the board (and edited or removed). Messages are displayed as **threads**, which can be added to by other users in an ongoing dialogue. Often responses to threads contain examples of framing, where another's post is used as a way of shaping a contribution. Some contributions can be modified into **stickies**, which remain at the top of the message board as foregrounded important posts that a **moderator** or members of the community want all other users to see. Posts remain on the message board over a series of pages until they are removed by a moderator. Threads are distinguished by a title that may also aim to draw attention to their importance through the use of emoticons, capitalisation and exclamation marks. In some cases, boards allow the posting of particular types of threads such as polls, to which users are invited to contribute.

- As a thread continues the original focus may shift as users **go off-topic**, though this may be frowned upon by other contributors.

- Many message boards are tight discourse communities and display a distinctive and idiosyncratic use of language, for example in the use of particular items or phrases in a form of **lexical accommodation**. Moreover the community feel often means that participants behave like close friends even if they have never met. Solidarity and shared interests and passions promote this sense of community.

Key terms

Asynchronous discourse: discourse in which there are delays between turns that participants take.

Synchronous discourse: discourse that takes place in real time.

User: an individual using a message board.

Username: the name chosen by a user of a message board that is known to all on that board and appears every time a post is made.

Thread: a topic area initiated by a post to which others can respond.

Stickie: a thread that is considered important and remains near the top of the message board regardless of how many times it is read or has responses.

Moderator: an individual or group of individuals who run the message board and have the right to edit or delete threads and posts.

Go off-topic: a term for posts that stray from the original topic of a thread.

Lexical accommodation: the way in which speakers mirror each other's lexical choices as a sign of community membership.

Flaming: the act of posting aggressive threads or responses to threads.

Lurker: a user who reads a message board as a member or guest but who rarely, if ever, posts.

Trolling: the posting of messages with the intention of irritating others.

Web log: a site that is set up to allow an individual or several individuals to post frequent entries.

Pragmatically, participants are expected to follow a set of conversational rules. **Flaming** involves posting a contribution aimed at another user that is deemed aggressive or inappropriate. In addition to off-topic behaviour that breaks the conversational maxim of relevance, excessively long or unacceptably brief responses that break the maxim of quantity, or those which appear untruthful (the maxim of quality) are also frowned upon. In sensitive situations, politeness strategies may be used when face threats are obvious. **Lurkers** (those who read message boards but rarely post themselves) and those guilty of **trolling** (posting with intent to irritate others) are seen as outcasts in the virtual discourse community.

Extension activity 18

Message boards and chat rooms provide fertile ground for further investigation. Some areas that you might wish to investigate include:

- usernames that participants use to identify themselves
- lexical and grammatical features of spoken discourse
- evidence of Grice's conversational maxims being adhered to or broken, including examples of flaming and trolling
- politeness strategies used by various participants
- the use of small talk within virtual discourse communities
- how power might be demonstrated by more senior members of a community, for example through responses to others' posts and in the case of chat rooms, topic management and control of the discussion (floor control)
- attitudes to new members (newbies) and lurkers that exist as a way of gauging the community ethos of a particular board or chat room.

Other genres

Web pages

Just as it is difficult to identify absolute features of email language, the enormous variety in functions of web pages makes identifying distinctive elements virtually impossible. Web pages may exist to provide information, entertain or persuade in the form of advertisements. In the light of this, they may use a range of language features in order to communicate with their implied readers and audiences. In terms of discourse structure, whilst many pages may resemble print documents, they also exist as complex sites of navigation, offering a range of resources, links and even encouraging reader participation.

Classroom activity 21

Access the Plain English Campaign's guide to designing and constructing websites, which can be found at www.plainenglish.co.uk. Compare its advice with a range of web pages. (Note that you will need Adobe Acrobat Reader to access this document.)

Web logs (blogs)

A **web log** is a site that allows individuals to post in a way that is similar to an electronic diary, accessible to anyone who chooses to navigate to the site. Blogs may contain links to other blogs and websites of potential interest and so are wide ranging in so far as they serve to provoke further discussion and exploration. Some blogs invite readers to post comments and some exist to share copyright-free downloadable material, for example MP3 music files. At the other end of the spectrum, many **bloggers** simply use their site as a personal diary space, albeit one that is accessible to the general public.

Linguistic features of blogs

Read through Text X, an extract from David Crystal's (2006) *Language and the Internet*, in which he analyses an example from a blog and comments on the unique form of personal blogging. Using Crystal's comments on *blog style*, investigate a number of personal and corporate blogs. Can you account for their style by considering their linguistic features and their intended audiences and purposes?

Text X

'Went out, stopped by the Mall to get some coffee – problem as usual with all the car parking, and as if that wasnt enough the lights controling the way into the car-park, you know the twostage green and red switching thingies werent working so it took ages. And theres never mechanics around when you want them, is there – tho I did see someone in a uniform lurking about – but come to think of it what would you need a uniform for to fix lights, so maybe they were just there for something else. Anyways it took me an hour instead of what I was expecting, 10 minutes.'

Here we have an example of a style of writing which has never been seen in a public, printed form, outside of literature, and even there it would take an ingenious novelist indeed to capture its innocent spontaneity and unpredictable thematic direction. It is difficult to know how to describe the style, because it falls uneasily between standard and non-standard English. It illustrates writing that is largely orthodox with respect to the main dimensions that identify standardness – spelling, punctuation, and grammar, but they depart from the norms in various ways.

In spelling, we see controling for controlling, tho for though, and twostage for two-stage; in punctuation, we see the avoidance of apostrophes. In vocabulary, we see criterium for criterion and anyways for anyway. There are several features of informal written English which would be eliminated in a copy-edited version of such a text for publication, such as the unconstrained use of the dash to mark a change in the thought or the use of commas to follow the rhythm of the 'speaker'. As regards grammar, stretches of text defy conventional grammatical analysis in terms of sentences. The discourse expresses a sequence of units of thought, but these do not correspond to the kinds of sentence division we have been taught to associate with 'elegant' writing. At lower levels of grammar, too, there are features which would be considered unacceptable in traditionally printed publications, such as to, of course, finally get (which automatically splits the infinitive), theres never mechanics (breaking a concord rule), and criterium on (wrong preposition). In its unconstrained flow, it is – I imagine – as close to the way a writer talks as it is possible to get. Certainly, the style drives a coach and horses through everything we would be told in the grammatical tradition of the past 250 years about how we should write.

David Crystal, Language and the Internet, 2006

Key terms

Blogger: an individual who uses a web log.

AQA Examiner's tip

Don't limit discussion of the features of web pages and blogs to their graphological features. Pay close attention to elements of discourse structure, lexis, grammar and pragmatics as you analyse.

■ Further reading

Beard, A. *The Language of Sport*, Routledge, 1998 (contains a very good chapter comparing television and radio sports commentaries)

Crystal, D. *A Glossary of Netspeak and Textspeak*, Edinburgh University Press, 2004

Crystal, D. *Language and the Internet*, Cambridge University Press (2nd edn), 2006 (an extremely detailed treatment of emails, message boards, chat rooms and blogs)

Wray, A., Trott, K., and Bloomer, A. *Projects in Linguistics: A Practical Guide to Researching Language*, Arnold, 1998 (a range of topics with some excellent ideas for further research and data collection)

Download phone-ins, interviews and sports commentaries in MP3 format from the BBC Radio Five Live website: www.bbc.co.uk/fivelive

A definitive source of information and statistics on mobile telephone use: www.text.it/home.cfm

The Guardian Unlimited – search for a range of articles on language and technology: www.guardian.co.uk

Examination preparation and practice

In this topic you will:

■ learn about the requirements of the assessed task in Section B

■ explore applying your learning from this section and have opportunities to assess your work against assessment criteria.

■ The data focuses

The following types of data could be set for each of the topics covered in this section. It is important therefore that you feel comfortable when handling each of these.

Language and power

■ A transcript of spontaneous interaction where one participant has a more powerful role than others.

■ A transcript of a speaker attempting to influence an audience.

■ A written or electronic document produced by an organisation in an attempt to influence an audience.

Language and gender

■ A transcript of spontaneous interaction from either same- or mixed-sex talk.

■ A transcript of same- or mixed-sex interaction through a medium for an audience.

■ A published document displaying the representation of gender issues in some manner.

■ A statement or summary of linguistic research of a set of beliefs for discussion.

Language and technology

- A transcript of interaction via landline or mobile phone.
- Examples of text messages.
- A transcript of a radio or television phone-in.
- A transcript of a radio or television commentary on any live event.
- Examples of emails, message boards, web pages and web logs.

Examples of examination questions

The following provide you with one example of a question from each topic in Unit 1, Section B. Read the questions carefully and look at the tips given to you to emphasise key points regarding what the examiner will be looking for.

Language and power examination-style question

1   This text is an advertisement for a charity that appeared in a national newspaper. How does this text aim to influence the audience?

> The question invites you to analyse various features of *lexis*, *grammar*, *discourse* and *graphological* features that the text producer uses to influence and persuade. In addition, what *pragmatic implications* and *assumed knowledge* are present?

> As this is an *advertisement*, you should consider how advertising sets up a relationship with and positions its implied readers. What *purposes* might a charity have for advertising?

He told his parents to f**k off. He told his foster parents to f**k off. He told fourteen social workers to f**k off. He told us to f**k off. But we didn't and we still haven't.

The UK is full of vulnerable children. Many of them with stories that would break your heart. Some of them capable of terrible things. But if you believe that no child is born bad, then you can't watch somebody get filed away as a problem. You can't let society play pass the parcel with a young person's life. If a child is referred to Barnardo's we stick by that child. We listen. We look for potential. We give practical support. And if we don't give up on the troubled, young boy, it's not because we enjoy being sworn at. It's because we believe in him.

Believe in
children
Barnardo's

Student's response

Here Nicola comments on a relevant graphological feature, which is explored rather than just stated as a feature and makes some good points on how the text producer's belief systems are evident through this (AO2).

This text is produced by the charity with the purpose of persuading people to support them achieve their aims of supporting young and vulnerable children. This purpose is achieved in a variety of ways.

Graphologically, the text is dominated by the large image to the left, which immediately attracts our attention as we read from left to right and in comparison to the smaller text. This consists of a forlorn-looking boy, obviously plagued by troubles. By using a child who appears to be vulnerable, the producer presents the fact that there are many susceptible children, who need to be helped. This idea of charitable giving as an, admirable if not essential, quality is of course is the ideology held by the charity, and by using this image their own held ideology is pushed forward on to the audience.

There is more developed discussion here using Fairclough's work on synthetic personalisation (AO2) together with key language features. Pragmatics is addressed through the comments on shared knowledge and Nicola fully supports her interpretations with reference to the data (AO3).

Synthetic personalisation, as identified by Fairclough, is used vastly in adverts; and here it is indeed used extensively. For instance, the pronoun 'you' is used throughout; its ambiguity (as to whether it is in the singular or plural form) allows the audience to feel they are being addressed directly and personally (which then allows the producer and receiver to establish a relationship), whilst still allowing the producer to address many. The producer also assumes a relationship with the audience through the use of shared knowledge; for example 'pass the parcel' which of course is the children's game in which a parcel is unwrapped, its layers cast aside, and passed to a vast number of others. This then creates the allusion that children are treated much like the parcel in the game, without consideration to their welfare.

Again there is sustained contextual discussion here with a firm linguistic foundation, for example the comments on pronoun use and verb processes (AO3). Nicola also identifies a range of ways in which the text producer attempts to influence the audience and assumes a powerful position. There are precise comments on syntax and lexical choices, linked to an explicit awareness of the text's purpose and context (AO3).

The modal auxiliary verb 'can't', in the sentences 'you can't let…' and 'you can't watch…', denies the audience the option of not helping Barnardos, and suggests that the situation is more disastrous than the audience knows; coupled with the aforementioned 'pass the parcel' reference, the audience are very much under Barnardos's influence.

Barnardos also shares their work with the audience, albeit not explicitly. For example, the parallelism in the sentences 'we listen. We look… We give…' emphasises how Barnardos is actively helping, through the repeated pronoun 'we'. The verb processes, such as 'look', show Barnardos to be caring and trusting; the pronoun 'we' shows them to be almost like a family unit; and the action process 'give' implies that they're providing the active help and support needed. Parallelism is also used 'he told… he told… he told…' which allows the subsequent 'but we didn't' to be foregrounded, thus highlighting that though everyone else left him, Barnardos will stay with him; this paints them as a reliable and compassionate charity. The shift, from 'he' in the subject position, to 'we' as the subject, shows that Barnardos also has control, and so will help him.

The answer ends with some more focused observations and a final evaluation of the context of reception, which pays close attention to and comments on the fact that the advertisement, unlike conventional charity ads, does not explicitly ask for a donation (AO3).

The use of the taboo term 'f***' in an advert usually would be rather shocking and offensive; however, here it is used to highlight the extent of the hurt and problems of the child; and so consequently to emphasise the good-natured work of Barnardos in transforming children.

The lexeme 'believe' is repeated in the text. It carries guilt with it in the sentence '…we believe…', when it is used in addition to the pronoun 'we' (which is here used as exclusive) to suggest that the audience should, too; it is then coerced into an imperative 'believe' to demand that the audience do; and then it is used in the sentence 'to show you believe…' which again uses an emotional impact to refuse the audience the chance to say no. This is a hard-hitting advertisement about what would be a serious subject for the vast majority of people. It needs to be so in order to raise funds. As charities often have to compete for funding, this advertisement aims to be as explicit as possible to gain supporters. Interestingly, although it does not explicitly ask for funding, most readers would understand that supporting the charity would mean parting with money (although of course there are other ways of supporting a charity).

Examiner's overall comments

Nicola shows a clear understanding of a range of language features, which she uses to analyse the text, aware very much of its purpose and context (AO3). She uses relevant ideas from her study of language (AO2) to help support her own analyses. She uses the data well and makes some perceptive observations on lexis and syntax to support her overall points about the text's purpose and methods of influencing its audience. These qualities would place her work high in the 11–14 band for AO2 and high in the 22–29 band for AO3.

Language and gender examination-style questions

1   This text is a transcript of a conversation between three women at a hairdresser's salon. S2 is being questioned by the hairdresser S1. S3 also works at the salon as a hairwasher. Comment on the significance of gender in this interaction.

> The *context* is important here. This is an example of *same-sex female interaction*, so you should look carefully at how the *speakers interact* and the various *discourse strategies* they use. You should also consider the women's statuses as employees and customer.

> How significant is gender? You could refer to *relevant research* into the way women behave in same-sex talk, for example ideas on cooperation through various linguistic strategies.

Key:
(.) indicates a brief pause;
numbers within brackets indicate length of pause in seconds;
underlining indicates emphasis in speech;
words between vertical lines are spoken simultaneously;
relevant contextual information is given within square brackets

S1:   how much do you want off
S2:   ermm (2) Well I like to keep the top quite long
S1:   yeah
S2:   ermm but I like the back nice and short and the sides nice and short it's just got a bit you know a bit grown out of shape
S1:   too heavy
S2:   yeah
S1:   do you like your sides feathered
S2:   yeah, yeah
S1:   so whispy there
S2:   yeah
S1:   now this back bit do you tend to have that bit clippered
S2:   yeah and I have (.) I tend to have it like graduated at the back (.) right at the bottom really short and then kind of graduated up (.) you know not like a line as such just
S1:   right
S2:   graded up
S1:   so right yeah
S2:   and I generally style it but it's cos it's got so I generally have like a maybe side (.) side-ish parting
S1:   parting going ‖ over that way ‖
S2:   ‖ Yeah   ‖ just to give it a bit more
S1:   do you have the front bit thinned slightly
S2:   yeah, yeah (.) it's got so heavy
S1:   how long would you say it is since you've had it cut

S2:   I know I had it done on the last day of January (.) so that's
S1:   right
S2:   but my hair grows really quickly and really thickly as well so
S1:   Do about six weeks or so
S2:   yeah
S1:   and then if I taper that out slightly so it's shorter there (.)
      clipper that slightly and taper it slightly down
S2:   yeah
S1:   so you haven't got such a line
S2:   yeah
S1:   and then just take a bit through your layers
S2:   yeah that would be great
S1:   [inaudible] for you
S2:   cos it just needs some more ‖ umph   ‖
S1:   ‖ it's just ‖ laying heavy
S2:   yeah
S1:   okay do you want to take a seat
S2:   thanks a lot
S1:   I'll pass you the bowl
S2:   thank you
S1:   take a seat in the middle
S2:   right thank you
(17 seconds)
S1:   here we are
S2:   thanks (4) thank you
(16 seconds) [laughter]
S2:   she's one step ahead of you in't she
(6 seconds) [phone rings]
S2:   thanks (6) Have you been busy today or has it just quietened
      down
S3:   well I didn't start until one (4) and I'm here till nine
S2:   oh yeah it's late night opening isn't it
(49 seconds) [washing hair]
S2:   the shampoos always smell so nice don't they
S3:   yeah (96) the conditioners are nice as well
S2:   yeah [inaudible]….[laughs]

R. Carter and *M. McCarthy*, Exploring Spoken English

Nicola's comments here identify the roles of the hairdresser and customer and begin to make some valid points about particular uses of language within this context, for example the point on deictic expressions (AO3).

Student's response

Most of the dialogue in this extract is between the main hairdresser and the customer. What is important to remember is that the hairdresser's role is to support the customer in making the right choice. She does this by asking most of the initial questions, which is a sign of her status, for example 'Do you have your sides feathered?' and 'Do you tend to have that bit clipped as well?' In some cases she builds on the rather vague instructions given by the customer such as 'I generally have like a side, side-ish parting'. Her response to this clarifies the customer's wishes. The use of deictic expressions such as 'over that way' and 'so wispy there' would of course be in the context of the hairdresser physically handling and pointing to the customer's hair. The hairdresser's comments are forceful but she needs to ensure that mistakes are not made.

Speaker support is also used extensively by the hairdresser. This could be a way of helping the customer feel at ease or in some cases to ensure that she is absolutely certain about what kind of haircut the customer wants. When overlaps do occur, they are more to support than examples of interruptions. The customer also uses minimal responses such as 'yeah' to indicate that she is in agreement with what the hairdresser is proposing to her. At one point she uses the adjective 'great', which has been cited as an example of an 'empty adjective' by Robin Lakoff and typical of a weakness in women's language. In this context, however, it clearly signals that she is happy with what the hairdresser is suggesting and could be seen more as a cooperative device in line with that suggested by Janet Holmes. Other examples of similar terms can be seen when the customer uses the intensifier 'really', 'but my hair grows really quickly and really thickly.' There is nothing weak about these words; they just exist to give relevant information to the hairdresser in this context.

> Again, Nicola sustains a close analysis of the interaction and makes some valid points on the use of speaker-support strategies used (AO3). She identifies particular lexical choices made and explains them in the context of the interaction. Her references to the work of Robin Lakoff and Janet Holmes are relevant and valid (AO2) and support her own comments well.

The hairdresser also avoids threatening the customer's face needs by using the indirect construction 'it needs some more umph'. Here she avoids criticising the current state of the customer's hair by using an informal term, which reflects the friendly atmosphere she wishes to maintain.

> The comments here on indirect strategies are valid, although Nicola could have made more of other politeness strategies used by the speakers in this extract.

When the customer speaks to the hairwasher, we notice a different type of communication. The customer tries to initiate small talk by enquiring about the hairwasher's day and uses tag questions to try to gain a response from the hairwasher (who seems reluctant to speak). Again this use of tag questions can be seen as a facilitative device aimed to develop social relationships (as suggested by Holmes and supported by my own investigation into all female talk where I discovered that tag questions were frequently used by female speakers to encourage others to speak). As the hairdresser has less status than the main hairdresser in the shop, she does not seek to comment on hairstyles but instead just carries out her role. She does however repeat the adjective 'nice', mirroring the turn of the customer before her. This example of speaker accommodation could be seen as another way that the females in this extract attempt to create a social relationship.

> Again, there is some good work on language features (in this case tag questions) with a clear understanding of the context of the interaction. Nicola again uses relevant ideas from language study (including results of her own investigations) to support her comments (AO2) and makes some insightful points about the role of the hairwasher and how that might affect her linguistic behaviour (AO3).

Overall, there is clear evidence of the female speakers supporting each other here, which would reflect much of the research on all-female talk as being collaborative and cooperative, for example Coates, whose study in 1989 suggested that all female speakers tend to negotiate discussions and support each other. Pilkington in 1992 also found that women aimed for more positive politeness strategies when engaged in conversation with each other.

Examiner's overall comments

Nicola identifies a range of language features and explores them with a good focus on contextual factors (AO3). She explores how the women use language to collaborate and cooperate, and hints at how a hierarchical power structure within the hairdresser's salon might also be responsible for some of the linguistic behaviours as the three women act out roles. Her comments are supported by relevant ideas from the study of language, for example on the researchers Lakoff and Holmes and on small talk and accommodation. She also uses her own investigations to strengthen her comments and arguments. These qualities would place her work in the 11–14 band for AO2 and just into the 22–29 band for AO3. The AO3 mark would be improved with a more focused set of comments on how collaboration and cooperation occur within the context of the hairdresser's salon.

Language and technology examination-style question

1   This transcript is an extract from a radio phone-in. The presenter (P) is speaking to a caller, Mark (C). How has the language of the text been influenced by technology?

> *P*: Mark's the Spurs fan on the line to kick us off (.) hi Mark
>
> *C*: hello er Mark down in Bexley mate I've just got back from that erm (.) you know what they've got this Spurs team now (.) they've got the bottle to fight er as good as Arsenal are (.) erm it it's something special that (.) er really really something special (.) they had all the all the rubbish thrown at them that we've taken erm [sighs] I really do think we can win the cup this year (.) you know we can beat Chelsea I reckon
>
> *P*: pick out a few players for us who have er really stood out tonight
>
> *C*: well that man (.) er Berbatov sensational (.) still think we need a goalkeeper but perhaps that's a little bit unkind (.) he's Robinson going to get back I think (.) Keane magic (.) but he he he's got them playing together hasn't he and the big lad up front erm sens absolutely sensational (.) I wouldn't have thought at the beginning of the year er the beginning of October we'd be struggling but er it's fantastic
>
> *P*: I just think Berbatov starts to look the (.) he's got that swagger about him and the the ‖ third goal ‖ and the turns the (.) maybe Jol was right maybe he
>
> *C*:   ‖ yeah   ‖
>
> *P*: will be the man for Spurs this year
>
> *C*: yeah well well Ramos you know again he's had his critics hasn't he but er perhaps Jenas bless him (.) erm the pace he he's like a rabbit a rabbit down that wing but erm (1) but er (2) fan fantastic game honestly and I er think they will really challenge for the top four next year I think it (.) with due respect to to Liverpool and Everton and Villa erm (.) But Arsenal (.) they've got the league and a two horse race do you agree (.) don't you agree
>
> *P*: who cares what I think (.) thanks Mark (.) Ron's an Arsenal (.) Ron good evening

Student's response

As this is a radio phone-in, the programme is happening in real time, although it is likely that the caller has already spoken to an editor and questioned about what he is going to say. This is a key feature of the phone-in and gives both the presenter and caller an understanding of how the interaction will proceed. Despite this, there are still many examples of naturally occurring spoken discourse and many language features are influenced by the medium of the radio phone-in.

The presenter's role is to maintain the interaction and allow the caller to express his view. The presenter begins with a metaphorical play on words 'kick us off' which is in keeping with a range of lexical items from the field of football that give the interaction cohesion. The greeting sequence 'Hi Mark' is a signal that the caller can begin to speak and he further initiates another exchange with his question on Spurs players who have played well.

The caller speaks to the presenter using informal terms such as 'hello' and 'down in Bexley mate'. He shows his position as a Spurs fan by using the first-person plural pronoun 'we' and addresses the presenter directly using the pronoun 'you'. He assumes shared knowledge on the part of the presenter by referring to the (again metaphorical) 'rubbish' that Spurs fans and players have had to take, which I assume means criticism from others.

The presenter's second turn, as well as initiating another exchange structure could also be seen as speaker support, encouraging the caller, whose pauses and fillers suggest he may be a little nervous at speaking live on air, to develop his opinions. The caller, because of the medium of communication is not constrained by the need to use standard grammatical constructions. Instead, he uses elliptical sentences, omitting verbs, 'Berbatov sensational' and again assumes shared knowledge on the part of the presenter and other listeners by referring to the Spurs player as 'the big lad up front' ('lad' is often used by footballers and fans to refer to a player). His comments on Berbatov are taken up by the presenter, again as a sign of speaker support. In this instance, the caller also uses back channelling 'yeah' to maintain the interaction with the presenter.

The presenter initiates a further question by referring to Jol (who was the previous manager), again expecting a degree of shared knowledge with caller and listeners, that further allows the caller to express some more views, particularly his opinion that Spurs could challenge for the league this year. He even uses a tag question at the end of his turn 'don't you agree' to get a reaction from the presenter. Interestingly, the presenter's response 'who cares what I think', which would normally break the conversational maxim of manner and threaten positive face probably doesn't do in this context as the caller is almost certainly aware that his contribution to the show will come to an end. Instead, the presenter finishes with an abrupt politeness marker 'thanks Mark' before moving on to his next caller. This may well be because of time constraints because in a short show, the production team would want to get the views of as many fans as possible. Overall then, the discourse of a radio phone-in is clearly evident in a greeting-question-farewell structure and the abundance of features of spoken discourse as well as the presenter and caller cooperating to ensure a worthwhile contribution has been made.

Nicola makes a good point about informality here in the context of what the show is attempting to portray. In addition she continues with her close focus on lexical items and makes some valid comments on shared knowledge in this context (AO3).

There are references to typical features of spoken discourse here with some attempt to explain why they may be evident (AO2). Nicola also draws attention to non-standard grammar and the referencing to the Spurs forward as the big lad up front, again with some insight as to why the lexical item 'lad' is chosen. She continues to comment on the way that the speakers cooperate to maintain the interaction (AO3).

The ending of this answer considers some aspects of politeness (AO2) and maintains a strong focus on context by considering the need for the presenter to move quickly on to his next guest (AO3). Nicola's response concludes with a summary of the discourse pattern commonly found in radio phone-ins (AO2/3).

Examiner's overall comments

Nicola maintains a good focus on this text, considering how the medium of the radio phone-in influences the language choices that speakers make. She is aware of contexual factors (AO3) and clearly and soundly analyses a number of language features. She makes insightful and relevant comments, with some valid references to ideas from language study (for example conversational exchanges, maxims and politeness strategies). These qualities would place her work clearly in the 11–14 band for AO2 and in the 22–29 band for AO3. Again some further attention to lexical and grammatical features in addition to those mentioned in paragraph four, would have made this a more secure answer.

Assessment objectives:

- **AO1** Select and apply a range of linguistic methods to communicate relevant knowledge using appropriate terminology and coherent, accurate written expression (5 per cent of the AS mark).

- **AO2** Demonstrate critical understanding of a range of concepts and issues related to the construction and analysis of meanings in spoken and written language, using knowledge of linguistic approaches (5 per cent of the AS mark).

- **AO3** Analyse and evaluate the influence of contextual factors on the production and reception of spoken and written language, showing knowledge of the key constituents of language (5 per cent of the AS mark).

- **AO4** Demonstrate expertise and creativity in the use of English in a range of different contexts informed by linguistic study (25 per cent of the AS mark).

In Unit 2 you will explore the skills required to produce your own creative writing. You will have been introduced to many of the skills required for this unit while you were studying GCSE English. For example, at GCSE you will have already analysed writers' use of language, and you will be familiar with the stylistic conventions of different text types such as autobiography and writing to persuade. You will also have used many of the technical terms used in Unit 2, such as *metaphor*, *simile* and *personification*.

Unit 2 builds on your existing knowledge and extends it so that your analysis of texts becomes more sophisticated and, in turn, your own writing becomes more controlled. The best pieces of original writing will use the structures and conventions associated with different genres. In addition register will be manipulated to meet the demands of specific audiences. A new skill that you will explore in Unit 2 is the ability to write a commentary on your original writing. The commentary provides you with an opportunity to explain to the examiner what process you went through to produce your pieces of original writing.

Section A of Unit 2 takes you through the intricate process of producing your original writing. Your first task is to choose a genre, such as creative writing or travel writing, and to analyse examples of writing from these genres. The extracts that you analyse are referred to as your style models. You will be shown how to identify the linguistic features associated with the genres that you choose to write. Section A then explores how you can use in your own writing the linguistic features that you have identified in your style models. At each stage of Section A you will explore the linguistic features of different genres and study students' and examiners' comments on a range of activities.

Section B of Unit 2 shows how to write an effective commentary on your original writing. You will be shown how to annotate your style models and how to refer in your commentary to the linguistic features that you have identified in them. You will then be shown how to discuss how you have used these linguistic features in your original writing. The requirement to comment on significant changes that you have made during the drafting process will be considered. Finally, you will see how important it is to include your judgement about the effectiveness of your original writing. At each stage of Section B you will judge students' commentaries and consider how the students' commentaries could be improved.

Complete coursework folders will contain:

- two pieces of original writing, totalling between 1,500 and 2,500 words
- two commentaries, totalling 1,000 words.

In addition you must submit:

- annotated extracts of texts that have influenced your writing
- drafts of your writing that illustrate the creative process that you have gone through, including evidence of early planning/preparation
- clear references of any sources that you have used.

A Original writing

Introduction

In this section you will:

- learn how to write effective commentaries on your own writing, in order to explain your stylistic decisions to the examiner
- explore the conventions of different styles of writing
- produce two pieces of original writing.

Section A supports you in your analysis of the stylistic conventions of eight different pieces of writing, which you will use to improve the quality of your own writing. Creative writers often deliberately challenge stylistic conventions for specific effects, but if you are going to do this, you must be confident about your reasons for doing so, and explain your decisions in your commentary. It is not advisable to challenge the conventions just to be different.

Each of your pieces of original writing should have a different audience, purpose and genre within the following categories:

- writing to entertain
- writing to persuade
- writing to inform
- writing to advise/instruct.

Within these categories you have a great deal of freedom. Table 1 below, taken from the examination specification, gives you an idea of some of the possibilities.

Table 1 *Examples of writing categories*

Writing to entertain	A soap opera script. An extract from an autobiography. A dramatic monologue.
Writing to persuade	An editorial. A letter to a head of centre about uniform issues. A speech delivered as a football captain.
Writing to inform	A piece of travel journalism. A leaflet focusing on a health issue. An extract from a motorbike maintenance manual.
Writing to advise/instruct	A leaflet focusing on 'How to choose a university'. A guide to texting for novices. An article on 'How to survive a music festival'.

Classroom activity 1

Add two more writing ideas within each of the four categories in Table 1: writing to entertain, persuade, inform and advise/instruct.

It is important to understand that this is not meant to be an exhaustive list. Other options might include a magazine article, a children's story or a review of a television drama.

To produce two pieces of writing for different purposes, audiences and genres within these categories you might **either**:

1 (a) write a letter to a head teacher persuading her that the imposition of school uniform is outdated, then (b) write a leaflet that informs teenagers about the dangers of smoking.

Or:

2 (a) Write a piece of autobiography in order to entertain other AS students, then (b) write an article for an adult audience, giving advice on how to support students who are going through a period of examinations.

Some other suggestions for your writing are:

- a book review
- a film review
- a music CD review
- a review of a live performance of a play
- a review of a concert
- a holiday brochure
- a short story
- a story written for children
- an audio guide to a museum or art exhibition
- a play script or radio script.

Style models

Before you start writing it is essential that you thoroughly analyse the **styles** of different pieces of writing. You need to understand how the following operate within texts:

- Register and style.
- Characteristics of genres and sub-genres.
- Impact of language choices (lexis and grammar) and **discourse strategies**.

You will also need to understand how to use primary sources within your own writing, and how to reference them so that your readers can refer to them. Planning, drafting, and redrafting are vital, and you should keep copies of all of your rough work. This will require you to print a copy of each draft that you write on a computer, in order to have a record of all the changes that you make.

Appropriate linguistic terminology

In this topic you will:

In this topic you will:

- revise some linguistic terms that you learnt in Unit 1
- learn some new linguistic terms.

AO1 requires that you:

- select and apply a range of linguistic methods, to communicate relevant knowledge
- learn how these linguistic terms are used when analysing texts using appropriate terminology.

Consequently, it is important that you understand:

- what the linguistic terms mean
- how to use them appropriately in your own writing.

If you understand these two things, your analysis of different authors' writing will be more sophisticated, your own writing will be more controlled, and your analysis of your own writing will be more systematic and reflective.

In this topic we will look at the key linguistic terms, identify the use of these features in different authors' writing, and see how you can use these terms when commenting on authors' writing and also your own writing. You will have learnt many literary terms at GCSE, and many others during Unit 1 of AS English Language. There will be very little new terminology to learn.

Some of the more common linguistic terms

You will probably have used all of the following terms in writing about poetry and prose at GCSE. Look back at your GCSE revision notes if you need to remind yourself about some of them.

Classroom activity 2

Match each of the linguistic terms below with its definition in Table 2.

noun	metaphor	second person
verb	simile	emotive language
adverb	alliteration	third person
rhetorical question	assonance	personification
adjective	colloquialism	analogy
pronoun	first person	

See page 199 for feedback on this activity.

Table 2 *Linguistic term definitions*

Linguistic term	Definition
	Word that provides information about a verb
	The use of a term to describe something that it does not denote, to suggest similar qualities between the two
	The use of the same initial sound in words close together
	Discourse that uses 'I' or 'We'
	Word that names a place, a person, a thing, a feeling or an idea
	Word used instead of a noun or a name
	Word that provides information about a noun
	Discourse that uses 'she' or 'they', for example
	Giving human qualities to a non-human object
	The use of a comparison between two cases, implying that if this comparison works, then the two cases have many similarities
	Language that encourages readers to respond emotionally rather than rationally. Many words have emotive connotations and readers may respond to these rather than their denotations.
	A question that does not require an answer because the answer is obvious
	Discourse that uses 'you'
	Informal use of language
	The use of the same vowel sounds in words close together
	A comparison of one thing with another, using the words 'like' or 'as'
	Word that describes an action or condition

■ **Classroom activity 3**

Here is a list of linguistic terms that you studied in Unit 1. Define each of them.

- determiner
- conjunction
- preposition
- proper noun
- abstract noun
- concrete noun
- personal pronoun
- possessive pronoun
- reflexive pronoun
- demonstrative
- pronoun
- relative pronoun
- lexical connector
- cohesion
- synonymy
- antonymy

Many of these terms will be used in this unit, so it is important that you are confident about their meanings and the effects that can be achieved by using them. Refer to Unit 1 if you are not confident about the definitions of these terms, or about using them in your own writing.

💡 Some new linguistic terms

Here is a further list of linguistic terms that you have met briefly and will become more familiar with. You will be expected to use them in the analysis of your own and others' writing.

Table 3 *Additional linguistic term definitions*

Linguistic term	Definition
Denotation	The literal meaning of a word or phrase. The sentence 'I gave her a rose' could denote a red flower.
Connotation	What is implied or suggested by a word or phrase. The sentence 'I gave her a red rose' could have connotations of romance or love
Declarative sentence	A statement: 'It is Tuesday today.'
Imperative sentence	An instruction: 'Close the door behind you.'
Interrogative sentence	A question: 'Would you like me to go through that again?'
Idiolect	The individual features of a person's language. A character in a novel might repeatedly use the phrase 'Alright now…' This will signpost to the reader which character is speaking.
Lexis	The language used in a text. Lexis can be appropriate or inappropriate, e.g. colloquialisms might be considered inappropriate lexis in a formal speech.
Lexical field	Lexical items that share certain semantic value. The lexical field of teaching might include the words 'differentiation', 'formative assessment', 'discipline', and 'rewards'.
Register	The level of formality or the subject-specific nature of the language of a text. The following sentence would be the appropriate register for a formal speech: 'I am delighted to have been asked to speak to this knowledgeable audience about energy conservation.'
Minor sentence	A sentence whose construction does not follow normal rules, e.g. the sentence 'Three roses' does not have a verb and so constitutes a **minor sentence**.

Key terms

Minor sentence: a grammatically incomplete sentence.

Classroom activity 4

Make a record of the terms in Table 3 that you feel confident about using in your own writing. Make a conscious effort to learn any terms that you do not understand, or are less confident about using in your own writing.

Text A overleaf is an extract from Charles Dickens's novel *Hard Times*, written in 1856. In this extract Dickens describes an industrial city. A student has annotated the text and written a commentary about it.

Text A

HardTimes

It was a town of red brick, or of brick that would have been red **if the smoke and ashes had allowed it**; but as matters stood, it was a town of **unnatural** red and black like the painted face of a savage.

It was a town of machinery and tall chimneys, out of which interminable serpents of smoke trailed themselves for ever and ever, and never got uncoiled.

It had a **black** canal in it, and a river that ran purple with **ill-smelling** dye, and vast piles of building full of windows where there was a rattling and a trembling all day long, and where the piston of the steam-engine worked monotonously up and down, **like the head of an elephant in a state of melancholy madness**. It contained several large streets all very like one another, and many small streets still more like one another, inhabited by people equally like one another, who all went in and out at **the same hours, with the same sound upon the same pavements, to do the same work**, and to whom every day was the same as yesterday and tomorrow, and every year the counterpart of the last and the next.

Margin labels: Personification, Adjective, Denotes/Connotes, Adjective, Simile, Parallelism

Student's commentary

The tone of this piece is depressing, with the industrial activity of the town oppressing its inhabitants. This is emphasised with the **personification** in the first sentence, 'if the smoke and ashes had allowed it'. It is as though the consequences of the industry, the smoke and ashes, have become more powerful than the humans. Dickens' criticism of this is evident in his description of the colours of the town being 'unnatural'. This seems to suggest that this way of living is also unnatural. The adjective 'ill-smelling' to describe the dye suggests the smell of rotting. But there is also a suggestion that the smell made people ill.

There is a clear sense that the people of Coketown live monotonous lives because of the monotonous industrial processes. The repetitive rhythm of the final sentence, with the **parallelism** in the sentence 'with the same sound upon the same pavements, to do the same work' reflects the never-ending repetitive nature of the people's lives. A simile describes the piston of the steam engine as an 'elephant in a state of melancholy madness'. While this image represents the continuous industrial process, it also suggests that the humans will have been driven mad in the same way as the machine.

Using the adjective 'black' to describe the canal denotes the filth of the industrial revolution, and also connotes the evil of this industrial environment. The use of vocabulary from the lexical field of industry creates the sense that work is more important than living.

This extract consists of three **complex sentences**. This echoes the relentless nature of the industrial process. For example, the final sentence contains over 10 clauses, adding successive layers of information. The repetitive rhythm created by these clauses suggests the repetitive nature of the people's lives.

■ Key terms

Personification: a figure of speech where an animal or inanimate object is described as having human characteristics.

Parallelism: the repetition of a pattern or structure in related words, phrases or clauses.

Complex sentence: a sentence containing a main clause with one or more subordinate or dependent clauses, often connected with a subordinating conjunction.

Extension activity 1

Copy and annotate Text B, taken from the same novel, then write your own analysis. The extract below is taken from the opening of the novel. To demonstrate your understanding of the writer's use of language you will need to use some of the linguistic terms mentioned so far in this unit. Try to comment on:

- a lexical feature, such as the use of words from the lexical field of nature to describe Gradgrind
- a phonological feature, such as the way Dickens uses the sounds of Gradgrind's words to suggest his dictatorial nature
- a grammatical feature, such as Dickens's repetition of patterns in his sentences
- a semantic feature, such as how the different nouns used to describe the schoolchildren illustrate Gradgrind's view of children and education.

Text B

Hard Times

NOW, what I want is, Facts. Teach these boys and girls nothing but Facts. Facts alone are wanted in life. Plant nothing else, and root out everything else. You can only form the minds of reasoning animals upon Facts: nothing else will ever be of any service to them. This is the principle on which I bring up my own children, and this is the principle on which I bring up these children. Stick to Facts, sir!'

The scene was a plain, bare, monotonous vault of a schoolroom, and the speaker's square forefinger emphasized his observations by underscoring every sentence with a line on the schoolmaster's sleeve. The emphasis was helped by the speaker's square wall of a forehead, which had his eyebrows for its base, while his eyes found commodious cellarage in two dark caves, overshadowed by the wall. The emphasis was helped by the speaker's mouth, which was wide, thin, and hard set. The emphasis was helped by the speaker's voice, which was inflexible, dry, and dictatorial. The emphasis was helped by the speaker's hair, which bristled on the skirts of his bald head, a plantation of firs to keep the wind from its shining surface, all covered with knobs, like the crust of a plum pie, as if the head had scarcely warehouse-room for the hard facts stored inside. The speaker's obstinate carriage, square coat, square legs, square shoulders, — nay, his very neckcloth, trained to take him by the throat with an unaccommodating grasp, like a stubborn fact, as it was, — all helped the emphasis.

'In this life, we want nothing but Facts, sir; nothing but Facts!'

The speaker, and the schoolmaster, and the third grown person present, all backed a little, and swept with their eyes the inclined plane of little vessels then and there arranged in order, ready to have imperial gallons of facts poured into them until they were full to the brim.

Learning from different styles of writing

In this topic you will:

- analyse a range of texts

- use linguistic terminology in writing about different texts.

AQA Examiner's tip

It is essential that you study the stylistic features of different genres and use them appropriately in your own writing. In your commentary you will need to explain how your writing has been influenced by the texts you have studied.

AQA Examiner's tip

The candidates who produce the best pieces of writing have a clear sense of audience and purpose.

Audience, purpose and context

A useful structure for approaching the analysis of texts is to consider the three contextual factors of audience, purpose and context. These will influence the language and style adopted by writers. Consider these factors in a leaflet about the dangers of drug-taking, aimed at a teenage audience.

Audience

Texts are likely to have more than one audience, but it will be possible to identify the primary audience. For example, the author of a leaflet designed to inform teenagers about the dangers of drug-taking will probably expect adults working with teenagers to also read the leaflet. In this case, the primary audience will be teenagers, while the adults working with teenagers would be a secondary audience.

The audience of a text will influence the lexical, phonological, grammatical and semantic features used by the writer. For example, the leaflet may use lexis that defines its audience, such as slang.

Purpose

The primary purpose of a leaflet informing teenagers about the dangers of drug-taking is clearly defined. It may be that the leaflet uses stylistic features associated with information writing, such as the active voice, or sub-headings to create cohesion.

Context

The literary context of the leaflet refers to stylistic features that might be expected of a piece of informative writing. However, the political context of the leaflet may be significant. In 2006 marijuana was declassified to a Class C drug, and the medical profession warned that this would give the wrong message to teenagers. This context might influence the content of a leaflet aimed at teenagers.

Producing your own pieces of writing

You know that you have to produce two pieces of writing within the four categories:

- writing to entertain
- writing to persuade
- writing to inform
- writing to advise/instruct.

You also know that you will need to choose two different *audiences* and two different *genres*.

Classroom activity 5

Copy and complete the table below by adding possible purposes, audiences and genres in the gaps. Many texts have more than one purpose; it is important that you identify both primary and secondary purposes.

See page 199 for feedback on this activity.

Task	Purpose	Possible audience	Possible genre
Creative writing	To entertain		
	To persuade		Editorial
	To inform	Yr 12 students	
How to survive a pop festival			Leaflet/flyer

AQA Examiner's tip

Use your own interests, knowledge and skills to inform your writing.

We will look at the four different categories of writing in turn. To be a good writer you need to have learnt from established writers, so there will be an analysis of texts to illustrate how we can learn from different writers, and how you can use this learning to direct your own writing. Finally, you will be asked to produce your own piece of writing in an appropriate style. You will be asked to think about providing commentaries on your own writing, but commentary writing will be developed more thoroughly in Section B.

Writing to entertain

In this topic you will:

- learn the stylistic features associated with writing to entertain

- analyse a piece of autobiographical writing, and a piece of dramatic monologue

- produce your own writing to entertain.

The Examination Board suggests three examples of writing within this category:

- a soap opera script
- an extract from an autobiography
- a dramatic monologue.

However, it is important to note that these are only examples of the genre. Some others might be: describing a place that has some personal significance; recalling a major event in your life; a radio programme.

Entertaining writing can take a wide range of forms, but at the moment we will focus on writing whose primary purpose is to entertain, whatever form it takes. For example, it could be argued that the primary purpose of fiction is to entertain. It might also be argued that the primary purpose of a piece of autobiography is to entertain. But can an editorial, whose primary purpose is to persuade, also be written to entertain? This final example shows that a piece of writing can have both a primary and a secondary purpose.

In this topic we will be specifically looking at three pieces of writing whose primary purpose is to entertain: a piece of autobiography; a dramatic monologue; and a radio drama script.

■ Classroom activity 6

List four more examples of writing that can be considered to have entertainment as their primary purpose. Is it possible to identify a secondary purpose for each of your examples? From your own reading, name a piece of writing that exemplifies each of them.

■ Stylistic features associated with autobiography and dramatic monologues

It is important to consider the linguistic features that autobiography and dramatic monologues might share.

Mixed-mode features

Texts in these genres often contain mixed-mode features. That is, they contain features that would be expected in writing and features expected in speech, for example:

Colloquialisms and slang

While Standard English might be used predominantly, colloquialisms and slang may also appear. The speaker's character may be created through the use of accent and dialect, so non-standard spellings might be expected.

Non-fluency features

Because there is some ambivalence about whether a dramatic monologue is spoken or written, non-fluency features expected of the spoken word may appear: incomplete sentences; minor sentences; ellipsis; hesitations; false starts.

Cohesion

The features to connect different parts of the text should be explored. The repetition of words or phrases, anaphoric references (reference to something already mentioned) and cataphoric references (reference to something that will appear later).

🔍 Autobiography

You will know that an autobiography is a person's account of an event or events from their own life. However, this genre needs to be analysed more thoroughly for your purposes. In fact, it is likely that if you produce a piece of autobiographical writing it would more accurately be defined as *literary autobiography*. This term suggests that the writing is not just a factual account of events, but has been consciously crafted for the reader's entertainment.

Let's look at the autobiography from the reader's point of view. First, the reader approaches an autobiography as an opportunity to look inside someone else's experience. Through this exploration the reader expects to learn something about the writer's personality, but also expects to be offered some significant insight or understanding.

From the writer's perspective, an autobiography is a voyage of self-discovery. Some critics see it as a confessional narrative, in which writers interpret themselves and their behaviour for a public audience. The writer has to make decisions about how much they are willing to reveal about themselves during their account.

Read Text C taken from a piece of autobiographical writing: *A Roof Over One's Head*. In it Jeanette Winterson explains how literature influenced her when she was a child. However, she also uses this piece of autobiographical writing to say something about the nature of literature, and about her relationship with her very religious mother. Jeanette Winterson had to be secretive about her love of literature because her mother was frightened of the potential of literature to corrupt. The author explains that while she was allowed to read library books, she was not allowed to own books; consequently she resorted to copying out library books by hand.

Text C

The book was a door. Open it. Pass freely.

Barriers there were; largely my mother, who always placed her ample frame in the way of my small doorways.

A pamphleteer by temperament, she knew that sedition and controversy are fired by printed matter. She knew the power of books so she avoided them, countering their influence with exhortations of her own, single-sheets pasted about the house. It was quite normal for me to find a little sermon in my packed lunch, or a few Bible verses, with commentary, stuffed into my hockey boots. Fed words and shod with them, words became clues. I hunted them down, knowing they would lead me to something valuable, something beyond myself, and whether that something was inside or outside, in action or imagination, hardly mattered.

My mother suspected me of harbouring print. She searched thoroughly but found nothing. Library books that were vetted and returned never worried her, it was close association that she feared – that a book might fall into my hands and remain there.

It never occurred to her that I fell into books. That I put myself for safe keeping inside them. When I copied them out later it was myself I was freeing.

Jeanette Winterson, A Roof Over One's Head, *found at www.abc.net.au*

Extension activity 2

This activity encourages you to be selective about the events in your life when writing a piece of autobiography. Think of a significant moment in your life. Imagine that you have to provide two accounts of this significant moment, for two different purposes:

Purpose 1: You want your readers to admire you.

Purpose 2: You want your readers to sympathise with you.

Copy and complete the table below by listing the aspects of the moment that you would include in each case to give the two different impressions of yourself.

You should be able to see from this activity that the details that you choose to describe can completely change the focus of your writing.

Purpose 1: You want your readers to admire you	Purpose 2: You want your readers to sympathise with you

1. Who is the intended audience for this piece?
2. What is the purpose of this piece of writing?
3. Select four verbs and comment on the effects each one achieves.
4. How does the structure of the complex sentence starting 'I hunted them down' match the content?
5. What can you say about Winterson's use of metaphor and simile? Choose one metaphor and one simile and explain what each of them suggests.
6. What effect is achieved by the sentence 'Pass freely'?
7. What effect is achieved by the foregrounding in the sentence 'Barriers there were'?

Notice that in this piece of writing Jeanette Winterson does not just recount an incident from her own life. She uses it to explore significant issues such as the nature of literature and the nature of her relationship with her mother. For example, what link does she make between the Bible and other literature? In what sense does she see herself in conflict with her mother?

Read Text D taken from a piece of writing, produced by Rosie Knight, a student. At first sight it appears to be a piece of autobiographical writing. In it she explores a relationship and hints at its demise. Six short passages have been underlined. After you have read the extract, you can read a second student's commentary on these.

Text D

If you go back to where we first met, it will only break your heart.

In this dim city light barely dressed girls eat Chinese food, drunken fools sing 80's tunes, and you keep your head down. <u>Clouds of warm breath fill the icy air ahead of us and it's really hard to keep up with you</u>. Those kitsch little dolly-shoes scuff on the uneven pavement and you push your hand up to your face, the silver glint of that ring reflects the flickering lamp light. <u>Don't cry</u>. Down by the river a wind picks up your perfectly straight, blonde hair and lets it go again reluctantly. You stop to light a cigarette and it takes me back.

When I go back to where we first met, it only breaks my heart.

It was hot and the shade of the beech tree was mottled. You asked me for a smoke and I told you it would kill you but you said it was inevitable. <u>Ironic really</u>. We sat there and just talked, for hours, and hours, just talking. We were so different but so intoxicated at the same time. <u>We lay there side by side, day after day</u>, just making daisy chains and arguing, all the while under some fairy-tale spell of infatuation.

It was good to hear your voice.

I'd grin from cheek to cheek with uncontainable pleasure when I saw you coming up over the hill, wearing the latest fad, <u>plugged into some indie tunes</u>, your trademark straight hair reflecting spring sun. It was all loose knit, no ties, no attachments, just a summer in the city and there were no responsibilities or obligations. And I liked it that way.

We'd just hang out in the heat and <u>it was cool</u>, but I didn't see that there were storm clouds overhead.

Rosie Knight, Firm

Student commentary

A second student has commented on the underlined text, reflecting on what they think Rosie was trying to achieve.

The imagery in the sentence 'Clouds of warm breath fill the icy air ahead of us and it's really hard to keep up with you' suggests both the warmth of the relationship, and the iciness of their future. The fact that the girl finds it difficult to keep up also suggests that the relationship will not last. At a semantic level, the antonymy of 'warm' breath and 'icy' air foregrounds the pivotal nature of this moment.

The sentence 'Don't cry.' is ambiguous. Why has this been placed here in the story? It suggests that there are multiple time perspectives in this piece of writing. Does this imperative belong to the time of the event being described, or the future?

The minor sentence 'Ironic really' adds further mystery. The colloquial declarative statement challenges the reader to predict why the phrase 'it's inevitable' is ironic.

The parallelism in the sentence 'We lay there side by side, day after day' emphasises the repetitive nature of what they were doing.

The phrase 'plugged into some indie tunes' serves two purposes. It connotes the boy's isolation, but the colloquial reference to the music genre also helps to place the story in a contemporary setting.

There is irony in the words 'it was cool'. It might be interpreted as a reference to the weather, but it could also be a contemporary colloquial term meaning *acceptable*. The reference to storm clouds obviously connotes emotional problems for the future.

The writer uses the first-person singular ('When I go back'), the first-person plural ('Where we first met'), and the second person ('You stop to light a cigarette'). This keeps changing the narrative perspective and gives the impression of turmoil.

■ Classroom activity 8

One of the things you are required to do in your creative writing coursework folder is to show how your own writing has been influenced by other authors' work. Identify four stylistic features from the extract above that you could use in a piece of autobiographical writing, for example ambiguity.

■ Extension activity 3

Try producing your own piece of autobiographical writing. Choose a significant moment in your life that illustrates something about your character, your personal values, or your relationships.

You will need to think about:

■ your intended audience

■ the tone of your piece

■ how descriptive or discursive your writing will be

■ whether you will include dialogue

■ how much of yourself you are willing to disclose to an audience

■ what insight or understanding you will offer your readers.

AQA Examiner's tip

Writing based on personal experience needs to be shaped so that it appeals to a wider audience.

You will also need to think of some linguistic features common to autobiography.

- Use of first-person narrative.
- Colloquialisms and slang.
- Accent and dialect.
- Non-fluency features.
- **Mixed-mode features**.
- Minor sentences.
- Ellipsis.
- Cohesion.

■ **Key terms**

Mixed-mode features: features expected in printed text combined with features expected in conversation.

■ The dramatic monologue

A dramatic monologue is a written speech by one person. The audience might be the speaker themselves, a defined third party, or even an implied audience. In fact, the reader takes the part of a silent listener.

It is common for the reader to identify a gap between the reality of the events described and what the speaker says about them. Through this identification the reader will also gain an insight into the speaker's personality. This provides the speaker of a dramatic monologue with many opportunities. The reader should also create, for themselves, the drama behind the monologue, through inference and through their own imagination.

Robert Browning is attributed with developing this genre through his poetry. However, there are many dramatic monologues in modern prose.

Text E is an example of a modern dramatic monologue. The speaker is a mother with a teenage daughter. She is writing a letter to her daughter, who has left home after a family argument. Read the extract and then work with a partner to answer the questions that follow.

Text E

I'm sure you'd never have left if you realised I'd be this upset. You didn't mean to hurt me, did you? You never meant to make me so unhappy I'm sure. It was that mob you got in with at school. That Vanessa for instance. I wouldn't be surprised to hear she's on drugs. She had that look. You're so innocent, you didn't realise. You're too trusting, too kind, you don't know what these people can be like.

People pretend to be kind but they're ghouls. They ring up to see how I am and I can hear them gloat. It's not their fifteen-year-old daughter who's left home and gone off God knows where. The doctor's given me something to help me sleep and I've taken a week's sick leave from school. I try to put on a cheerful face. Oh, I say: she'll be back soon. I'm sure of it, why, she hasn't even taken her new shoes!

I don't think that you have a clue how we feel. Just because we're not the ones for letting it all out in public doesn't mean we don't live with this terrible pain. We don't speak of it much. But of course we know how each other feels. We have to be brave, we have to get on with living. The doctor told me: try to live from day to day. That's what they tell dying people too, I've heard it on a radio programme on hospices.

Michele Roberts, During Mother's Absence, *1993*

With a partner, answer the following questions:

1. What effect is achieved by using so many short sentences?
2. What effect is achieved by the use of the first-person plural in the final paragraph?
3. What examples of textual cohesion are there?
4. What examples of mixed-mode features are there?

Extension activity 4

Write the opening paragraph of a dramatic monologue giving an account of a conversation you have recently had with an adult. Show how there is a gap between the reality of the event and what the adult says about the event. In addition, use the following linguistic features:

- Anaphoric reference.
- Cataphoric reference.
- Colloquialism or slang.
- Mixed-mode features.

In the 1980s, Alan Bennett wrote a series of dramatic monologues depicting five ordinary people. Bennett explains that dramatic monologues cannot be objective because the narrator does not tell the whole story. In a play there would be other voices to provide a more balanced perspective, but with a dramatic monologue there is only a single point of view. Because of this, the dramatic monologue gives the reader opportunities to interpret things differently from the speaker.

In *A Lady of Letters* Bennett presents the reader with a character who thinks she is 'a public-spirited guardian of morals'. However, the reader is likely to interpret things differently. Read the extract below and think about the three key features of a dramatic monologue:

- What gap is there between the reality of the events that are described and what the speaker says about the events?
- What do we learn about the speaker's personality?
- What can we speculate about the drama behind this monologue?

Text F

A Lady of Letters by Alan Bennett

Angie her name is. I heard him shout at her as I went by en route for the Post Office. He was laid out underneath his car wanting a spanner and she came out, transistor in one hand, kiddy in the other. Thin little thing, bruise on its arm. I thought, 'Well, you've got a car, you've got a transistor, it's about time you invested in some curtains.' She can't be more than twenty and by the look of her she's expecting another.

I passed the place where there was the broken step I wrote to the council was a danger to the public. Little ramp there now, access for the disabled. Whenever I pass I think, 'Well, that's thanks to you, Irene.' My monument that ramp. Only some dog has gone and done its business right in the middle of it. I'm sure there's more of that than there used to be. I had a little Awayday to London last year and it was dog dirt everywhere. I spotted some on the pavement right outside Buckingham Palace. I wrote to the Queen about it. Had a charming letter back from a lady in waiting saying that Her Majesty appreciated my interest and that my letter had been passed on to the appropriate authority. The upshot eventually is I get a long letter from the Chief cleansing officer in Westminster City Council apologising profusely and enclosing a rundown of their Highway and Maintenance Budget. That's been my experience generally... people are only too grateful to have these things pointed out. The keynote is participation. Of course I wrote back to thank him and then blow me if I didn't get another letter thanking me for mine. So I wrote back saying I hadn't been expecting another letter and there was no need to have written again and was this an appropriate use of public resources? They didn't even bother to reply.

Alan Bennett, Talking Heads, 1987

Classroom activity 10

Working with a partner, answer the following questions based on the above extract:

1 What examples are there of mixed-mode features?

2 What examples of non-fluency features can you find?

3 What nouns are used to imply the speaker's importance?

4 Identify three examples of non-standard grammar. What effect do these have?

Extension activity 5

We can learn about someone's personality from what they say and do. Write the opening paragraph of a dramatic monologue, making use of mixed-mode features and non-fluency features.

💡 🔍 The radio drama play script

The radio drama script is another genre of writing to entertain. In more recent times this genre has also branched out to include the podcast. If you choose to write a radio drama, you will first need to study the conventions associated with setting out the script. There are no universally agreed conventions, but it is possible to define appropriate principles to guide your writing. Text G is taken from Steve Walker's *The Dolphinarium*, a play that has been broadcast on the BBC World Service and Radio 3. It aims to draw your attention to the conventions of setting out a script.

Text G

1) PLAY IN WITH Saint-Saens's 'Piano Concerto No. 2'.

WHEN THIS HUMAN MUSIC IS ESTABLISHED, BRING UP DOLPHINS SINGING INSIDE IT. THEN FADE AWAY HUMAN MUSIC, LEAVING THE DOLPHINS ALL AROUND US, AND SWIMMING BETWEEN OUR EARS. THEY ARE ANXIOUS, THEN FRIGHTENED.

SLOWLY BRING UP THE SOUND OF WAVES CRASHING ON TO A BEACH. THE MANY DOLPHINS DIE AWAY UNTIL THERE IS ONLY ONE, CLOSE. THIS STOPS ALSO. JUST THE WAVES, SOFTLY LAPPING.

SUDDENLY:

RADIO NEWSREADER: The death has been announced in Copenhagen of the great Danish mountaineer and explorer, Henning Bleeze. He was sixty-four years old and had been ill for some time. Dolphins all over the world... (RADIO IS TWIDDLED OFF STATION)

COCKNEY NEWSVENDOR: Henning Bleeze snuffs it! Read awl abart it! Henning Bleeze is a goner!

'March of Time' MUSIC FROM CITIZEN KANE.

AMERICAN REPORTER: Today, as it comes to all men, death came to Henning Bleeze. Mountaineer. Explorer. Ecologist. Hero...

TIXOVER SPEAKS DIRECTLY TO US. A SPLASHING OF WATER AROUND HIM, BUT WE MUST NOT KNOW EXACTLY WHY UNTIL THE END OF THE PLAY.

TIX: Who would believe it, me, Hartley Tixover, with only a few weeks of his life left to go, there I was, being interviewed yet again by that shifty bastard, Duncan Macnab. (LAUGHS) No, I don't hate him any more.

1) A RADIO INTERVIEW

TIX: For God's sake, shut up about Henning Bleeze! Tell them about the dolphins. That's what I'm here to talk about! We've just found out, you see, they're all dying... Sod Henning Bleeze!

MACNAB: (A GAMESHOW HOST USING THE VOICE OF A SUBTLE SCOTS PSYCHIATRIST, VERY CLOSE AND INTIMATE) He was like a father to you, wasn't he, Tixover?

TIX: Don't you put that headshrinking voice on with me, Macnab! You old ginger fraud! You just want to make me cry on your bloody radio programme! (HIS VOICE BREAKING WITH EMOTION) And I won't! Oh, God!

MACNAB: (MORE SLY YET) He took you under his wing when you were just a wee boy, didn't he?

TIX: (WIPING AWAY TEARS, ANGRY) Yes, yes, yes! Me and Gary Wopfner and Jiddu Dutt, the giant Indian.

Setting the scene

Delivering direction

Technical direction

Sound effect

Paralinguistic feature

Delivery directions

Each of the annotations deserves further explanation.

1. Stage drama precisely describes the visual appearance of each scene. This is clearly inappropriate for radio drama, as listeners have to imagine the visual scene for themselves.

2. Delivery directions are usually presented before the dialogue. Here, they are in upper case. It is important not to use unnecessary delivery directions. If a character emerges from a hospital ward and announces 'Mother has died', it would not be necessary to direct them to deliver this line emotionally. However, if the family had been waiting impatiently for their inheritance, delivery directions such as '(CELEBRATORY)' would be required.

3. Sound effects can be placed within the dialogue or as separate instructions. They are often used as signposts to lead the listener from one place in the script to another. It is conventional not to use redundant sound effects, for example, if the sound of a cup against a saucer will not add any significant detail to the radio play it is unlikely to be included in the script. However, the sound may have connotations of social cohesion and so may need to be included.

4. Radio scripts require non-speaking dialogue such as grunts, groans and gasps. These are a significant feature of natural dialogue and provide valuable information about the characters' thought processes.

The linguistic devices that we have explored in the autobiographical extracts and the dramatic monologues have been predominantly mixed-mode features. It is possible to see that this radio play script makes use of similar linguistic features.

Colloquialisms

The Cockney news vendor uses 'snuffs it' and 'is a goner'. Notice how the spelling of 'awl abart it' has been used to suggest the cockney accent.

Ellipsis

This is used in the utterance, 'We've just found out, you see, they're all dying... Sod Henning Bleeze!' The ellipsis is used to denote a pause, but in this case it might also add a sense of the speaker's frustration.

Elision

Elision is common in dialogue. In this extract there are a number of examples, including 'don't', 'that's' and 'they're'.

Vulgarisms

Tixover expresses his anger and frustration with 'shifty bastard' and 'bloody'.

■ **Key terms**

Elision: the missing out of sounds or parts of words in speech or writing.

■ Classroom activity 11

Copy and annotate Text H taken from *The Dolphinarium*, identifying (a) the conventions associated with setting out the script, and (b) the linguistic devices used. Explain clearly what the writer has achieved with each of the linguistic devices.

Text H

NOW WE'RE IN THE LAKE DISTRICT. A JOURNALIST IS KNOCKING ON A DOOR. DOOR OPENS.

TIX: (VEXED) What is it?

JOURNALIST: Excuse me, sir, are you perhaps Sir Hartley Tixover, the famous mountaineer?

TIX: Yes, yes. Yes!

JOURNALIST: I'm from *The Sun*.

TIX: I'm from Basingstoke. GOODBYE!

HE SLAMS THE DOOR. CREAK OF LETTERBOX.

JOURNALIST: (BENDING DOWN) Excuse me, sir, I don't mean to letterbox you, but could I have a few words? About the death of Henning Bleeze. I believe he was a close associate of yours. When you were young.

DOOR IS PULLED OPEN AGAIN.

TIX: (BREATHLESS, ANXIOUS) What did you say?

JOURNALIST: Henning Bleeze, sir. Hadn't you heard? Oh, I am sorry. He's rumoured to have killed himself. Any comment?

Classroom activity 12

Using the following scenario, write the opening scene of a radio drama play script.

A young teenage boy is in a graveyard, looking at the gravestones of his mother, father and siblings. A scruffy man, with an iron shackle on one leg, appears. He shakes the young boy upside down, shaking food from the boy's coat pocket. As the man eats the food he demands to know where the young boy lives and who he lives with.

Further reading

If you want to read more radio play scripts, visit:
www.simplyscripts.com

If you want to read some more autobiographical writing, you might enjoy some of the following:

Angelou, M. *I Know Why The Caged Bird Sings*, Bantam, 1969

Brittain, V. *Testament of Youth*, Virago, 1994

Greene, G. *A Sort of Life*, Vintage Classics, 1971

Guest, T. *My Life in Orange*, Granta Books, 2004

McCourt, F. *Angela's Ashes*, HarperCollins, 2004

Pelzer, D. *A Child Called It*, Health Communications, 1995

If you want to read more dramatic monologues, you might enjoy some of the following:

Bennett, A. *Talking Heads*, BBC Books, 1987

Becket, S. *Krapp's Last Tape*, Faber & Faber, 1959

Henley, B. *Monologues for Women*, Dramaline Publications, 1992

Writing to persuade

In this topic you will:

- learn the stylistic features associated with writing to persuade
- analyse a persuasive speech and a newspaper editorial
- produce your own writing to persuade.

The exam syllabus offers the following suggestions of pieces of writing to persuade:

- An editorial.
- A letter to a head of centre about uniform issues.
- A speech delivered as a football captain.

Again, it is important to stress that these are only suggestions, and that there are many more examples of writing that attempt to persuade, such as: a leaflet persuading teenagers to change their lifestyle; a political pamphlet; a radio advertisement. This topic will analyse two types of writing whose primary aim is to persuade: the persuasive speech and the editorial.

What makes a good persuasive speech?

This genre offers a range of opportunities as there are so many potential audiences, and so many lexical choices to make. While all speeches will share some stylistic features, each audience will require subtly different features. For example, a speech for a group of doctors and a speech for teenagers will require different lexis and grammatical features.

Persuasive speeches combine two related features:

1 The features of persuasive writing.
2 The features of a speech.

You are familiar with the following features of persuasive writing: analogy; emotive language; metaphor; simile; personification; and rhetorical questions. Definitions of these appear in Table 4. It is important that when you write about writing, both your own and other people's, these terms do not become mere labels. At all times you must be aware of the effects achieved by the use of these devices.

Table 4 *Features of persuasive writing*

Feature	Definition
Analogy	The use of a comparison between two cases, implying that if this comparison works, then the two cases will have many similarities
Emotive language	Language that encourages the reader to react emotionally rather than rationally; many words have emotive connotations and the reader may respond to these connotations rather than their denotations
Metaphor	The use of a term to describe something that it does not denote, to suggest similar qualities between the two
Simile	A comparison of one thing with another, using the words 'like' or 'as'
Personification	The use of human qualities to describe an inanimate object
Rhetorical question	A question that does not require an answer because the answer is obvious

Fig. 1 *What makes a good persuasive speech?*

To briefly revise these rhetorical devices, identify them in Text I, which aims to persuade people that there are impending breakthroughs in artificial intelligence.

Text I

It is absolutely clear to me that artificial intelligence will ultimately lead to thinking computers. Technological developments have increased tremendously over the past twenty years, and scientists have laid the foundations for the next significant breakthrough. The human brain is only like a sophisticated computer, so it will be easy to replicate its behaviour. In the near future machines will be able to make decisions as easily as a photoelectric cell does today. I envisage a time when your home computer will be able understand your voice commands, and will even be able to politely remind you what document you were last working on. A subsequent development will be robots at home that will be able to jump to your every command. These realistic, but necessary developments in artificial intelligence will transform the quality of our lives and cement the marriage between humans and machines.

Classroom activity 13

Complete the table below by providing an example of each of the devices from Text I, and then explaining what effect is achieved by the use of each one.

See page 199 for feedback on this activity.

Rhetorical device	Example	Effect
Analogy		
Emotive language		
Metaphor		
Personification		
Simile		

🔍 New terms for describing persuasive writing

You are likely to be confident about the features of persuasive writing that we have considered so far. If you are going to write a persuasive speech, or even a piece of persuasive writing, the rhetorical devices defined below will improve it and/or help you to explain the effects that you have achieved.

Anaphora

This is the deliberate repetition of a word or phrase at the beginning of successive phrases or sentences. An example is found in Churchill's speech to the House of Commons on 4 June 1940:

> We shall fight on the beaches, we shall fight on the landing grounds, we shall fight in the fields and in the streets, we shall fight in the hills.

This rhetorical device is used to create a rhythm, and also to emphasise the relationship between ideas. It is also used for cohesion, to connect parts of the speech.

Antistrophe

This is the deliberate repetition of a word or phrase at the end of successive phrases or sentences. An example is found in Franklin D. Roosevelt's speech declaring war against Japan on 9 December 1941:

> In 1931, Japan invaded Manchukuo – without warning. In 1935, Italy invaded Ethiopia – without warning. In 1938, Hitler occupied Austria – without warning. In 1939, Hitler invaded Czechoslovakia – without warning. Later in 1939, Hitler invaded Poland – without warning. In 1940, Hitler invaded Norway, Denmark, Holland, Belgium, and Luxembourg – without warning.

This rhetorical device is used in the same way as anaphora, to create a rhythm and to emphasise the relationship between ideas. Like anaphora, it is used for cohesion, to connect parts of the speech.

Hyperbole

This is the use of exaggeration for effect. An example would be: 'If he sits next to me I will die.' This rhetorical device is used to emphasise a point, or to emphasise someone's feelings about something.

Tautology

This is the repetition of the same sense in consecutive words. An example would be, 'If you look back, retrospectively, you will find the answer.' This device can be used to emphasise a point, but generally its use should be avoided.

You will be easily able to identify these rhetorical devices in Text J, an extract from a speech to be delivered to a group of adults. However, it is more important that you are able to say something about the effect that each of the devices achieves.

Text J

It is essential that we band together and use our combined force to tackle the riotous teenagers of our town. For too long now we have been subjected to the nightly noise of hordes of drunken teenagers, intoxicated on alcohol. For too long now we have been intimidated by their speeding cars racing down the high street. For too long now we have let them get away with it. Mothers with young children are frightened to go out over the weekend, while the older members of our community have resorted to locking themselves in their houses. There has been a massive increase in crimes associated with drinking, and there has also been a huge increase in the number of traffic violations identified by the Police. Official statistics show that at least two people per night are being arrested for drunk and disorderly behaviour, while there is at least one arrest per week associated with a traffic offence. For too long now the responsible majority has been too inactive. It is now time to make a stand. We need to protest resolutely. We need to demonstrate resolutely. We need to exhibit our displeasure resolutely. Only in this way will we be able to reclaim the tranquillity and safety of our beautiful town.

Classroom activity 14

Complete the table below by providing an example of each of the rhetorical devices in Text J and explaining what effect you think the writer wanted to achieve by the use of each one.

Rhetorical device	Example	Effect
Anaphora		
Antistrophe		
Hyperbole		
Tautology		

Classroom activity 15

1 Read Text K overleaf taken from Franklin D. Roosevelt's inaugural speech, delivered in 1933. His primary aim was to persuade the American people that together they could overcome the devastating consequences of the Great Depression.

2 Copy Text K and annotate the text to highlight the persuasive language and the rhetorical devices. You should also write something about the effects achieved by each of the devices that you identify.

Text K

> This is predominantly the time to speak the truth, the whole truth, frankly and boldly. No need to shrink from honestly facing conditions in our country today. This great nation will endure, as it has endured, will revive and will prosper. So, first of all, let me assert my firm belief that the only thing we have to fear is fear itself – nameless, unreasoning, unjustified terror which paralyses needed efforts to convert retreat into advance. In every dark hour of our national life, a leadership of frankness and of vigour has met with that understanding and support of the people themselves which is essential to victory. And I am convinced that you will again give that support to leadership in these critical days.
>
> In such a spirit on my part and on yours we face our common difficulties. They concern, thank God, only material things. Values have shrunk to fantastic levels; taxes have risen; our ability to pay has fallen; government of all kinds is faced by serious curtailment of income; the withered leaves of industrial enterprise lie on every side; farmers find no markets for their produce; and the savings of many years in thousands of families are gone. More important, a host of unemployed citizens face the grim problem of existence and an equally great number toil with little return. Only a foolish optimist can deny the dark realities of the moment.

🛈 An editorial

The newspaper or magazine editorial is an example of persuasive writing. As with all the writing considered within this unit, there are stylistic conventions.

The structure of the editorial

Let's look at an example of an editorial and see what can be said about its structure. Text L is an editorial that was written for a school magazine, to persuade people that students should not be set homework.

Text L

> Every school in the country piles homework onto its students. So, every night students are trapped in their homes working instead of socialising with their friends or playing sport. This has to stop. It is unfair and it is unhealthy.
>
> Parents and teachers seem to have ganged up on the youth of today and decided that we are so rebellious that we need to be kept off the streets at night. On the one hand we are told that our generation is too fat and lazy, while on the other hand we are prevented from going out to improve our health. We are forced to sit at a desk for most of the day and then we have to sit at a desk at home all evening. No wonder the Government has labelled us couch potatoes.
>
> Also, it is not clear what value this homework has. Most students will agree that they rush work at home, or even copy their friends' work the following day. This is not educationally valuable. Teachers might be able to persuade themselves that the students are continuing their education at home, but there is very little evidence to support this. In fact, the setting of homework seems to imply that teachers have not covered enough work during their lessons.

Punctual teachers and better planning of lessons would do away with the need for homework.

It has been argued that homework is set to consolidate our learning – that we do homework to practise the skills that we have been taught at school. However, this is clearly not the case. How many times have you been given homework that just fills up your free time? Colour in the flags of Europe; print off some facts about a composer that you find on the Internet; draw a poster warning about the dangers of drugs. These aimless activities have not been designed as part of the curriculum but are thought up just to waste our time.

It is increasingly important for our generation to do well at school and to obtain good examination results. However, homework does not contribute to this. The tasks that are set are usually trivial and they seem to be set purely to waste our time in the evenings. Make sure teachers arrive to their lessons on time, and teach well planned lessons, and we wouldn't have to do homework – we could go out in the evening, socialise and get fitter.

Susan Hayward, 'Homework is a Crime'

Classroom activity 16

Text L has five paragraphs. For each one, give a summary of the content and explain its purpose.

See page 200 for feedback on this activity.

Extension activity 6

Read a range of editorials from national newspapers. How far do they adopt the same structure as the editorial that you have studied?

The style of the editorial

More important than the structure of the editorial is its style. Remember, an editorial's primary purpose is to persuade. Consequently, many of the stylistic features that you explored in the persuasive speeches will be relevant to the editorial, namely:

- analogy
- emotive language
- metaphor
- personification
- simile
- anaphora
- antistrophe
- hyperbole
- tautology
- connotation.

Text M overleaf is an editorial that was written by Chris Pearce, a student, and is more typical of the length that you should produce if you choose to write an editorial. Read it and think about its structure and use of persuasive language.

Text M

Has the Government Failed the Poor?

In 1997, Tony Blair stated: 'Yes, We are the party of Middle Britain, but if we don't raise the standard of the poorest people in Britain, then we will have failed as a Government.' Well, recent research shows that this Government has failed.

Blair's pledge can only be fully analysed once we have a clear definition of Poverty. The Government says people are living in Poverty when the income of a family is below 60% of the nation's median disposable income. And far too many children fall below this line. According to the Joseph Rowntree Foundation (1998), the number of children living in Poverty in 1997 was between 3 and 4 million, which is triple the number in 1979.

Poverty has both national and individual consequences. For example, recent research has found that Child Poverty is associated with such things as physical abuse, teenage pregnancy, homelessness, smoking, lack of self-esteem and suicide (Economic and Social Research Council, July 2000). Every year these problems are costing the country billions of pounds. More importantly, Poverty affects a child's education and life chances. This causes the problem referred to as the Cycle of Poverty. This is when a child is born into Poverty, and a poor diet causes them to miss lots of school due to consequential illness. In turn, the child is more susceptible to illness as they have a weaker immune system. This means that they do not go on to further or higher education, which leads them into a low wage, manual job. Also, due to a lack of education, they have children young, and these children are born into Poverty, and the Cycle is maintained.

Furthermore, having so many people living in Poverty could pose a threat to the majority of the population's well-being. Recently in France there were massive riots. These were due to one group in society being excluded, which is what is happening to those in Poverty. People in Poverty cannot afford to do the things that most privileged people get to do. This leaves them excluded from their peers. Should this happen on a massive scale, such as in France, the riots will be horrendous.

As Britain is one of the richest countries in the world, there should be many more nets to help catch those falling into the Cycle of Poverty. Such nets as Second Chance Homes, help pregnant teens and offer these young mothers a supportive environment. Support of this kind could help to stop people falling into the Cycle of Poverty and could also help families to break it.

Many charities are doing everything in their power to help combat child Poverty. However, they cannot do it alone. They need the help of the government.

Many politicians from the Right believe that it is the responsibility of the parents to help their children out of Poverty, yet this view is too simplistic. The State and parents are both to blame when looking at children in Poverty. The State must educate parents, allowing them to get higher paid jobs, allowing them to break out of the Cycle of Poverty.

Chris Pearce

Classroom activity 17

1. Summarise the ideas and explain the purpose of each paragraph in Text M.

2. With a partner, look at the student's use of persuasive language. Identify any rhetorical devices and comment on what has been achieved by each example you identify.

3. How many of the linguistic features that you have studied in this section can you identify in this editorial?

4. What can you say about the effects they achieve?

Student commentary

Since we have the student's commentary on this editorial, we can see what decisions Chris Pearce made, and what effects he hoped to achieve. Read this analysis, which gives an insight into the thought behind a piece of persuasive writing.

There are four main purposes for editorials: to explain, to criticise, to persuade and to praise. The editorial I wrote was 'to criticise'. This style of editorial should constructively criticise someone's actions while offering solutions to the problems that the actions have caused. This was achieved by considering the current position, without coming from an overtly right-wing point of view. This allowed a seemingly non-biased view on the subject, adding to the validity of the argument.

A 'critical' editorial's purpose is to inform the audience about the problem, and then offer solutions to it. I chose to write an editorial as it let me present my views on an issue that is topically important. However, while the piece is meant to inform, there is a sweeping statement at the start: 'Recent research shows that this Government has failed.' This is to gain the reader's attention while simultaneously informing them of the topic of the editorial.

The piece follows a structure that is defined by the conventions of the genre. It first points out the problem, then gives an opposing viewpoint which is refuted, and finally gives realistic solutions to the problem. The extent of the problem was not overtly pointed out until the end of the second paragraph. This can be seen in the words: 'The number of children living in Poverty in 1997 was between 3 and 4 million'. This was followed by the opposing point of view, which is clear in the declarative sentence: 'Many politicians from the Right believe that it is the responsibility of the parents to help their children out of Poverty', but this was refuted and the text went on to talk about what needs to be done to improve the state of things, which can be seen in the last paragraph, but most clearly in the sentence: 'A drastic reform in the welfare system is needed.'

There was very little use of interrogative sentences, and much of the declarative mood, in the editorial. This was so that what was being read would seem more like fact than opinion, in order to strengthen the authoritative tone of the piece. Also, Standard English was used. This was to help the author maintain an authoritative tone.

A range of sentence structures was also used. 'Should this happen on a massive scale, such as in France, the riots will be horrendous.' This is a good example as inversion has been used so that 'horrendous' comes last, adding emphasis to the severity of the sentence. A further example of a different sentence structure is 'They need the help of the government'. This sentence was used to create a sense of urgency.

There were many non-standard capitalisations used in the editorial such as the abstract noun 'Poverty'. This is capitalised to bring it to the audience's attention. The non-standard capitalisation makes it stand out from the rest of the text, and acts to highlight the repetition, to help emphasise the issue in the reader's mind.

Extension activity 7

Chris was quite specific in his commentary about the effects he wanted to achieve with his writing. How successful do you think he was in achieving his aims?

Rewrite his analysis, adding five points of your own.

Further reading

If you want to study some more persuasive speeches, consider the following:

The Suffragettes. (Tracks 16 and 21 of CD ROM 1. *Voices of History*. British Library)

Recording of Martin Luther King:

www.americanrhetoric.com

Winston Churchill announcing the start of the Second World War:

www.history.com/media

A range of American speeches can be found at:

www.history.com/media

The text of Tony Blair's speech to mark the bicentenary of the end of the slave trade:

www.number10.gov.uk/output

If you want to read more editorials you could visit online newspapers and read their editorials, or their leader articles. Two examples are:

www.guardian.co.uk

www.independent.co.uk

Using source material and plagiarism

Most non-fiction writing will require you to use source material, so it is essential that you understand the difference between using sources and plagiarism. This topic goes through the process of writing an editorial in order to illustrate some research techniques, consider ways to avoid plagiarism, and show how to reference your sources. Although these skills are introduced within the framework of editorial writing, they apply to all academic research.

Researching your subject

Imagine that you have chosen the subject for a piece of editorial writing. Your first task is to carry out some research into your subject. To make your argument more convincing you need some influential support. This could be:

- statistics
- facts
- expert opinion.

Some helpful sources

- Government websites can provide statistical evidence on a number of subjects such as health, transport, education, law and order.

- The CIA World Factbook provides military, health and population information.

- Charities such as Oxfam and the RSPCA provide facts and figures on topical issues.

- Pressure groups such as Ash, which campaigns about the dangers of smoking, and League Against Cruel Sports will provide facts, figures and opinions, although you are likely to find that pressure groups, generally, do not provide a balanced view. However, this may suit your purposes as you will not want to provide a balanced view in your persuasive editorial.

- National and local newspapers often have online databases where you can search for reports and opinions on a wide range of issues.

Using sources

You probably learnt at GCSE that there are problems with using sources that you have found during your research. This is a problem that you will have at AS and even at degree level: how far can you use a source without being accused of plagiarism?

Plagiarism can be defined as: copying someone else's work and then presenting it as your own. So you need to know how you can make intelligent use of other people's writing. There are a number of ways.

"He plagiarizes so much that he has a fence instead of an agent."

www.cartoonstock.com

Study the list of potential subjects for editorials in the table below. Copy out the table, and in the right-hand column write where you might find some information to support each subject.

You may be able to record specific websites that you think, or know, will provide appropriate information. Alternatively, you may need to record information sources more generally as 'Greenpeace' or 'local newspaper archives'.

Subject for editorial	Potential information sources
Individual responsibility for global warming	
The use of animals in medical research	
A proposal to charge students for parking in your school/college	
The raising of the age at which people can drive a car to 18	
The problems of binge-drinking amongst teenagers	

Take the following piece of information that appears in *Teenage Lifestyles*, a book written by John Smith in 2007:

> It has been estimated that every day 450 children in the UK start smoking. Because nicotine is so addictive this does not bode well for the future; it means that every year 165,000 children choose to die prematurely.

How should you treat this if you want to use it in your own writing?

1 You could credit your sources. There are two common ways of doing this. First, you could write:

> 'It is frightening to think that despite all of the scientific evidence that smoking kills, the youth of this country still chooses this evil habit. In his book *Teenage Lifestyles*, John Smith reports that "every day 450 children in the UK start smoking. Because nicotine is so addictive this does not bode well for the future; it means that every year 165,000 children choose to die prematurely." The government needs to do more to prevent children getting access to cigarettes.'

In this example you have explained where you have got your information from before you have used it. The quotation marks let your readers know that the words that you have used are directly copied from your source.

2 Alternatively, you could write:

> 'It is frightening to think that despite all of the scientific evidence that smoking kills, the youth of this country still chooses such an evil habit. Every day "450 children in the UK start smoking. Because nicotine is so addictive this does not bode well for the future; it means that every year 165,000 children choose to die prematurely." (Smith, J., 2007) The government needs to do more to prevent children getting access to cigarettes.'

In this example you have explained where you have got your information after you have presented it. Again, the quotation marks tell your readers that the words that you have used are taken directly from your source.

In both cases you will have to explain your source more precisely in a bibliography. How to reference sources is explained on page 148.

3 However, you could rework the details to make them your own. For example, you could write:

> 'It is frightening to think that despite all of the scientific evidence that smoking kills, the youth of this country still chooses such an evil habit. It has been estimated that over 150,000 children every year fall victim to this addictive habit. The government needs to do more to prevent children getting access to cigarettes.'

In this example you have used the information from John Smith's book without copying it word for word. Again, you would reference John Smith's book in your bibliography so that your readers could follow up your sources.

So, you can use sources within your own work, without being accused of plagiarism, provided you can:

- tell the reader what your source was, and then quote from it
- provide the reader with a quotation and then provide them with the source
- rework the information from the source to make it your own.

Under no circumstances should you ever copy directly from any source: a simple internet search can reveal exactly what sources you have used.

Text M

Illness caused by smoking

Smoking harms nearly every organ of the body, causing many diseases, and reduces quality of life and life expectancy. It has been estimated that, in England, 364,000 patients are admitted to NHS hospitals each year due to diseases caused by smoking. This translates into 7,000 hospital admissions per week, or 1,000 day. For every death caused by smoking, approximately 20 smokers are suffering from a smoking-related disease. In 1997/98, cigarette smoking caused an estimated 480,000 patients to consult their GP for heart disease, 20,000 for stroke and nearly 600,000 for COPD.

Half of all teenagers who are currently smoking will die from diseases caused by tobacco if they continue to smoke. One quarter will die after 70 years of age and one quarter before, with those dying before 70 losing on average 21 years of life. It is estimated that between 1950 and 2000 six million Britons, 60 million people worldwide, died from tobacco-related diseases.

Non-lethal illness

Smokers face a higher risk than non-smokers for a wide variety of illnesses, many of which may be fatal (see 'Deaths caused by smoking' below). However, many medical conditions associated with smoking, while they may not be fatal, may cause years of debilitating illness or other problems.

www.ash.org.uk

Extension activity 9

Imagine that you are writing the text for a leaflet that is trying to persuade teenagers to stop smoking. The leaflet will be placed in doctors' surgeries.

Read the information that is presented in Text M and then write a paragraph of text for the leaflet, using some of the information appropriately.

Referencing your sources

With your own non-fiction writing it is essential to reference your sources in a bibliography. The most commonly used referencing system is the Harvard Referencing System. This can easily be found using a search engine. However, some of the main points are included here.

■ If you are referencing a book, you should present the details like this:

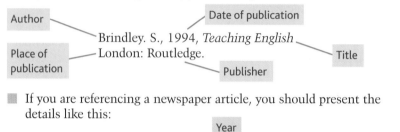

■ If you are referencing a newspaper article, you should present the details like this:

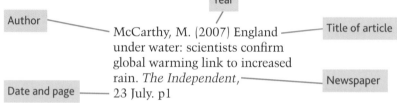

■ If you are referencing a website you should present the details like this:

Extension activity 10

Use a search engine to find web pages on the topic 'The danger of taking banned substances.' Try to reference three websites using the model above.

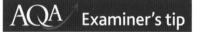

AQA Examiner's tip

Fully reference all of your sources so that you cannot be accused of plagiarism.

Searching the internet

The internet is a useful research tool. However, two big problems you have when researching on the internet are:

1 the amount of information that is available
2 how reliable the information is.

Searching for information on the internet is similar to searching for information in a library:

■ First, you think of your research question.
■ Next, you write down as many key words as you can.
■ Then you use the key words to find information.

However, search engines can help you find the information you want.

1 Using the words and/or your key words can help you to find information:
   ■ Foxes **and** hunting would list all the articles that contain both the words 'foxes' and 'hunting'.
   ■ Foxes **or** hunting would list all the articles that have the word 'foxes' in them and all of the articles that have the word 'hunting' in them.

2 If two words need to appear next to each other in your search, place them inside speech marks: 'global warming'.

3 Placing an asterisk at the end of a word will find articles that contain words with the same root. For example, teach* would list articles with the key words: 'teach', 'teaching', 'teacher', etc.

Judging websites

While the examiners will not reward you for the reliability of the information you use in non-fiction texts, for your own sense of pride you need to be confident that material you use from websites is reliable. Additionally, your non-fiction text will be more convincing if the information it contains can be seen to be trustworthy.

Millions of websites on the internet are private websites; the information on these might be completely wrong. For example, you could set up a website about Somerset and just make up all the details. How would someone in America know that everything you had written was wrong? One thing you can do when you visit a website is to study its address (URL). You should also ask yourself some questions:

1 What can the URL tell us about the information on a website?

- If a website has ~ in the address, it is probably a personal site.
- If a website has % in the address it is probably a personal site.
- If a website has **edu** or **ac** in the address it is probably an educational site.
- If a website has **com** or **co.uk** in the address it is probably a company site. This company might be using the site to sell you something.
- If a website has **net** in the address it is probably a company site.
- If a website has **org** in the address it is an organisation that does not make a profit. However, it might be trying to persuade you to change your opinion about something.
- If a website has **gov** in the title, then it is a government site.

2 Is the information up to date?

Some sites are not updated as regularly as they should be. This might mean that the facts on the site are wrong. Can you imagine checking the Premiership league tables, only to find out that the last four games had not been put on the site? Look for a date that tells you when the site was built. Look for a statement about how often the site is updated.

3 Who is the web page written for?

You should read one or two paragraphs of a website to see whether you are going to be able to use the information on the site. Some sites contain a lot of technical information that you might not understand.

4 What is the purpose of the site?

You need to think about why a website has been created. For example, is it giving you information, or is it trying to persuade you to change your mind about something?

5 Are there any links to additional sites?

A website's links to other sites often tell you something.

6 Can I cross reference this information with that on other websites?

It is often worth cross referencing several websites to check the validity of your information.

Extension activity 11

Experiment with a search engine to see how efficiently you can search for:

- reality TV
- teenage obesity
- the health dangers posed by mobile phones
- information on how to recycle more household waste.

■ Classroom activity 18

Look at the URLs in the table below and comment on how reliable each site is likely to be. Explain each of your comments.

See page 200 for feedback on this activity.

URL	How reliable do you expect the site to be? Why?
www.library.uq.edu.au	
www.elsevierdirect.com	
www.rspca.org.uk	
www.diaries.co.uk/article%	
www.standards.dfes.gov.uk	
www.gwt.edu~space.htm	

■ Extension activity 12

Research websites that provide information about GM foods. Make a list of sites that are:
- probably personal sites
- probably serious sites
- probably company sites
- probably sites of organisations that do not make a profit
- government sites.

■ Further reading

If you want to read more about referencing your sources follow the link for citing references on the following website:

www.bournemouth.ac.uk

Writing to inform

In this topic you will:

- learn the stylistic features associated with writing to inform
- analyse a piece of travel writing, a magazine article and a leaflet
- produce your own writing to inform.

The Examination Board gives three different examples of writing to inform:

1 A piece of travel journalism.
2 A leaflet focusing on a health issue.
3 An extract from a motorbike maintenance manual.

These examples are offered to illustrate the wide range of types of writing whose primary purpose is to inform. Some other examples are:

- an album review
- a magazine article
- publicity material for a teenage community group.

As with all created texts it is important to consider:

- the purpose
- the target audience
- what the target audience should be told
- the most appropriate medium
- the most appropriate style.

Classroom activity 19

To explore these issues further, study the table below carefully. Make a copy and fill in the empty cells.

See page 200 for feedback on this activity.

Purpose	Target audience	What the target audience should know	Possible media	Most appropriate style
Information about the dangers of illicit drugs				
How to save energy in your home				
Alternative guide to your school or college				
How to predict the weather				

There is a wide range of information writing, and each type has different stylistic conventions. However, it is also possible to see that **all** information writing has some shared qualities. In this section we will analyse travel writing and a magazine article.

💡 🔍 Travel writing

Travel writing provides you with many creative opportunities. It is often seen as writing to inform. However, as we see here, travel writing can also have entertainment as its primary purpose.

You may think that travel writing could just be an account of your last summer holiday, but good travel writing is much more than that. First we need to consider what makes a good piece of travel writing, and then see if we can identify these qualities in different pieces of writing. We then need to think about how you could produce your own piece of travel writing – even if you have never travelled abroad.

What makes a good piece of travel writing?

Good travel writing focuses on a place and provides the reader with a unique view. To do this, it focuses only on the interesting aspects and describes details that are significant in some way. The writer will also choose a central theme and focus their writing on this theme, for example, a writer might want to write about a visit to San Francisco. There are many interesting things to describe in San Francisco, including the trams, the underground, the Golden Gate Bridge, Alcatraz, and Fisherman's Wharf. But if you were going to describe these places, how could you decide on a central theme? One theme to link them all might be transport: the traditional trams; a bicycle ride over Golden Gate Bridge; and the view of the city from the boat to Alcatraz.

Travel writing is usually written in the first person and the past tense. This has two effects: using the first person makes the account more personal, and the past tense lets the reader see that you have reflected on your experience before you have written about it.

Read Text N taken from Ayun Halliday's *A sarong in my backpack*. This is the opening paragraph of her account of Tanzania.

Text N

> The mosquito must have bitten me the first night. Lots of mosquitoes bit me that first night in Tanzania, but this one was special. This one had a snoutful of malaria, or some jungle crud that caused me to stagger across our campsite two weeks later like a lion-felled gazelle, erupting at both ends.

Ayun Halliday, A Sarong in my Backpack, *2005*

The use of the first person and the past tense are clear. Notice also how the lexis and tone of the piece suggest a younger audience. The terms 'snoutful' and 'crud' are non-standard lexis and would not be expected in a formal register.

The opening paragraph of a piece of travel writing needs to have a hook, such as an interesting fact or observation. The style may be humorous, and the writer may exaggerate for effect. Above all, the writer needs to adopt a style that reveals something about the place they are describing, rather than just writing a report about it.

Look at the opening paragraph of Mark Moxon's account of his walk across Hinchinbrook Island in New Zealand in Text O.

Text O

> Quite why I got drunk on the Tuesday night, I don't know; the excuse was something about it being my last night in Cairns, and the next thing you know... but whatever the justification, Wednesday morning was a struggle, boarding the 8.45am coach while still quite drunk. I slowly surfaced throughout the day, but there was one good thing: I was out of Cairns, camping again, and looking forward to some good walking.

www.moxon.net

Notice that this opening paragraph has very little to do with informing the reader about Hinchinbrook Island, but it does serve to catch the reader's attention. Moxon uses non-fluency features such as ellipsis and incomplete sentences which suggests that he is having an informal conversation with the reader.

So, some of the stylistic conventions associated with travel writing are that:

- it focuses on a place and provides a unique view of that place
- it chooses a central theme
- it is usually written in the first person
- it is usually written in the past tense
- it often directly addresses the reader
- the opening paragraph has a hook
- the style may be humorous
- the writer may use exaggeration for humorous effect
- the writer will reveal something about the place.

In addition:

- The writer may address the reader by using the first-person plural ('we'), or the second person ('you').
- Borrowed words may be used to reveal something about the place that is being described, or about the writer's focus. For example, borrowed words such as 'bunny chows', 'mealie' and 'fufu' suggest that the writer's focus is on the ethnic population of South Africa.
- Other lexical experimentation may be seen, such as non-fluency features and mixed-mode features. In this example, 'I was, you know, in cahoots with three of the most officious Government officials I had ever met,' the phrase, 'you know' is a non-fluency feature, while the combination of 'cahoots' with 'the most officious Government officials' can be seen as mixed-mode features.

How writers use stylistic devices

Let's look at a piece of travel writing and see how many stylistic conventions we can identify. Text P comes from another of Mark Moxon's travel books entitled *A Million Mosquitoes Can't be Wrong*. Moxon makes all his travel writing available online at http://www.moxon.net/ebooks/index.html

■ **Extension activity 13**

Write the opening paragraph of a piece of travel writing that focuses on the village, town or city where you live. Capture the reader's interest by using the first person plural, or the second person. In addition, include an insightful observation.

Text P

I'm a little loath to ascribe such importance to the language barrier when travelling, but it's amazing how much difference crossing the border from Senegal into the Gambia has made. The Gambia – one of the few countries whose official name starts with 'the' – is a long, thin and very small country that follows the bends of the River Gambia due east from the river's mouth on the Atlantic coast, and apart from this coastal region, the country is entirely surrounded by Senegal. From end to end the Gambia is about 300km long but it only averages 35km in width, but even more bizarre is the fact that they speak English here, as it used to be a British colony.

At the border the linguistic change is instant. In Senegal, English isn't a great deal of use, and without at least basic French, communication is tough. But as soon as you cross into the Gambia, English takes over with an almost imperceptible transition; signs are in English, the locals speak English, and for the English-speaking traveller it instantly feels less alien and more comfortable.

The difference it makes is amazing. Within a couple of minutes of entering the Gambia I felt completely at ease, and it wasn't long before I was joking with the Gambian touts as they tried to sell me dalasis, something I'd find hard to do in French (the dalasi is the local currency in Gambia; being an ex-British colony, it doesn't use the CFA). When you're speaking your native language it's so much easier to understand subtleties of communication, and for the first time in a fortnight I feel as if I can actually talk to people. Irritating salesmen stop being annoying and become targets for a bit of banter, and I immediately feel happier and more relaxed in the Gambia than I did at any time in Senegal. I'm looking forward to exploring the place.

www.longdistancewalks.com

Classroom activity 20

Copy and complete as much of the table below as you can by finding examples of the stylistic features in Text P.

See page 200 for feedback on this activity.

Stylistic feature	Example
1 A unique view of a place	
2 A central theme	
3 First person	
4 Past tense	
5 Directly addresses the reader	
6 A hook in the opening paragraph	
7 Humour	
8 Something is revealed about the place	
9 Range of register	

Linguistic features of Moxon's text

Drawing our attention to the determiner 'the' in the country's name serves at least two purposes. Firstly, it seems to assign status to the country (although as the country was once a British colony, this may reflect its colonial past). Secondly, the determiner draws the reader's attention to the country being different in some way from other countries.

Notice, at a lexical level, how Moxon incorporates Gambian vocabulary into his own writing. He refers to 'dalasi' (plural 'dalasis') the Gambian currency. This is an illustration of how successful travel writing is influenced, lexically, in this instance, by its location. Further evidence of this is Moxon's use of 'CFA'. This is the official currency of 14 central African countries, all of which were once French colonies.

The abrupt sentence that starts the second paragraph, 'At the border the linguistic change is instant,' reflects the sudden switch. Cohesion is achieved with the minor sentence that opens the third paragraph, which echoes this.

If you choose to write a piece of travel writing, you need to be aware of what you are trying to achieve. The list of stylistic and linguistic conventions will help you to plan the content and style of your writing. However, it is essential to reflect on what you have written and to judge how successful you have been. It is only in this way that your writing will improve.

Read Text Q overleaf, an extract from a piece of travel writing produced by Fee Grammar, a student, then answer the questions about her use of language.

Text Q

> I decided to visit Madame Tussaud's on one of those lovely archetypal red rear-entrance double deck buses, the first of which was fifty years old in 2004. I was mildly surprised I managed to find one, since their numbers have dwindled due to their spectacular age. However, one cannot claim to have experienced all the delights of London unless one has taken a ride in a big red bus.
>
> Madame Tussaud's has been moulded like its figures, and has experienced a fair amount of change, not least when a fire broke out and the place had to be rebuilt, but mostly when a German bomb was dropped and the place was blown up. Ironically, the model of Hitler was one of the few that survived. But in 1958 a planetarium was opened which just marked the ongoing success and rebuilding of Madame Tussaud's. And thank God for it. I mean, how can you better spend a day than getting 'close to your favourite celebrities', and watching slightly-over-weight-peroxide-blonde-gum-chewing-big-earring-wearing girls who have draped themselves around Brad Pitt or Robbie Williams, or the lanky-greasy-cover-your-hair-in-gel-and-your-neck-in gold-chains lads who have an arm around the A-lister like Jennifer Lopez whist smirking at the camera as if they have achieved something impressive. As far as I can tell this delightful species have fairly recently gathered in the darker corners of the city occasionally venturing out for their new pair of Adidas trainers. But in fairness you can do a lot worse than a day at Madame Tussaud's, as long as you are able to ignore the shrieking girls as they see yet another figure of 'Oh My God he is the most bloody gorgeous man alive!'

Fee Grammar

Classroom activity 21

Working with a partner, answer the following questions as thoroughly as you can. Provide evidence from Text Q to support each of your answers.

1. What lexical features can you comment on? For example, from what lexical fields does the student take words? What can you say about the complex adjectives that the student experiments with?

2. How has the student used mixed-mode features?

3. How has the student used connotation to describe the visitors to Madame Tussaud's?

4. What effect is achieved by juxtaposing the minor sentence 'And thank God for it' and the complex sentence that follows it?

AQA Examiner's tip

Students who write a magazine article for a teenage audience should avoid adopting a roughly colloquial style, as it does not allow them to demonstrate their full control over their style.

■ Magazine article

Read Text R, a piece of information writing by Nigel Slater, then answer the questions that follow in as much detail as you can.

Text R

The juice is running through the cream and over the meringue like blood from a deep cut. The berries are stingingly tart, a more or less perfect contrast to the sweet, brown-sugar notes of the meringue's shattered crust. Puddings like this come but once or twice a year.

We don't do much in the way of creamy, billowing puddings in our house. Maybe a pavlova once a year, the clouds of egg white smothered in wincingly sharp passion fruit seeds, the occasional trifle with its layers of syllabub, fruit and booze-soaked sponge cake, and perhaps a pale gooseberry fool on a warm July afternoon. As a rule, dessert tends towards the understated – a ripe mango maybe, a bowl of strawberries flecked with mint, a ripe peach or nectarine splashed with sweet wine. Yet it just wouldn't be summer without at least one over-the-top, take-no-prisoners fruit and cream pudding.

If such an extravagant finish is going to delight rather than cloy, then the fruit should be sharp rather than sweet. Loganberries, tayberries, red and blackcurrants, raspberries and passion fruit will give a more interesting result than, say, strawberries or peaches. You need that prick of tartness to balance the sugar and cream. Blackberries succeed too, especially with a hazelnut meringue or almond shortcake to keep them company.

Loganberries and mulberries (the latter so rare I can't remember the last time I spotted one) contain the most spectacular juice of an almost arterial red. Sharp and sweet at the same time, they appear briefly in the shops in midsummer. This summer's rain has not been kind to such fragile fruit and sadly, like their friend the tayberry (a cross between the raspberry and the blackberry), they do not travel well and often resemble jam by the time you get them home. None of which matters if they are to end up rolled in a meringue.

I rather like the idea of the rolled meringue – a pavlova-type mixture where the meringue is used to wrap up the cream and berries rather than wear them on its head. The sugar-crusted roll looks extravagant, the sort of thing to bring out at a summer birthday party, but appears much more difficult than it actually is. And should it fail, then you simply dump it in a bowl and call it a meringue fool.

The one in front of me now is one of several fruit puddings I have made this week. (I went a bit mad with berries at the market, like a kid in a sweet shop.) There were white currants suspended in a pale sugar syrup, strawberries sliced and marinated in passion fruit juice, and a sweet stew of berries spooned over toasted bread. A little rosewater found its way into the meringue, but although it goes well with the scarlet berries I only mention it in passing, rather than making it part of the recipe.

The fruit I love finding above all others at this time of year is the white currant. So difficult are they to locate that I planted several bushes – White Versailles – and six years on they produce enough fruit for a decent-sized tart (a crisp pastry base, then a layer of fromage frais and double cream) and make a very peaceful-looking compote. Resembling a bowl of pearls, they produce perhaps the most calm and understated end to a meal I have ever had. Eaten shortly after cooking, the sharp currants are startling to find in the same mouthful as the warm, sweet syrup. If you let them cool, the fruit takes up the sweetness of the syrup and produces a very pleasing compote if served chilled. A striking contrast to the dessert I am eating right now.

Nigel Slater, '*The sweetest feeling*', The Observer magazine, *22 July 2007*

Extension activity 14

Although the primary purpose of Text R is to inform, the writer also wants to entertain. In the table below you will find an example of how Nigel Slater uses figurative language to entertain. Choose three more examples of Slater's figurative language and explain what effect you think each one achieves.

Figurative language	What it achieves
'The juice is running through the cream and over the meringue like blood from a deep cut.'	Because the verb 'running' is such an active verb it suggests something exciting about the pudding. The phrase 'The juice is running' is also sexually suggestive and so the pudding sounds exotic and physically exciting. The simile 'like blood from a deep cut' is shocking in this context. It obviously refers to the rich colour of the juice, and possibly its thick texture – however, it also reminds the reader of the dangers of the kitchen.

Classroom activity 22

Although the lexis is generally formal, Nigel Slater also uses humour. Choose three further examples of this and explain what you think each one achieves.

Example of humour	What it achieves
'I went a bit mad with berries at the market, like a kid in a sweet shop.'	'mad' is exaggeration for effect, while the simile 'like a kid in a sweet shop' mocks his excitement

Classroom activity 23

Information writing provides factual details. List four facts that you learnt from this article.

Classroom activity 24

This piece of writing has very few **connectives** or **discourse markers** to signpost the reader through the text. What cohesion features does Nigel Slater use?

See page 200 for feedback on this activity.

Key terms

Connective: a word, such as a conjunction, that connects words, phrases, clauses, sentences or paragraphs.

Discourse marker: a word or phrase that signposts the structure of a text.

We have looked closely at the lexis, the discourse structure and the information of Nigel Slater's piece of information writing. Can we use these features to analyse other pieces of information writing? Do we need to refer to other features when analysing different styles of information writing? We will explore these questions when we analyse a leaflet.

◤ Leaflet

Study Text S, a page from a government transport information leaflet, and consider what you could say about:

▪ the lexis

▪ the discourse structure

▪ the style in which the information is provided.

Also, think about what additional features of the text you would like to refer to in an analysis.

Text S

For the provision of information electronically, equipment and systems are available and being developed for both light and heavy rail and form buses.

The two key types of information are:

● Journey planning and information

● In-journey information (including at stop [or station] information)

Journey planning for heavy rail is available through a range of network owner and service operator websites and from the National Railways Telephone Enquiry Service.

Journey planning information for multi-mode public transport (including bus and light rail) is available through the Traveline initiative (formerly PTI 2000).

Traveline is a service that provides public transport information via a series of linked regional centres. Users can obtain information either by ringing a national number or via a web site. The regional centres are funded by a partnership of local authorities, bus operators and passenger transport executives. The individual systems will be developed and linked over the next few years to enable the provision of national real time information.

GOVERNMENT OBJECTIVES

A key objective of the Government is to make public transport a viable alternative to the car. To support this, the intention is:

● Make public transport services accessible

● Provide confidence that services are predictable and appropriate

The development of journey planning systems, integrated with fare information and electronic ticketing will support the accessibility of public transport services.

Public transport information systems will increase passenger confidence and satisfaction with services by informing travellers when their vehicle will arrive, and by providing a reason if it is late.

BACKGROUND

The improvement and development of public transport if an essential objective of the Government's ten-year plan to deliver a UK network that is safe, efficient, clean and fair. The provision of information on public transport services by operators and passenger transport authorities is recognised as being key to this objective.

The Transport Act 2000 requires local authorities to consider what information should be provided and how it should be made available. They must also consult with both Bus User Groups and the Traffic Commissioner on the issue.

Most information will still be delivered on paper, but a great deal of information can be delivered electronically. Electronic delivery provides the benefit that information can be real time taking into account delays and incidents.

http://www.dft.gov.uk

Over the page is a student's analysis of the government transport leaflet (Text S). It considers the lexis, the presentation of information and the discourse structure. While you are reading it, think about:

■ how far you agree with the analysis

■ whether you would like to add any further comments

■ what other features you would like to comment on.

Copy and annotate the text and the analysis with your own responses.

Student analysis

Lexis

The leaflet uses formal and technical lexis. Phrases such as 'Electronic delivery provides the benefit' and 'service operator websites' are extremely formal, while phrases such as 'journey planning systems' and in-journey information' come from the lexical field of transport planning. The formal and technical lexis suggests that the leaflet has been written for educated readers who have professional knowledge of transport systems.

Presentation of information

The leaflet provides a great deal of information. It is set out clearly in the section 'Government Objectives' and then developed more thoroughly in the section 'Background'. The declarative sentences encourage the reader to accept the authority of the information.

Discourse structure

The information tends to be presented like a list, with few connectives linking the paragraphs. This reduces the sense of structure, or narrative. Consequently, it is unlikely to be read by people other than those involved in transport planning, who probably require the information. However, some discourse markers do help to structure the information.

The opening section 'Government Objectives' sets out the structure for the rest of the page. The phrase 'To support this, the intention is to…' signposts the significance of the information that follows. In the 'Background' section, discourse markers such as 'The two key types of information are…' also signpost to the reader that significant information is to follow. These are examples of cataphoric references.

This brief analysis of the lexis, presentation of information, and discourse structure provides a valuable overview of the leaflet. However, there are many other features that require analysis. These features can be grouped under the heading 'graphology'.

🔍 Graphology

You learnt about the graphological features of a text in Unit 1 (page 45); they are the visual features that structure the text and make it more interesting to look at. Graphological features include:

■ headlines and sub-headings

■ pictures and captions

■ typographical variations

■ colour

■ presentation of the text.

What can you say about the graphological features of the government transport leaflet?

Below is a transcript of three students' discussion on this topic.

Text T

> **John**: The layout is extremely formal. The use of three columns and short paragraphs gives the impression of a formal newspaper article, or a textbook page. There is very little typographical variation, which adds to this formality.
>
> **Emily**: Yes, but bullet points are used to highlight important information.
>
> **George**: The two photographs break up the intensity of the text. Both are relevant, illustrating the information provided in the text. The formality of the pictures, with little use of vibrant colours, and no human beings, complements the formal tone of the piece. The captions anchor the unusual pictures.
>
> **Emily**: Also, look how the page uses one colour other than the colour of the text – green. The illustrations have green bars to separate them from the text, and the two sub-headings use the same colour. If the page had used a range of vibrant colours it might have given the impression of frivolous content. I also wonder whether the green has been used to subliminally suggest that the Government's transport policy is environmentally friendly?

Extension activity 15

What other graphological features of leaflets are you familiar with? Copy and complete the table below by listing as many graphological features as you can, and see what you can say about the impact each one might have.

Graphological feature	Impact
Cartoon characters	Makes the leaflet look lively and cheerful. Suggests a younger target audience.
Wide range of typographical variation	

Classroom activity 25

The discussion above is a reasonably exhaustive analysis of the leaflet's graphological features. Could you add anything else? Study the front page of the Royal Observatory web page in the online resources, and write about the graphological features: www.nmm.ac.uk/astronomy.

We have identified the following stylistic features that help us to analyse information writing:

- Lexis.
- Discourse structure.
- The style in which information is presented.
- Graphological features.

It is now important to explore how this framework can be used to analyse other information texts. It would be possible, for your coursework, to write

AQA Examiner's tip

If you produce a leaflet, avoid subjects that are too far outside your personal experience. You are likely to have to research any subject that you choose, but researching an unfamiliar subject is extremely time-consuming.

a textbook page for students of your own age. However, an alternative assignment would be to simplify the technical demands of one of your own textbooks and prepare the information for a younger audience.

Extension activity 16

Use the framework that we developed when analysing the transport leaflet to analyse the science textbook page (Text U). Comment on the lexis, the discourse structure, the style in which the information is presented, and the graphological and linguistic features.

Text U

3.3 DESCRIBING THE EARTH'S MAGNETIC FIELD

It will be clear to you by now that the simplest possible magnetic field that the Earth could have is that of a bar magnet which, unlike that in Figure 44, is inclined at about 11° to the axis of rotation. The field is essentially that of a **magnetic dipole**; in other words it is associated with *two poles*, like a bar magnet. No one has yet observed an isolated pole, whether north or south. For the moment, let us make a simplifying assumption and consider the characteristics of the field produced by a dipole lying at the centre of the Earth and aligned along the Earth's rotational axis. This is called an **axially geocentric dipole**, which is exactly as shown in Figure 44. We have defined the places towards and away from which compass needles point as the *geomagnetic poles*: M_N in the Northern Hemisphere and M_S in the Southern Hemisphere.

Further reading

If you want to read some more travel writing, you might like to try:

www.moxon.net/australia

Bryson, B. *Notes From a Small Island*, Black Swan, 2005

Chatwin, B. *In Patagonia*, Vintage Classics, 1997

Fermor, P. L. *A Time of Gifts*, John Murray, 1997

Fleming, P. *News From Tartary*, Jonathan Cape, 1936

Naipaul, V. S. *Among the Believers: An Islamic Journey*, Alfred A. Knopf, 1981

Thesiger, W. *My Life and Travels*, HarperCollins, 2002

If you want to read more magazine articles, visit:

http://observer.guardian.co.uk/magazine

www.nationalgeographic.com/siteindex

http://home.q4music.com

www.empireonline.com

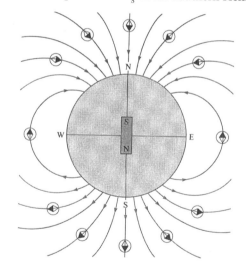

FIGURE 44 Field lines (red) with compass needles oriented correctly (cf. Figure 38) around a bar magnet located at the centre of a sphere. The geographic directions N, S, E, W are marked for ease of comparison with Figure 38.

☐ Where are ghe geomagnetic poles M_N and M_S located in an axially geocentric dipole model of the Earth's magnetic field?

■ Since *in this model* the dipole axis and rotation axis coincide, M_N and M_S coincide, respectively, with the north and south geographic poles.

Now imagine that you are standing on the Equator (i.e. the geographic equator) with an ordinary compass and that you walk along a line of longitude from the equator towards the north geographic pole.

The Open University, 1989

Writing to advise/instruct

In this topic you will:

■ learn the stylistic features associated with writing to advise/instruct

■ analyse a leaflet and a recipe

■ produce your own writing to advise/instruct.

The Examination Board mentions three examples of writing in this category:

1 A leaflet focusing on 'How to choose a university'.

2 A guide to texting for novices.

3 An article advising 'How to survive a music festival'.

However, as with all of the writing categories that we have studied, the list of types of writing is almost limitless. Some more suggestions of different types of writing to advise/instruct are:

■ a study guide for new AS Level students

■ a leaflet about healthy living

■ an article that provides instructions about how to change a tyre.

The distinction between writing to advise and writing to instruct is blurred, but as we have seen through this unit, many texts have more than one purpose.

Through an analysis of a range of texts we will be able to identify the stylistic features of writing to advise and writing to instruct, and be able to see where the distinctions are blurred. If you choose to produce a piece of writing to advise/instruct, you will need to identify your primary purpose, and also understand whether you have used features of both styles of writing.

i An advice leaflet

Read Text V, an extract taken from a leaflet provided by Childnet International. While you are reading, think about:

■ how far the leaflet provides advice and how you can identify advice

■ how far the leaflet provides instructions and how you can identify instructions

■ what the target audience is.

Text V

Advice

Take care in what you share online, e.g. pictures and passwords

Blogs are great. They help you keep in touch with friends and let the world know your thoughts. Which is all well and good, but you have to make sure you're sensible about it. What you think may be a harmless piece of information, like the school you're from or the local football team you play for, could be all someone needs to be able to trace you in real life. You know all the horror stories – just take care in the details you're posting and think before you click 'Submit'.

Choose good passwords and keep them closely guarded

We seem to live in a world where everything has a password – your bank account PIN, email accounts, mobile phone codes... the thing is, all too many people use the same password for everything online. That's their email account, their blogging login, instant messaging programs, and whatever else they get up to. Don't be one of these people – use different passwords for different activities to make sure you're safe if someone finds out. It's a good idea to use a combination of letters and numbers for extra safety, change it regularly, and make it something less obvious than your dog's name. Apparently that's the most common password chosen.

Take care and disguise your e-mail address online

Sometimes it seems a mystery how spammers get hold of your address in the first place. Often, they send what's called a spider out, which crawls web pages looking for email addresses. So, if you've got your email posted on somebody's Guestbook or on your own personal website, it might be the source of some of the spam. There's one easy way you can protect yourself here – disguise your email address when you post it online. Humans will be able to interpret it correctly, but spiders won't. Here are some examples:
rob@~deletethis~email.com
rob[at]email[dot]com
rob@ *SPAM* email.com

Don't reply to spam and don't click 'Unsubscribe'

You might think it makes sense to click the 'Unsubscribe' link at the bottom of Spam emails. But think of it this way: if these spammers are willing to send you advertisements without your consent, are they really going to care if you ask them not to? In truth, clicking Unsubscribe merely confirms that your email address is a valid one. Most web-based email clients allow you to click a 'Report Spam' button that will move the offending message into your junk mail folder. Doing this will also train the spam filters to reject this kind of message in the future. If you don't have this feature, simply delete the message.

Childnet International leaflet, 2006

Extension activity 17

Write the text for a leaflet informing GCSE students about the best way to prepare for their exams.

Classroom activity 26

We have already seen how the distinction between advice and instruction is blurred. One way of telling them apart is that:

- instructions are likely to use declarative and imperative sentences
- advice is likely to give options, and to explain why it is good advice.

1. In Text V, identify writing that could be seen as instructional, and writing that could be seen to be writing to advise.

2. Write six sentences about sixth-form education: three giving advice and three that provide instructions.

See page 200 for feedback on this activity.

Classroom activity 27

Identify two personal pronouns in Text W and say what effect they have. Does this tell you anything about the target audience? What can you say about the way the leaflet has been structured? Does each section follow a similar pattern? Identify any other linguistic features used in the leaflet, and comment on their effects.

See page 201 for feedback on this activity.

■ Instructional writing

The step-by-step instructions in Text W explain how to use the Beat Crime website, and illustrate some of the stylistic features of this genre. This extract is used to illustrate the stylistic features of instructional writing. If you choose to produce a piece of instructional writing, you will need to tackle a much more challenging task.

Text W

Here is your step-by-step guide on how to use www.beatcrime.info:

Step 1   Either type in your postcode or click down through the maps to find the area you are interested in.

Step 2   Choose a crime type from the drop-down menu *'Which crime type would you like to see*?' The map will then change to display the frequency and location of this crime type in the last month in your area.

Step 3   Click on *'As a chart showing trends over time'* underneath the crime types menu to check police performance in your local area for this crime type. The map display will change to show a chart containing monthly crime figures for the last two years.

Step 4   Click back onto the *'Displayed as a map'* option and use the zoom bar next the map to see the picture of crime at divisional and district level too.

Step 5   At any time, use the *'Which crime type would you like to see*?' drop down menu to see the picture of crime for each of the different crime types available.

Step 6   At any time, click on the *'What can I do about crime in my area?'* link to access advice and information about how to protect yourself and others from being a victim of crime.

www.beatcrime.info

Classroom activity 28

Make a copy of the following table and complete it with brief notes about the stylistic features found in the Beat Crime instructions (Text W).

See page 201 for feedback on this activity.

Stylistic feature	Commentary
Lexical choices	
Discourse structure	
The way instructions are given	
Linguistic features	

■ Further reading

If you want to read more information leaflets, visit:

www.centerparcs.co.uk/villages

http://campaigns.direct.gov.uk/firekills

www.cityoflondon.gov.uk/corporation

Search for Information leaflets

You have engaged in a detailed analysis of a range of non-fiction texts. At each stage you have generalised about the stylistic features associated with a different style of writing. It is now possible to draw all of this analysis together.

You have analysed different texts using the following categories:

■ Lexical choices.

■ Linguistic features.

■ Discourse structure.

■ The way instructions are given.

■ Extension activity 18

Look closely at Text X. Look back at all the analysis you have engaged with in this unit. Draw all your studies together to write a detailed analysis of the leaflet, commenting on:

■ the use of language

■ the use of graphological features

■ the structure of the text

■ who the target audience might be.

Use as many of the technical terms as possible that you have become familiar with in this unit.

Text X

The scheme supports children and young people who:

- have special educational needs
- are disabled
- have emotional and behavioural difficulties

To access inclusive leisure, play and childcare opportunities;

- Pre-school (playgroups)
- Private day nurseries
- Early Years Centres
- Children's Centres
- Summer play schemes.
- Uniformed groups i.e. scouts & brownies.
- Out of school clubs.
- Arts & recreation groups i.e. sports & art clubs.

Application & Grant Process

1. Parents /Carers find a setting or group that meets both their needs and their child's. You can offer the family support by contacting the Children's Information Service tel 0113 2475487 www.leeds.gov.uk/childcare

2. Family visit setting or group and discuss their child's needs. If the setting needs to enhance its staffing levels to enable the child to benefit fully, then the setting should apply to Leeds Inclusion Support Scheme.

3. **Pre-school age children** will need to meet EYFFI criteria and a 'suitable' professional will need to apply depending on the criteria band.

4. **Holiday or out of school setting** should complete an application form for additional funding which could be for resources or enhancing staffing. All applications are presented to a monthly panel.

5. Social Workers may need to support parents in providing evidence for the application (for school aged children).

What happens next?

1. The setting or group will be informed of the panels decision.

2. The setting is responsible for completing the grant claim forms on a regular basis.

3. Support will be monitored by the 'virtual team' - the Early Years SEN Service, Inclusion Workers at Leeds Play Network & Special Needs Development Worker at PsLA.

Remember this all takes time. Parents and professionals need to plan at least 6 - 8 weeks in advance. This sometimes needs to be longer to enable settings or groups to recruit appropriate staff. Play schemes may have a booking deadline for the holiday schemes.

Leeds Inclusion Support scheme

Coursework preparation and practice

☑

In this topic you will:

- consider the writing process
- study a writer's experience
- produce your own writing.

AQA Examiner's tip

Choose different genres, purposes and audiences for your two pieces of writing.

The process of writing

This unit has explored writing within each of the categories:

- Writing to entertain.
- Writing to persuade.
- Writing to inform.
- Writing to advise/instruct.

It has also been stressed that your final portfolio will include:

- two pieces of original writing
- two commentaries.

How to approach a piece of writing

This topic will explore a piece of writing by Chris, an AS Level student. We will go through the process that Chris went through when he produced a piece of creative writing.

- We will learn from Chris what decisions he made before he started writing, how he chose texts to annotate, how he annotated them and what he learnt from them.
- We will learn how he transferred this learning to his own piece of writing.
- Chris will explain his redrafting and what he hoped it would achieve.

Decisions made before writing

There are three important things that must be considered when writing any form of text. These are audience, purpose and genre (APG). First, you must find an audience you can comfortably address. I chose late teens, as I felt that my style of writing suited that age group. However, audience doesn't have to be age related, as you can have an audience with a common interest.

Purpose can seem a straightforward concept, but what has to be taken into account is maintaining the purpose of the text consistently throughout. My purpose was to entertain. To entertain, the piece of text must grip the audience and suit their interests.

Genre is the centre point of the APG. When choosing a genre you must keep in mind both your audience and purpose. I chose a story, as it allows you to convey a message whilst maintaining a fictional feel. By doing so, you can show your underlying message as horrifically or as pleasantly as you feel necessary to get your point across.

Extension activity 19

Re-read the list of suggested writing tasks provided on page 118. Imagine that you are going to write one of the suggested texts. Choose one and define an audience, a purpose and a genre.

Annotating texts

Chris analysed a number of texts written in the first person, including *Dracula* by Bram Stoker, *Frankenstein* by Mary Shelley, and *The Wasp Factory* by Iain Banks. Text Y is an example of one of his annotated extracts.

Text Y

Frankenstein

Sounds epic

First person

It was on a dreary night of November that I beheld the accomplishment of my toils. With an anxiety that almost amounted to agony, I collected the instruments of life around me, that I might infuse a spark of being into the lifeless thing that lay at my feet. It was already one in the morning; the rain pattered dismally against the panes, and my candle was nearly burnt out, when, by the glimmer of the half-extinguished light, I saw the dull yellow eye of the creature open; it breathed hard, and a convulsive motion agitated its limbs.

Complex sentence to suggest his complex thoughts

Pathetic fallacy used to create atmosphere

Pronouns to show creature is not human

How can I describe my emotions at this catastrophe, or how delineate the wretch whom with such infinite pains and care I had endeavoured to form? His limbs were in proportion, and I had selected his features as beautiful. Beautiful! – Great God! His yellow skin scarcely covered the work of muscles and arteries beneath; his hair was of a lustrous black, and flowing; his teeth of a pearly whiteness; but these luxuriances only formed a more horrid contrast with his watery eyes, that seemed almost of the same colour as the dun white sockets in which they were set, his shrivelled complexion and straight black lips.

Question engages the reader's sympathy

Lexical field of science

Ambiguous. Blasphemous or respectful?

The niceties have a contrast with the watery eyes, adding to the grotesqueness of the creature

Grotesque description of body parts, in direct contrast with stereotypical literary style, e.g. love poetry

Extension activity 20

Imagine that you have already chosen a genre for your next piece of personal writing. Select a text from that genre as a style model, and annotate it like the example above.

Student commentary

Chris explains how his analysis of the different texts influenced his writing.

The style models that I analysed have been influential. First of all, I used the first person, as it was used in all of the texts that I analysed. I used the first-person perspective in order to explore the inner feelings of the main character. However, while annotating the *Frankenstein* extract, I found myself wondering how 'the creation' would feel throughout the story, and this inspired me to introduce a second character into the story to add a history to the main character, and to add irony to the child's beliefs.

In my final draft, I chose to write in a formal style, without colloquialisms, even fluency features might have been appropriate for a first-person narrative. I chose to write in this register to allow the narrator to tell the story with conviction and authority. Sentences such as 'My solitude has driven me to hate all things about the beings of the Mainland' illustrate the formal register. However, there also seems to be some influence from the *Frankenstein* extract, as my expression does appear archaic at times.

When the father reveals his thoughts I use the lexical field of science, with some scientific jargon; I adopted this idea from *Frankenstein*. This gives the father's ideas some authority, but because it is such a different style from the one used when the son speaks, it is easy to distinguish between the two. Also, as the text moves between characters so does the graphology. The italics used for the father help to suggest that he is talking from beyond the grave.

I adopted the interrogative sentences used in *Frankenstein*. For example, 'Why should you allow rules to make you live your life in misery when changing them could make it much more pleasant?' The rhetorical questions help to engage the reader in the son's philosophical argument. I also adopted the exclamatory mood of *Frankenstein* in sentences such as 'No one to fight!' This helps to suggest the son's passion.

Extension activity 21

Using the annotations that you made to the text that you chose in Extension activity 20, write two paragraphs of a text that is influenced by your style model. Afterwards, explain how your style model has influenced your writing.

AQA Examiner's tip

You need critical feedback on all stages of your writing, and you should address the feedback in subsequent drafts and redrafts.

■ The drafting process

It is essential that you see the writing process as a series of drafts and redrafts. Good writing is crafted, with conscious decisions made about ways to improve it. You need to draw on your linguistic knowledge and your understanding about the stylistic conventions associated with different genre.

Ask for the opinions of others. While this can feel threatening, or even intrusive, readers can often give advice that will improve your work.

Chris explains some of the drafting decisions that he made.

Originally, I wrote the story with only one character and it contained quite a lot of simplistic language. However, in my second draft, I altered the simplistic language into a form that helped show a tone or mood, rather then just telling the plot. For example, the sentence 'The lack of company has driven me to hate all things about The Mainland' became 'My solitude has driven me to hate all things about the beings of The Mainland'. 'Solitude' is more sophisticated than 'lack of company', and suggests that the narrator is more sophisticated.

Also, I rewrote the ending of the story to provide a bigger impact. Originally, the deaths at the end of the story were not written about in great detail, but then the second draft improved that from one line to a paragraph. This gives the story more excitement and will, hopefully, grip the reader more.

However, the third draft showed the biggest changes by far. In the third draft I introduced another character, who would tell the story from another perspective. This then added a back plot to the story and gave the main character a history. It also put other twists into the story, which were also aimed at gripping the audience.

At a lexical level I chose the lexical field of science to help distinguish the father. For example, in the opening section from the father I used 'haemorrhaged' and 'transfusion'. This was in response to readers finding the two characters too similar. I also used two different fonts to identify the two characters.

My earlier drafts adopted many of the linguistic features associated with first-person narratives: mixed-mode features and non-fluency features for example. However, I felt that this prevented the narrator from exploring his emotions as thoroughly as I wanted him to, and so I removed these features and adopted a more formal register.

■ The final piece of writing

Read Chris's final piece of writing (Text Z). This has largely been included for your interest – you have learnt about the process so you may be interested in the outcome. While you are reading the piece, think about what Chris has achieved.

Text Z

As I run from my past I realise how different I am, how I am so close to those on The Mainland, and yet so far away. This solitude may be good for someone who has lived in the city for decades but not for a child, not for me.

Long before the land took me, I used to live in a city on The Mainland. I had grown up there and I had hated it. The people were cruel and I was not free. I was being confined to a life that I had not wanted. Therefore, as soon as I had saved enough money, I bought a small island off of the coast of The Mainland. I moved out there with my wife, my adulterous wife. She just gave me another reason to leave that place. But she died in childbirth. She haemorrhaged 6 hours into labour, and died of blood loss, despite the transfusion we gave her. She left me with a son to raise on a remote island. I did the best I could with Him, I even tried to get Him an education. But he was stubborn and refused to do anything that He didn't like.

Long ago, my father decided that he no longer liked the city that he had lived in for his whole life, so he moved out here. Here is my prison. Here is loneliness. Here is a small island off the coast of The Mainland. The name of this place is not important, but what is important is that the only people to ever have lived here are my father and I. My solitude has driven me to hate all things about the beings of The Mainland. They are different. They don't live as they want to, they have rules. This seems strange to me. Why should you allow rules to make you live your life in misery when changing them could make it much more pleasant?

Two months! That is all it took Him to be expelled. Two months. I was in peace for two months, but I knew it was too good to last. Not that I don't love Him. I love Him as if He were my own.

There was once a time when I went to The Mainland. My father insisted that I needed an education better than he could provide so I was sent off to boarding school, only to return two months later, with a letter stating how I was uncontrollable and refused to learn. But I didn't refuse to learn. I was happy to learn, but I wanted to learn the truth, rather than the lies that they taught there. From that day onwards my father taught me how to cultivate the land, how to live off it. How naive he is. Humans don't live off the land, they live with it. The land will not support humans unless we learn to respect it, learn to love it. Man has tried to rule nature in the past and Man has lost. They try to bend the will of nature to suit their lives, feel that they are dictating how this world is to be altered. But they don't see the truth. They don't see how it is nature who dictates how we alter the Earth. How we are ruled by nature. This is one of my main doubts about the beings on The Mainland. They don't love the Earth. They must hate it to poison it so much. Roads stop it breathing; toxins stop its heart beating. These beings on The Mainland cannot be considered human, they merely impersonate humans. Humans could never be so unkind to something that keeps them alive. But my father and I are human, for we love the Earth. For we are almost one and the same. We share a bond that is only brought by blood.

Eventually time came to pass and I moved from His world, and into the next. However, I was given the job of watching over my adopted son, making sure no harm came to Him. Shortly after my death, some men came to the island from a mining company. They would have made millions exploiting Him. But I could not let this happen. I knew that He would try to protect the island but would never succeed without my help.

Inevitably, the Earth decided to repay my father for looking after it, by bringing him to the eternal happiness that is Death. For in Death we are one with the Earth. We will live on in the trees, in the soil, in life.

This was when the men came back. They came to try and steal our haven, our fortress. They claimed that I could not live on the island by myself and that they would take it off my hands and send me to live with a relative. They wanted to ship me to The Mainland like an animal, but even animals don't deserve that punishment. They said to me that they would get my island no matter what, now that my father was dead there was no-one to protect it, no-one to fight for it. At this threat I felt my father's spirit rise in me. I felt our bond, the bond that only comes between father and son, a bond that comes in blood. I did something that I thought I would never do; I killed. With anger in my heart and a knife in my hand, I struck out. The first man fell to the ground, for I had struck him in the head, the second ran for the door, forgetting that he had locked it behind him, to stop me escaping. All he could do in his state of panic was to keep trying to open the door without using the key that was in his pocket. I walked over to him, my knuckles white around the grip of the bloody knife, and as I struck him, I felt myself think; 'No-one to fight! No-one to protect it!'

With this done I took their bodies to the hidden coast, where The Mainland cannot see, and I burnt them. I stood and watched how the flames rose from beneath them, slowly engulfing them. I watched how their clothes did not resist the flames, but how their skin fought, and lost, eventually fuelling the fire that would shrivel their bodies, and keep them from the bliss that is reserved for those who have earned it. I burned them so that they could not poison the Earth with their Death. This is my secret. This is my demise…

Chris Pearce

Classroom activity 29

In his commentary Chris sets out unambiguously what he hoped to achieve in his piece of writing. However, has he achieved what he hoped to achieve?

1 Has Chris created a tone in this piece of writing?

2 What sort of impact has been achieved with the conclusion?

3 What twists has the second character added to the piece?

4 Does the use of the lexical field of science help to identify the father?

5 Does the formal register help the main narrator to explore his emotions?

See page 201 for feedback on this activity.

Extension activity 22

Think about the texts that Chris analysed, what he said that he learnt from them, and what he said he hoped to achieve with this piece of writing. If you were to analyse this piece of writing, what linguistic features would you focus on?

B Writing a commentary

Introduction

In this section you will:

- analyse a range of texts
- study different commentaries
- evaluate commentaries against the assessment criteria
- produce a commentary on each of your pieces of writing to explain how you wrote it and the stylistic decisions you made.

Key terms

Style model: a text that is used as a model for original writing.

In Section A of this unit you saw how important it was to analyse text types in order to define stylistic devices that are commonly associated with different text types. For example, you saw that imperative sentences are associated with information writing, while figurative language is commonly found in creative writing. You then saw how important it was to learn from this analysis and to use this learning in your own writing.

To let the examiner see how your own writing has been consciously crafted, you need to write a commentary. In this commentary you will make explicit features such as the way your writing has been influenced by the writing of others, the lexical choices that you have made, the discourse structure of your writing, and any graphological decisions that you have made. Your commentary will illustrate that you are a reflective writer.

You read a number of analyses in Section A, and it is at this level that you need to comment about your own writing. This section of the unit encourages you to think more explicitly about the way a commentary is constructed and how you can express your ideas purposefully. You will analyse a range of texts, read analyses and study examples of different people's commentaries.

Your two commentaries are almost as important as your two pieces of original writing. You need to keep this in mind while you are going through the writing process, because within your commentaries you will be expected to explain in detail how your writing evolved. Specifically, the examiner will be looking for:

- Discussion of the **style models** that you used in the planning process.
- Discussion of any significant changes that you made during the writing process.
- References to any reading materials that you used and discussion of how they were adapted to suit the new text.
- An analysis of the stylistic devices used in the text, with exemplification from the text.
- Reflection on the effectiveness of the final piece, including, where relevant, feedback from a variety of sources.

Purpose, audience and genre

☑

In this topic you will:

■ consider the purpose, audience and genre of different texts

■ consider the purpose, audience and genre of your own writing.

A good way to start your commentary is to clearly identify the purpose of your writing, the subject, your target audience, and the genre you have chosen. Although you may think that these things are apparent in your text, the examiner wants to know that you understand these features. The Chief Moderator's report for 2006 observed that many candidates' work suffered from being aimless, and advised:

> **Audience** | It is virtually a truism that if the writer can identify **WHO** the piece is for, **WHY** it is being produced, WHEN and WHERE the piece might be found and **HOW** it will be delivered, then the language choices made in the production of the task are more likely to be effective. | **Purpose** **Genre**

This comment makes an essential point. You should make these decisions about who, why, when, where and how *before* you start writing your text. Your commentary is just making explicit the decisions that you made during the writing process. From this starting point you should go on to discuss the language choices that you made in reference to your purpose, audience and genre.

Look at Text A taken from a leaflet:

Text A

> ***Who's the youngest person you've seen with liver problems?***
> The youngest woman we've seen was 19. She had severe pancreatitis, which is inflammation of the pancreas, an organ you need for digestion. She'd drink white cider and strong lagers all through the weekend and then eat very little at the beginning of the week while she recovered.
>
> We get a lot of women in their 30s and 40s with severe liver disease. Most people will have been drinking heavily (more than 35 units a week) for at least six to 10 years before they end up in hospital with serious problems. A couple of large glasses of wine a day could take you up to 35 units by the end of the week.
>
> There was a bad spell recently when we saw around one fatality a month of women under 40. The youngest female death we had here was a woman in her early 20s who died of liver damage.
>
> The problem with liver damage is there aren't any warning signs. Often you don't know you've got it until you've got a bad case as there may well be no pain. Liver disease may cause jaundice and this can cause severe health complications – or even kill you.

www.nhs.uk

Classroom activity 1

Is it possible to conjecture who Text A is for, why it has been produced, when and where the piece might be found and how it will be delivered?

If the author of this leaflet was to explain the who, why, when, where, and how of the extract, they might say something as simple as this:

I wrote the **leaflet** for a **teenage** audience in order to **persuade** them to reduce their drinking.

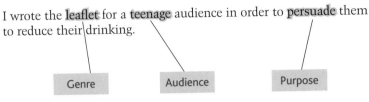

| Genre | Audience | Purpose |

Text B is an extract from a piece of writing by Sophie Taylor, a student.

Text B

> You never gave me any freedom. Just like the spotless crystalline shoes: locked in a dull unsightly cupboard, crushed under a cold sandpapery duvet not being able to see the distinct, gleaming world.
>
> Dad was never there; never when I needed him. Where was he when I needed an apology because he lost his temper with me, and I woke up in an unwelcoming strange hospital? Swamped at work or down the forsaken pub. How do you put up with him? Being violently hit by an overgrown ogre? Forced into being a deprived slave, battered to a pulp?

Sophie Taylor

Student commentary

This is what Sophie said about the piece's purpose, audience and genre:

> This is a piece of creative writing. Its primary purpose is to entertain, but I wanted it to go further than that; I wanted to engage the audience with the social issues that are raised, such as the way parents should bring up their children. I tried to write for an educated audience who enjoyed demanding literature, but I couldn't be more specific than that.

Notice that Sophie has not been completely specific about her audience, but she has still defined its boundaries. However, she could have been more specific, by, for example, identifying educated teenagers as her primary audience. She has also made an explicit statement about the primary and secondary purposes of the piece.

Extension activity 1

Commentaries should illustrate your understanding and appreciation of purpose, audience and genre. Revisit each of your pieces of coursework writing. Define the purpose, audience and genre of each of the pieces.

Style models

In this topic you will:

- ▪ evaluate how students have explained the influence of their style models

- ▪ explore how to discuss the influence of style models more analytically.

It is necessary to discuss the style models that you use in the planning process. In this discussion you should thoroughly analyse the linguistic choices that you made, referencing them back to your style models, and provide examples from your own texts to exemplify the points that you make.

🔲 Using travel writing as a style model

The following commentary by Fee Grammar analyses a piece of travel writing describing a visit to London, that you studied on page 162. While you are reading, think about the following questions:

1 How far does the writer discuss the way her style models influenced her own text?
2 How far does the writer analyse the linguistic features of her writing?
3 How thorough is this analysis? Could it be improved?

Student commentary

'City Travels' is in written mode with a formal register and it is literary in tone. It starts similarly to Bill Bryson's *Notes From a Small Island* with 'My first sight of London…' and is quickly followed by a metaphor 'breeze… parent'. This links to the idea of the parents and children in the station.

Being travel writing, it used lots of information about London, starting with the pavements and 'their fabled gilded construction'. The words 'fabled' and 'gilded' are higher-order lexis and more literary, showing that the piece has been consciously crafted. I included some dialogue with a Londoner to give an idea of the people, using typical London jargon like 'mate', which is an informal politeness strategy.

I used the first-person narrative which echoes Bryson and creates a personal feel as if talking directly to the reader. I also used direct address in the second-person pronoun 'you' to directly involve the reader. The use of a humorous comment and ellipsis 'When in Rome…' further this tone. I have used elision in the speech like 'can't' and 'I'd' to show an informal register.

Similar to Bryson's style, I have linked ideas throughout the piece. I mentioned Somerset at the beginning, and referred to it again at the end. I also discussed London's 'multicultural atmosphere' with the different countries, which I mentioned again at the end to link back. I used a semantic field of travel as it's a travel-writing piece, with words such as 'coach', 'fast paced', 'walk', and 'big red bus', which is also one of the typical London icons.

Classroom activity 2

With a partner, answer the following questions in as much detail as you can.

1 Has the writer made valuable references to her style models in this extract?

2 What linguistic choices has the writer discussed?

3 Which linguistic choices has the writer related back to her style models?

4 Has the writer used examples from her own text to exemplify her analysis?

5 Could you give the writer any advice about how she might have improved her commentary?

See page 201 for feedback on this activity.

So, could Fee Grammar have made more explicit references to the way her style model influenced her own writing? The key stylistic features of travel writing have been defined earlier in the unit:

- It is usually written in the first person.
- It is usually written in the past tense.
- The style may be humorous.
- The writer may address the reader by using the first-person plural, 'we', or the second person, 'you'.
- Borrowed words may be used to reveal something about the place.
- Other lexical experimentation may be seen, such as non-fluency features and mixed-mode features.

Text C is an extract from Fee's style model: Bill Bryson's *Notes From A Small Island*. Which stylistic features associated with travel writing can you identify in Bryson's writing?

Text C

I spent a couple more days in London doing nothing much. I did a little research in a newspaper library, spent most of the afternoon trying to find my way through the complex network of pedestrian subways at Marble Arch, did a little shopping, saw some friends.

Everyone I saw said, 'Gosh, you're brave' when I revealed that I was planning to travel around Britain by public transport, but it never occurred to me to go any other way. You are so lucky in this country to have a relatively good public transport system (relative, that is, to what it will be when the Tories finish it) and I think we should all try harder to enjoy it while it's still there. Besides, driving in Britain is such a dreary experience these days. There are far too many cars on the road, nearly double what there were when I first came here, and in those days people didn't actually drive their cars. They just parked them in the driveway and buffed them up once every week or so. About twice a year they would 'get the car out' – those were the words they used, like that in itself was a big operation – and pootle off to visit relatives in East Grinstead or have a trip to someplace like Hayling Island or Eastbourne, and that was about it, apart from the buffing.

Student commentary

Fee Grammar's analysis of Bryson's style illustrates the semantic and linguistic features that he has used.

> Typical of travel writing, Bryson writes in the first person, and in the past tense. To suggest a relationship between himself and the reader he uses the first-person plural 'we', as though he is writing about a shared experience. To suggest that Britain is a quaint, outdated country Bryson borrows words such as 'buff' and 'pootle', words not commonly used today. The anaphoric reference to buffing in the final sentence adds humour as it suggests that the British spend inordinate amounts of time cleaning their cars. Frequent use of place names such as Marble Arch and Eastbourne anchors the text in Britain.
>
> Although the text has been largely written in a formal register, there are some non-fluency features and mixed-mode features. For example, in the opening sentence the phrase 'a couple more days' is almost colloquial, while in the second sentence, the omission of a conjunction at the end of the list helps to create a conversational tone. The use of complex sentences, which gives his writing a sense of being rambling recollections, adds to the sense that the writing is a conversation between writer and reader.

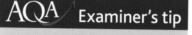

AQA Examiner's tip

You should be able to write texts that imitate examples from real life in terms of lexical, semantic and grammatical choices, as well as significant discourse features.

A number of semantic and linguistic features have been identified in Bryson's writing. Is it possible to find any of these linguistic features in Fee's description of her visit to London? In fact, the following linguistic features appear in both:

- The text is written in the first person and the past tense.
- The first-person plural is used.
- The text has largely been written in a formal style.
- Non-fluency features, such as the chains of adjectives, are used.
- Mixed-mode features are used ('and I mean', 'as far as I can tell').
- Complex sentences are the dominant sentence form.

It can be seen that Fee uses a number of the linguistic features used by Bryson. If she had deliberately used these linguistic features in response to her analysis of the Bryson style model, she could have added to her commentary by saying:

> To suggest a relationship between myself and the reader I used the first-person plural. Although the tone of my text is largely formal, with phrases such as 'However, one cannot claim to have experienced...,' there are examples of mixed-mode features. The two phrases 'I mean' and 'as far as I can tell' are more likely to appear in spoken language than written. This helps to give the impression that my writing is a conversation with the reader. Complex sentences are the dominant sentence form, which gives my writing a sense of being rambling recollections, and adds to the sense of the writing being a conversation between myself and the reader. For example, 'Madame Tussaud's has been moulded like its figures, and has experienced a fair amount of change not least when a fire broke out and the place had to be re-built, but mostly when a German bomb was dropped and the place was blown up.' The subordinate clauses provide additional information but also provide a conversational tone.

Using autobiography as a syle model

Text D comes from a piece of writing to entertain by Lucy Edwards. The extract has been selected because in her commentary Lucy made some insightful comments about her use of linguistic features and their effect in context. These have been underlined in the text. (The use of underlining is a good strategy to highlight the key features of your writing that you are going to discuss in your commentary.)

Text D

I pushed my way apprehensively through the porch doorway and I was immediately swamped by that intoxicating musty smell and engulfed by the dust we had unsettled as it rose like a tornado up around us. We discarded our bags and flopped onto the sofa with relief. Once we settled in, anxiety masked mum's face as she handed me the keys and finally repeated the rules for the last time 'No drinking, smoking, going out with boys or at night, and always stick together…?' Nodding sweetly and waving, we stood shakily on the crumbly old garden wall and watched until she and Rupert had retreated back up over the hill and were out of sight and on their way back home. Our four bodies collided as we all jumped down and ran, bumping and scraping up the tiny staircase, into the main bedroom, the bed creaking pitifully under the weight of our bodies as we crashed down in hysterical laughter.

Celebration was in order. We cracked open the beer and sat outside on the dustbins to have a smoke. I slipped from the conversation into contented satisfaction that I had finally escaped him. I had my best friends beside me without even the slight comprehension of the disturbance in my mind. It was better that way, they'd only worry if they knew what he had done to me, or worse, pity me. I'd hidden those old scars for so many years, worked so hard to build my life up – I wasn't about to let all of this go.

High on natural excitement, the time whizzed by until we realised it was by now 8pm and we were restless. A walk to the beach seemed to be the only sensible cure. Taking only a bag with our phones and cigarettes we strolled down through the secluded forest path, chatting and laughing. Eventually, breaking through onto the road we caught the sun as it was just disappearing beyond the horizon. We rested on a bench tucked away in the cliff and looked out at the pink sky that glimmered above the water, we watched in satisfied silence as the waves tumbled and wrestled their way to the shore. The sun now gone, a sign that day was over.

Eventually we continued our way down to the shore and found a large rock that had a perfect space for us all to squeeze onto.

In this surreal world of retreat and peace, only my thoughts remained in turmoil; echoing through the silence only worries plagued relentlessly against my happiness. I was crushed with the realisation that he was still in control, and as each cloud seemed to form his bulky shadow it seemed the bruises now faded from my skin were still darkly imprinted within my mind.

Lucy Edwards

Extension activity 2

What comments could Lucy make in her commentary about the underlined words, phrases and sentences in Text D? For example, could she say anything about:

- semantic fields
- sentence variation
- language choices.

See page 202 for feedback on this activity.

What could Lucy have said about her use of non-standard grammar and her range of sentence structures?

Read Lucy's analysis of the extract from her piece of autobiographical writing. Consider how far you predicted the comments that she makes.

Student commentary

The audience for this piece is young adults/students, the same audience intended for the stimulus material. I use colloquial language with an informal sense of humour, which gives lots of attention to small detail to lighten the tone of the overall text. This is seen clearly in the use of the verbs such as 'flopped', 'cracked' and 'scampered'. This allows younger readers to be involved with the text and masks the undertone of violence, making it appear less harsh. Language appears complex yet delicate. The sentences vary from short, snappy declaratives such as 'celebration was in order' to more complex sentences such as 'It was better that way, they'd only worry if they knew what he had done to me, or worse, pity me.'

There are various semantic fields throughout, from the overall theme of vacations such as nature 'the hillside had become wild and overcome with life', 'secluded forest path' to sitting contentedly on the beach. The descriptions and images bring the environment to life and emphasise how small details matter.

I used personification to bring the waves alive as they 'tumbled and wrestled their way to the shore,' this also creates strong imagery as well as being a metaphor for the writer's thoughts; as 'In this surreal world of retreat and peace only my thoughts remained in turmoil… echoing through the silence only worries plagued relentlessly against my happiness'. This conveys how even though she is so far away and with her closest friends, 'his bulky shadow' still haunts her, the audience can now share her deeper and most intimate secrets.

Using a radio play as a style model

The same level of analysis can be undertaken with radio play scripts.

Text E

FADE UP BOXING MATCH, ABE AND TOM. BARE KNUCKLE PUNCHES. CHEERS OF CROWD. CRASH AS TOM IS FLOORED BY A PUNCH.

ABE: (*in background*) I beat your pappy, I's goina beat you so bad. (*laughs big*)

MASTER: You aint hardly thrown a fist. I'll be ruint, ruint boy...

TOM: (*breathless*) You think on that, masser, and I shall be back presently...

MORE FIGHT. WE STAY WITH MASTER AND CROWD. TOM TAKES A BEATING. FALLS AGAIN.

HENRIETTA: Tom, what you doing to yourself?!

TOM: Henrietta, I knows wot I am doing here.

TOM TAKES A BIG HIT. FALLS HARD.

MASTER: Hit him, stomach him. Sakes alive, Tom, fight the evil black dog!

TOM: (*sudden, ice in his tone*)... I want my freedom. My free-dom if I puts Abe down. My free-dom and 500 silver dollars in my pocket. My freedom for your plantation, (*in victorious contempt*) masser.

MASTER: Yeah, sure, okay. You do that, Tom, uh-huh, and I'll give you your paper, I swear I will.

TOM: Your hand on the transaction, sir. (*slap of their hands, delighted arrogant chuckle*) Now just you watch this, how a slave becometh a freeeeee man today.

ENERGY OF FIGHT. REPEATED FAST PUNCHES. LAUGHTER FROM TOM. CHEER OF CROWD.

You are likely to have noted the following linguistic features:

■ Colloquialisms.

■ Incomplete sentences.

■ Ellipsis.

■ Elision.

■ Non-standard grammar.

■ Dialect.

Student commentary

Read the following commentary and compare it with the notes that you made about the effects achieved by these linguistic features.

> This radio play is set in Virgina in 1810, and the dialogue has been used to give the impression of dialect and accent. Non-standard grammar such as 'I's goina beat you so bad', 'knows' and 'wants' helps to create a sense of dialect, while the hyphen in 'free-dom' and the spellings of 'masser' and 'wot' help the actors with pronunciation. Colloquialisms in the phrase 'stomach him. Sakes alive' also help to place the script in Virginia.
>
> Linguistic features are used to create realistic dialogue. Ellipsis is used, for example, in 'I'll be ruint, ruint boy...' to indicate incomplete sentences, and is also used at the beginning of the sentence, '...I want my freedom' to suggest the character's hesitation. Elision is a common feature of dialogue and is used in the words 'I'll' and 'I's' and 'goina'.
>
> Non-speaking dialogue is also used. Instructions such as 'delighted, arrogant chuckle' and 'laughs big' work in a similar way to dialogue as they communicate the character's feelings at the time. Delivery directions such as 'breathless' help the actors.

Judging students' commentaries

Here are four extracts from students' commentaries. Study them closely to see how far the commentaries analyse the students' use of linguistic features, and how successful they have been in using examples from their writing to illustrate the points that they are making.

Commentary A

> I used adjectives to improve the descriptions, as in, for example 'grey, dark streets'. I used the first-person narrative to create a relationship with the reader. This relationship is helped with my use of a mixed register – formal register to suggest my authority, informal register to talk to the reader. I have used complex sentences, such as 'I got off the train, looked about me at the deserted platform, and immediately regretted my decision' to develop my argument. However, I have also used minor sentences such as 'Wait!' for variation.

Commentary B

> My holiday brochure's purpose was to persuade a teenage audience to visit Cuba. I appealed directly to the reader using the second-person pronoun which built up a relationship. An informal register was adopted, with colloquial words and some slang. I used imperatives to give the impression that they had to visit Cuba, and some rhetorical questions to engage the readers. The text was presented in an informal font to give the impression of the fun that teenagers would have in Cuba.

Commentary C

The register is largely formal, with descriptions such as, 'The hotel door opened and light gleamed off the glittering marble floor', but to engage the reader there is use of informal register in the humorous moments, such as 'The seat groaned in surrender as the rotund doctor collapsed into its cushions.' Cataphoric references give structure to the story and lead helpfully to the final joke. Exaggeration is also used for comic effect.

Commentary D

The text is very formal, and follows the discourse structure of a formal letter. This is emphasised by the formal layout of the addresses. The letter's purpose is to persuade people to donate money to the 'Distressed Dogs' charity. Lexis is taken from the lexical field of charities, such as 'suffering', 'help', 'relief' and 'donation'. Rhetorical questions are used to engage the reader: 'Would you let your dog suffer like this?' Facts and figures emphasise the problems that the charity wants to address. The background image of the distressed dog should help to persuade people to donate.

■ Extension activity 4

See if you can place these four commentaries in rank order, from best to worst. Explain the strengths and weaknesses of each one and why you have placed them in the order that you have.

See page 202 for feedback on this activity.

The drafting process

In this topic you will:

■ consider the importance of drafting your writing

■ evaluate students' comments about their own drafting.

In your commentary you should explain any significant changes that you make to your text during the drafting process.

The importance of drafting and redrafting has already been stressed in Section A of this unit. However, it is equally important to analyse in your commentary some of the significant changes that you make. Clearly, you will not be able to analyse all of the changes that you make during the drafting process, so some judicious selection is called for. It is also important that you make some insightful comments about what effects you hoped to achieve by your changes. You should not focus exclusively on semantic changes such as changes of vocabulary to create specific effects, but should also consider linguistic changes, such as your choice of verbs for effect, or your use of analogy, or your use of rhetorical devices. You should also explain any decisions that you have made relating to structure, such as your use of anaphoric and cataphoric references, and your use of syntax, the way you have organised words within your sentences.

The importance of drafting can be seen from this facsimile of the first page of George Orwell's novel *Nineteen Eighty-Four*. Orwell's handwritten annotations show how carefully he has crafted these paragraphs.

Text G

www.netcharles.com

Text H

It was a bright cold day in April, and the clocks were striking thirteen. Winston Smith, his chin nuzzled into his breast in an effort to escape the vile wind, slipped quickly through the glass doors of Victory Mansions, though not quickly enough to prevent a swirl of gritty dust from entering along with him.

The hallway smelt of boiled cabbage and old rag mats. At one end of it a coloured poster, too large for indoor display, had been tacked to the wall. It depicted simply an enormous face, more than a metre wide: the face of a man of about forty-five, with a heavy black moustache and ruggedly handsome features. Winston made for the stairs. It was no use trying the lift. Even at the best of times it was seldom working, and at present the electric current was cut off during daylight hours. It was part of the economy drive in preparation for Hate Week. The flat was seven flights up, and Winston, who was thirty-nine and had a varicose ulcer above his right ankle, went slowly, resting several times on the way. On each landing, opposite the lift shaft, the poster with the enormous face gazed from the wall.

George Orwell, Nineteen Eighty-Four, *1949*

It is likely that many of the changes you make to your writing will be semantic ones, but it is important also to analyse your linguistic choices. Your analysis of the changes that you make during the drafting process should demonstrate your understanding of semantic, linguistic and, where relevant, graphological features. In discussing these changes you have an opportunity to draw to the examiner's attention the conscious choices that you have made. This discussion should be illustrated with examples from your text.

> **AQA Examiner's tip**
>
> Thoughtful changes during your drafting process could form an interesting basis for discussion and analysis in your commentary.

Extension activity 5

Below are four examples of students' commentary of changes that they made during the drafting process. They were asked to:

- identify key semantic and linguistic features that they added
- comment on the effects that they hoped to achieve with these changes
- give illustrations from their texts to elucidate their analysis.

Using these criteria to judge these four extracts, place the extracts in order of quality, and make notes about why you place them in the order that you do.

See page 202 for feedback on this activity.

Student commentary

1 A magazine article about preparing for university life

In my first draft I wrote the text for my magazine article as a straightforward Word document. While I was pleased with the content of the article it did not appear very professional on the page. The simple strategy of putting the text into two columns transformed the presentation as it made the text look like a professional piece of journalism. However, the most important change that I made was to the article's cohesion. Each paragraph seemed to exist in isolation. Consequently, I changed the text so that each paragraph started with some reference to the previous paragraph. For example, the first paragraph dealt with financial matters, so I started the second paragraph about accommodation with the sentence. 'Finance is not the most important thing that you have to sort out.'

2 A charity leaflet

I was really pleased with my first draft. I put lots of effort into the graphology, with bright colours and appropriate pictures that I took from the internet. Some of the pictures didn't come out very well because they were originally black and white and when they were photocopied they became even less clear. I was a little bit worried that the text of the leaflet wasn't very persuasive, so I added some persuasive phrases. I was pleased with some of the language that I used and I think that it might have persuaded some people to give money to the charity, but I think that overall I should have worked harder at this aspect of my leaflet.

3 A piece of travel writing

I chose to write about Australia because some of my relatives live there and it is a place that I want to travel to in the future. My initial draft was a piece of writing to inform, but it sounded like a geography textbook. There was lots of information, with facts and figures that I got off the internet, and I did include an appropriate map. However, the text was almost all declarative sentences, just giving information, so I added a range of other sentence types. I wanted to entertain my audience as well, so I made the decision to add some humour. Obviously this was all just fiction because I have not actually travelled to Australia yet. Mostly, this was by using exaggeration.

4 An interview with the college Principal

I recorded the interview, and then transcribed it. Initially I wanted to capture the complete flavour of the interview, and present it exactly as I witnessed it. So, I put in all of the non-fluency features such as incomplete sentences, ellipsis and false starts. However, while this might have been effective in a piece of creative writing, the feedback I received showed that these features distracted the reader. That is why in the final draft I have taken these features out but still captured honestly what the Principal said.

Reading materials

You should make reference to any reading materials that you use, and discuss how you adapt these reading materials to suit your own text. You have already seen how it is necessary to analyse your style models and show how they have influenced your own writing. It is also important that if you create a piece of non-fiction you must be able to explain how your text is significantly different from your reading material. This could be achieved, for example, by explaining how you have used the information provided in your reading material, but have changed its register: facts and figures could be taken from government websites, but used in a persuasive editorial; you might take health information from NHS leaflets and adapt it for a younger target audience.

This section of your commentary is important because it will help you to show that your work is original and that you have not been guilty of plagiarism.

Effectiveness

You should reflect on the effectiveness of your writing. This reflection should include reference to any feedback that you get from people who read your writing. While this section of your commentary is likely to be brief, it is still necessary to say something significant and analytical. For example, you might say something about the stylistic devices of your style model: the lexical field or fields used; any non-fluency features used to create dialect; anaphoric references to achieve cohesion. You could also talk about the tone of your writing and comment on the semantic and linguistic choices that you have made.

AQA Examiner's tip

A full bibliography should be appended to coursework, including full citations and URLs of websites.

Coursework preparation and practice

In this topic you will:

■ become familiar with the coursework assesment criteria

■ assess student's work using the coursework assessment criteria.

Coursework assessment criteria

It is important that you become familiar with the coursework assessment criteria. In that way you can consciously craft your commentary to meet as many of the criteria as possible. In this topic we will look at the criteria and use it to assess four commentaries, so you can see how to produce successful commentaries yourself.

Mark	Coursework assessment criteria: Unit 2 – Creating texts ENGB2 Commentaries		
	AO1: 5% Select and apply a range of linguistic methods, to communicate relevant knowledge using appropriate terminology and coherent, accurate written expression.	AO2: 5% Demonstrate critical understanding of a range of concepts and issues related to the construction and analysis of meaning in spoken and written language, using knowledge of linguistic approaches.	AO3: 5% Analyse and evaluate the influence of contextual factors on the production and reception of spoken and written language, showing knowledge of the key constituents of language.
0	Nothing written	Nothing written	Nothing written
1–2	Linguistic methods applied inaccurately, or not at all. Rudimentary linguistic knowledge. Lapses in written communication.	Elementary understanding of chosen genre and related language choices. Little attempt to explain use of genre characteristics.	Broad understanding of purpose and audience. Generalised, everyday awareness. Likely to paraphrase/summarise own writing.
3–4	Basic linguistic methods applied – often not convincing. Limited knowledge and understanding. Inconsistent clarity and accuracy in communication.	Limited understanding of chosen genre and related language choices. Superficial understanding of the parameters and key characteristics of the genre.	Broad understanding of purpose and audience, possibly concerned with content rather than effect – likely to be descriptive in focus. One or two contextual factors identified – often over simplified.
5–6	Applies and explores some linguistic methods – some exemplification. Some appropriate linguistic knowledge. Generally accurate written communication.	*Some awareness and understanding of the links between chosen genre and language choices.* A number of issues explored demonstrating the beginnings of better understanding – some exemplification.	Awareness of purpose and audience – demonstrated by isolated references to relevant language features from writing and style models. Some awareness of the links between context and language features.
7–8	Uses linguistic methods in a systematic way – some evaluative comment though not consistent. Appropriate and accurate linguistic knowledge. Controlled, accurate expression.	Sound, sometimes perceptive, understanding of the genre requirements considering a range of language concepts and issues. Developed discussion of ideas showing some conceptualised knowledge – often helpful exemplification.	Reliable, sometimes sensitive, awareness of purpose and audience – demonstrated by reference to a range of significant features from writing and the style models. Sound, occasionally sensitive engagement with context.
9–10	Systematic and evaluative exploration of data selecting appropriate linguistic methods – suitably tentative conclusions drawn. Accurate and perceptive linguistic knowledge. Appropriate, controlled and accurate expression.	*Clear, perceptive understanding of the genre requirements considering a judicious range of concepts and ideas.* Conceptualised discussion which illuminates writing and drafting process – integrated exemplification.	Sensitive, consistently insightful awareness of purpose and audience – systematic reference to salient features from writing and style models. Analytical and systematic interpretation of context.

Below are two extracts from different commentaries, annotated to illustrate the assessment criteria that have been achieved.

Text I

Persuasive editorial for intelligent teenage audience

The lexis that I have used gives the impression that the narrator is intelligent. Phrases such as 'the latest accusation' and 'he acknowledged his frustration' have connotations of eloquence. However, the lexis is not too complex for teenagers to understand. Elisions have been avoided, as have other non-fluency features, because they would challenge the academic authority of the narrator's argument. Cohesion was important, as the reader needed to be led logically through the argument if they were to be persuaded. This was achieved with anaphoric references, referring back to something mentioned earlier in the text, and cataphoric references, referring to things that will be mentioned later. For example, in the third paragraph the following anaphoric reference is used: 'Again, it can be seen how important the evidence was.' In the same paragraph the following cataphoric reference is used: 'It will soon be seen how the defence lawyer used the evidence to mislead the jury.'

> Accurate and perceptive linguistic knowledge

> Sensitive awareness of purpose and audience

> Sensitive awareness of purpose and audience

Although it is not possible to formally assess a commentary from a short extract like this, it is possible to see which assessment criteria have been achieved. The student's comments about purpose and audience fall in the 7–8 band of AO3 with sensitive awareness of purpose and audience. Reference to a broader range of significant features would be required to move this into the highest band. Their linguistic knowledge falls into the 7–8 band of AO1, with linguistic methods used in a systematic way. More evaluation of the linguistic methods would have moved this aspect of the commentary into the highest band. Their use of integrated exemplification falls into the 8–9 band of AO2.

Text J

Magazine article to inform a teenage audience

My article is to inform and entertain teenagers. It is an interview with Susan Hill, the lead singer of the band The Normans. The language that I have used comes from the lexical field of music interviews, such as 'performance', 'vocalist' and 'albums'. I have used the colloquial language that teenagers use, so that I build up a relationship with my target audience. I have also used slang for the same purpose.

> Appropriate and accurate linguistic knowledge

My style model, an interview with Sonya Hartnett, showed how complex sentences are used when a speaker is trying to explain a complicated idea, while minor sentences are often used when an answer to a question is emphatic. A complex sentence from my interview is where Hartnett says, 'I think that because the fans have paid so much money for the concert, sometimes too much, I have a responsibility to give a good performance every time – however I might be feeling.' Interviews in music magazines often include the non-fluency features associated with conversations, such as unfinished sentences, ellipsis and false starts. I have used these linguistic features in my own interview to capture the moment of the interview.

> Some exemplification

> Reference to significant features from writing and the style models

Text J has similar qualities to Text I. The candidate's comments about style models falls into the 7–8 band for AO3; more analysis and interpretation would have moved this aspect of the commentary into the highest band. Their linguistic knowledge falls into the 7–8 band for AO1, with appropriate linguistic knowledge, and some evaluative comment. More evaluation would be required to move this aspect of the commentary into the highest band. However, the candidate offers little exemplification in this extract and the one example places this aspect of the commentary in the 5–6 band for AO2. To move this aspect of their commentary into a higher band the candidate would need to give more examples from their text to illustrate the valuable linguistic comments that they made.

■ Extension activity 6

Copy and annotate the following two extracts from students' commentaries. Identify the assessment criteria that they have satisfied for AO1, AO2, and AO3 and then place their comments in the appropriate band: 0, 1–2, 3–4, 5–6, 7–8 or 9–10.

Student commentaries

Michael Owen and Wayne Rooney

I wrote a magazine article to go into a teenage football magazine. This will be predominantly read by boys. My two style models were *Shoot!* and *Glovers* – the Yeovil Town fanzine. These magazines used graphological features like photographs, headlines, bright colours and columns. I used these features in my article. For example, I took photographs of Owen and Rooney from the internet. I also wrote my article in columns and used bright colours. My headline, 'Wayne's World', should have caught people's attention.

The purpose of my article was to inform. This meant that most of my sentences were declarative sentences, such as 'Owen first played for England in 1998.' However, I also wanted to be a little bit provocative so I used superlatives when describing both footballers. I claimed that 'When Rooney burst on to the scene he was the most exciting prospect England had ever produced' and I said that 'The most important goals ever scored for England were scored by Rooney.'

Obviously, my lexis came from the lexical field of football. I had to use words like 'score', 'goal', 'match', 'team', and 'sponsorship'. However, I also took lexis from the lexical field of hero-worship, with words like 'hero', 'brave', 'fighting spirit' and 'fearless'.

The drafting and redrafting process was very important to me. I got all of this information about Owen and Rooney and first of all I just wrote it up as information. This was dull. I had to think of a way of making it more interesting to the reader. One way was to include graphological features. Another way was to introduce the controversial comments; people could react to them with their own opinions.

I thought the article was quite successful. The piece of information writing provided lots of information. My feedback was positive, but this might have been because I showed it to all of my friends and they wouldn't have been too critical. But the graphological features didn't work very well. This was because I'm not very good at art.

Real life stories

I read lots of magazines, such as *Woman's Own* and *Hello!* So I thought that it would be a good idea to write a 'true-life story' for one of these magazines. I looked through the newspapers to see if an unusual event had been reported, and loosely based my fictional story on these details.

My audience was women and teenage girls. I knew that my story had to be about 1,000 words long, which was about the same length as the stories that appear in women's magazines. My research showed that women and teenage girls like to read articles that have some shock value, and are hard to believe. The readers like someone to feel sorry for. They also like it if the stories have a positive ending, something that is uplifting. In my story a girl was abandoned by her single mother and they lost contact. The girl had an awful life, being used as a slave by a family who adopted her. But when the girl was nearly sixteen a picture of her was put in the local newspaper and people commented to the mother how much the girl in the photograph looked like her. The mother investigated, found out that it was her daughter, and on her daughter's sixteenth birthday the mother turned up. They are now as close as they could be. I wrote the story in the first person, as though I was the girl – even though I wasn't.

Because the story was about 1,000 words long the discourse structure was very important. I started each paragraph with a connector so that the reader was signposted through the story. I also used anaphoric references, such as 'As I have mentioned, not knowing where your natural mother is can be a frightening feeling.' I also used cataphoric references, such as 'But a much more important thing happened to me the next year.'

The story has been written in an informal register – like a conversation with the reader. However, it does have mixed-mode features. Some of the writing is formal, with sentences like 'The following two years were the most complicated I would face.' But at other times I have engaged the reader with things like rhetorical questions, or colloquialisms. For example, I asked, 'Is this fair?' and 'He was such a dear.' I used emotional adjectives and adverbs deliberately to make the reader sympathise with 'me.' For example, I described my bedroom as a 'squalid, cramped room' and I admitted that at night I would 'cry passionately'.

Examiner's overall comments

Michael Owen and Wayne Rooney

This candidate demonstrates some generalised awareness of purpose and audience. He has identified the audience as boys but has not said how this has influenced his writing. He has also identified his purpose: to inform, although there is an interesting secondary purpose: to be provocative. This secondary purpose would be appropriate for a magazine article about footballers, however, there is very little understanding of his chosen genre and the related language.

The candidate has applied some basic linguistic methods. For example he refers to declarative sentences but unfortunately there are no examples. He does provide examples of his use of superlatives, and his references to lexical fields are relevant.

The candidate is aware that graphological features are important in a magazine article but there is no exploration of the candidate's use of graphological features beyond the observation that they were not successful.

Overall, this candidate's work falls into the 3–4 band.

Real life stories

This candidate is aware of her target audience and the purpose of her writing. The target audience is women and teenage girls, and although there is no specific statement about the purpose of the article, the candidate has made reference to 'shock value', 'someone to feel sorry for' and 'a positive ending'.

Unfortunately, there is little analysis of the linguistic choices made in her style models. However, the candidate does seem to have made some appropriate linguistic choices. She refers to informal register, mixed-mode features and colloquialisms. All of these features are exemplified.

The candidate has made sound references to linguistic methods, such as discourse structure, anaphoric and cataphoric references. These are also exemplified.

Overall, this candidate's work falls into the 5–6 band.

Summary

You have now studied what makes a good commentary. In your commentary you are required to:

■ define the purpose, audience and genre of your text

■ show how your text has been influenced by style models

■ use examples from your text to elucidate points that you make

■ comment on significant changes that you make in your text during the drafting process

■ explain how any reading materials have been adapted for your own text

■ judge the effectiveness of your text.

It cannot be stressed enough that your commentary needs to be selective. The best commentaries are not formulaic, but demonstrate discriminating focus on significant issues.

Practise the skills that you have developed during this section by selecting a range of texts and writing commentaries on them. You might select different texts from the list below.

■ A radio play script.

■ A newspaper editorial.

■ Creative writing.

■ Travel writing.

■ A leaflet.

■ An autobiography.

■ An information article.

■ A guide.

■ A speech.

Feedback on the activities

Unit 1, Section A Text varieties

An introduction to classification

Classroom activity 1

Your observations may have included some of the points listed below:

Suggested grouping	Basic similarities and differences	Further comments and potential problems with groupings
Shape and structure	A, B and C feature prominently placed images. D formally draws attention to its status as a government document. The layout of E and F shows that there is more than one speaker/writer.	A contains a great deal of other information, positioned near the bottom, and includes the company's logo. B and C are easily recognisable as a recipe and a children's story.
Use of images	A, B and C all use images to support written text.	C relies on an image to support the narrative. This is common in children's stories. B uses its image to entice the reader with an attractive 'finished product'. A's image is in line with the theatre programme where it appeared and helps to play on the versatility of the product advertised.
Written texts	A, B, C, D and F are all written texts. However, they have been written for different reasons.	A and especially D use specialised terms as they are intended for a specialist and mature audience. B and C are more 'chatty'; B in particular tries to establish an intimate bond with its reader through some of its word choices. F has features that we might expect to see in spoken language; it also displays features associated with communication via the internet.
Spoken texts	E and F could both be considered texts that are, or are close to, what we might expect to see in spoken language, C also contains examples of speech.	F is actually written, although the writers are communicating in real time, as in E. F contains abbreviations, informal features and spelling mistakes – suggesting that the writer composed spontaneously and did not redraft. Both show signs of their writers/speakers pointing to shared knowledge and things in their immediate location. They also know each other, but there is a closer relationship in F. The speech in C uses 'said' and is fictional.
Function of text	A and D and F are providing information; C is to entertain; B gives details; E appears more geared towards completing a personal task.	A is advertising a product and tries to sell a certain idea about the company, whilst D is purely informative. C might be read to a child; its purpose could be educational or to maintain a social relationship between a parent and child. B is structured like a set of orders but is relaxed in tone and is also informative. Although the writers of F are sharing information, they also use the opportunity to maintain a friendship bond.

Classroom activity 2

There are many problems with this oppositional view. Text F is written but contains examples of language that you might expect to find in a spoken text and fulfils many of the criteria of the right-hand column. Equally, Text E could hardly be termed 'loosely structured', as the exchanges between the vendor and customer follow a clear pattern. Text C could well be read aloud and therefore might exist in spoken form. Moreover, it is not complex like Text D and is informal in the same way that Text B is. No doubt you will have found other examples to question the validity of this model.

Classroom activity 3

You may have focused on the information given to you and tried to contextualise the lines, based on the fact that they were part of the chorus to a pop song. In this case, you may have focused on the fact that pop songs tend to be about love and that this lyric represents the speaker's joy at having found a loved one, the 'you' of the lyric. Equally, you may have recognised the lyric as being part of the number-one hit 'Things Can Only Get Better' by D:Ream and elaborated on this by considering Text G together with the remainder of the song (its **co-text**). You may have personalised it by placing yourself as the speaker and thinking of someone close to you, a friend or even a pet! You may even be an expert on D:Ream and attach some significance to the lyric in the context of the songwriter or singer's own life.

You may know that Text G was used as a campaign song by the Labour Party in 1997, its meaning changed to reflect the message that things would get better under a Labour government. A quick internet search will also reveal that these lines have since been quoted ironically by critics of the Labour government.

In another context, they were used by some supporters of Manchester City Football Club in the summer of 2007 when the club appointed the international manager Sven-Goran Eriksson in the hope of ending years of underachievement!

Classroom activity 5

Your rewriting should have demonstrated that an inappropriate level of formality can have drastic and have perhaps comical effects. Generally, writers and speakers think carefully about their register, ensuring that it is appropriate for the social context in which a text is produced. The use of an inappropriate register can, depending on the context, make a writer or speaker appear clumsy, unintelligent or unsophisticated. At the other end of the scale, an inappropriate register can seem arrogant, rude or pompous.

Classroom activity 6

The phrases 'eeh bahgum' and 'nowt' are stereotypical features of Yorkshire speech and are at times used for supposedly comical effect. This type of representation of a dialect and those who speak it is usually far removed from speakers' actual language use.

Lexis and semantics

Classroom activity 11

All the lexical items here have been chosen for their impact and effect.

In the first example, 'boost' is a strong alternative to other verbs of movement and growth, emphasising the strength and effectiveness of the product. The abstract noun 'radiance' has connotations of extreme brightness and beauty and aims to persuade the reader that his or her skin will really stand out when this product is used.

In the second example, the text producer uses an adverb to modify an adjective in a parallel structure reversing the use of the adjectives 'simple' and 'beautiful' with their derived adverb counterparts 'simply' and 'beautifully'. The text producer uses a narrow range of lexical items with a complex morphological manipulation to emphasise the product's stylish, modern look and its complex yet easy-to-use set of features.

The final set of lexical items conjures an image of optimum production for the coffee plants from which the text producer's instant coffee is manufactured. Notice that the choice of lexical items shifts between the technical ('well-drained soil') and the aesthetic ('sunny slopes').

Classroom activity 12

Your list may have included: 'wet'; 'dry'; 'sun'; 'rain'; 'cloud'; 'sleet'; 'snow'; 'wind'; 'gale'; 'storm'; 'cold'; 'heat'; 'shower'; 'drizzle'; 'thunderstorm'.

Some of these appear to be similar in meaning, for example 'rain' and 'showers', whilst others, such as 'wet' and 'dry', hold opposite meanings. In addition, there is a hierarchical relationship between certain lexical items such as 'thunderstorm' and 'storm', where we might say that 'thunderstorm' is a member of the larger category 'storm'.

Classroom activity 13

In example one, we might have expected B to say 'MP3 player' instead of the more general 'electronic appliance'. In not doing so, we have an example of **under-specificity**. The equally absurd second example is an example of **over-specificity**, where the lexical item 'car' would be more likely.

Grammar and syntax

Classroom activity 14

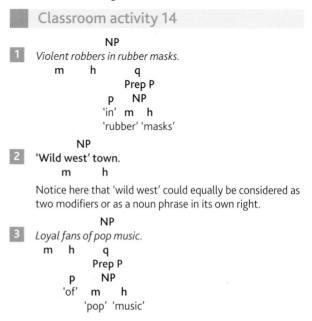

1. *Violent robbers in rubber masks.*

2. 'Wild west' town.

   Notice here that 'wild west' could equally be considered as two modifiers or as a noun phrase in its own right.

3. *Loyal fans of pop music.*

4 NP
Three record hot years predicted *before end of decade*.
m   m   m   h   h   q
                                 Prep P
                                 P   NP
                                      h
                                 'of' 'decade'

5 NP
Superb collection of coloured prints.
m   h   q
           Prep P
           p   NP
          'of' m   h
          'coloured' 'prints'

Classroom activity 15

Although this article aims to give an independent review of its chosen football boots, there is much subjective opinion here. It is clearly aimed at the knowledgeable football player and uses a combination of modified noun phrases (modifiers are italicised).

Comfort and design

lightest boot
ultra-thin fabric
smooth, moulded upper
seamless upper
pared-down boot

wasp-coloured boot
added comfort
snug fit
tucked-away laces

Technical ability and proficiency through wearing the boot

quick touches
long passes
greater accuracy
sweet spot
long-range passes
swerving, defence-splitting passes
true contact
good touch
precise distribution

Classroom activity 16

This text is typical of mailings from companies that aim to persuade the reader that their product will be both better and cheaper. The main modal auxiliaries used here are 'can', 'will' and 'could'.

Whereas 'can' and 'will' are used to express certainty: 'We can give you £60 cashback' and 'our excellent claims service will be there for you'; 'could' is more of a hedging device, 'that could save you money', where the company suggests a possible outcome rather than a definite one. A kind of *projection* occurs, where readers are asked to imagine a situation where they are financially better off. A key function of modal constructions in such mailings is to cue up a more attractive world involving the company's products. To explore this in more detail, look at similar texts or other advertisements and annotate them for your scrapbook.

Classroom activity 18

C and E are simple sentences; B and D are compound sentences; A and F are complex sentences; G is a compound-complex sentence.

Classroom activity 20

Some of your alternatives may have included:

A The door is still open.

B Can you shut the door?

C Please shut the door.

D Shut the door!

These examples correspond to the sentence functions we saw on page 38, **A** being grammatically a declarative, **B** an interrogative, **C** an imperative and **D** an exclamatory. They all, however, act as imperatives, with the desired result being that the addressee will shut the door. You may also have noticed that **A**, although grammatically a declarative, would be perceived as an order, unless the *implication* was missed. You might have also felt that **A** was ironic to the point of being sarcastic! Equally, although grammatically **B** is a question, you would not expect the answer 'Yes' or 'No' unless your addressee failed to understand what you were implying. Whereas **A** and **B** are more subtle ways of ordering, **C** and **D** are more direct, although the politeness marker 'please' suggests a level of respect and cooperation that the more direct exclamatory **D** lacks. You may also have decided that **B** and **C** are indicative of a formal relationship between speakers while **A** and **D** suggest a closer one. Using **A** and **D** to someone you do not know well could seem rude and threaten what is known as face. (See pages 76–77 for more on politeness and face.)

Phonetics and phonology

Classroom activity 21

All four examples use sound patterning for effect. Text S uses the fricative /s/ sound in an alliterative line to foreground a quiet yet eerie atmosphere found once the harsher-sounding affricates have vanished. (Notice here how syntactically the main clause beginning 'The silence' is also foregrounded before the subordinate clause – you might like to consider what difference shifting the two around might make.) In Text T, a similar contrast is used with fricative sounds in 'shells' and 'drizzling' mirroring the physical sound of the shells in the air before the run of /b/ plosives marks their explosion. Text U also relies on fricatives, here the extensive use of /s/ might be said to reflect the skaters moving across the ice. Extensive use of the /s/ phoneme is sometimes known as **sibilance**. In Text V, the stream is imagined through a cluster of plosives and approximants. 'Rollrock' is not an actual word, but try saying it to yourself a couple of times and you will no doubt begin to see why Hopkins chose to use it in the context that he does.

Of course, all of the above rely heavily on an individual interpretation of these sounds and there is no such thing as a sound that conveys a certain emotion or atmosphere in all contexts. What we can say is that sounds and meanings often interact to intensify an experience for a reader and that contextually readers will also be aware of how this interaction is appropriate. If, for example, you had never heard a shell exploding, you would struggle to come to the conclusion that fricatives were an important phonological feature in intensifying the experience of warfare for a reader.

Pragmatics

Classroom activity 23

This text contains a number of deictic terms designed to guide the listener by pointing out reference points. The spatial deictic terms 'left' and 'right' act as reference points for the listener with an assumed deictic centre somewhere on the river Seine. This is maintained through the proximal deictic term 'here', which acts both spatially, *at this point*, and temporally, *at this time*, to give the text a close and immediate feel. Another proximal deictic 'these' points to the booksellers from the listener's perspective and the deictic pronouns 'they' and 'their' cohesively refer back to the booksellers, again all from the deictic centre of the listener. The use of the present tense supports the text's immediate feel. Even if you are not floating down the Seine, the text positions you as though you were. It is easy to visualise what is being described as we are placed at the centre of a range of reference pointers; deictic terms play a big part in enabling this.

Graphology

Classroom activity 25

B and D are iconic as they are pictures of the things they represent. A and C are symbolic as they rely on conventional association. In the case of A, the colour red represents prohibition (in a similar way to a red traffic light) whilst the horizontal bar works in a similar way. The exclamation mark in C is symbolic of impending danger. It is important to note that A and C rely on cultural models of convention; in some cultures and societies, red and an exclamation mark may indicate something other than prohibition and danger.

Classroom activity 27

You probably noticed that you could place the messages along a formal–informal continuum, with 1 and 3 being more formal than 2, 4 and 5. You might also expect that the meeting referred to in example 1 is more formal and serious than that of example 4. You would not expect a summons to discuss your overdraft with your bank manager to use those informal fonts. Fonts may therefore be important features of *linguistic register*.

Discourse

Classroom activity 29

In Chattanooga, Tenessee, last November I watched Takeru Kobayashi devour a record 97 hamburgers with buns, onions and mustard in eight minutes flat – one every five seconds. It was a repulsive, riveting and astounding feat.

Participants in the annual World Hamburger Eating Championships had sought to persuade me that competitive eating was a sport requiring extraordinary physical ability and mental toughness.

I was deeply sceptical until I watched the baby-faced wisp from Japan in action. The 13 'gurgitators' lined up, the MC counted down, and they were off – a blur of flying hands, bobbing heads and gaping gullets.

Mr Kobayashi wetted each burger before stuffing it into his mouth. After two minutes, he had consumed 23, leading Joey Chestnut, America's great hope by one.

Within five minutes both had smashed the previous record of 69, and the 3000 spectators were roaring.

I felt sure that they would vomit, but they kept going – each bun a triumph of mind over rebellious body.

Finally the buzzer sounded. Mr Chestnut had devoured 91 – 21 more than the world record but six fewer than Mr Kobayashi. 'Awesome', muttered my neighbour.

You probably used your knowledge of genre to help you with this activity. Newspaper reports generally begin by detailing the main information. However, there are other important textual clues that should have helped you to re-weave this text:

- Paragraph 3 relies on an anaphoric elliptical construction 'I was deeply sceptical (of their claims)' to link back to the second paragraph.

- Paragraph 4 continues with narrative detail from paragraph 3 'they were off…', 'Mr Kobayashi wetted each burger'.

- The temporal adverbial 'within five minutes' connects paragraph 5 to paragraph 4 as a logical progression from the narrative detail there.

- The final paragraph is marked by the enumerative connector 'finally', which marks the end of the narrative.

Classroom activity 30

The speaker provides a clear *orientation* (which may also act as an *abstract* in this example) by explaining the time *from the age of two every single year*, the place *Cornwall near Redruth*, and those involved *myself and my sister and brother*. These provide important contextual details. The speaker then elaborates on a range of events that may be considered the *complicating action*, speaking of her time at the beach and on the farm. There is some *resolution* within parts of the complicating action, for example in her comments about collecting water. Her final comment *it was just a different world* is an *evaluative* one; it also acts as a *coda*, signalling that she has completed her narrative. Other moments that evaluate the narrative action include *which wasn't very fast at all* when speaking about the cow riding, *they just about had electricity where we used to go* and *it seemed like it took us all day to get there cos it was I suppose in a Ford Popular*.

You may have also noticed pauses, either natural or where the speaker is thinking about what she will say, and abbreviations and colloquialisms, *cos* and *every now and again*. In addition she uses another fixed expression *I suppose* as part of an evaluative comment.

Unit 1, Section B Language and social contexts

Language and power

Classroom activity 1

You will have probably identified the following as conferring power on individuals:

- Political power that government members hold in making decisions and which is enforced through the law by individuals such as the police and judges.

- An individual's position in an organisation: the higher an individual's position in any hierarchical structure, the more powerful that individual will be, for example a manager in a corporate organisation.

- The degree of knowledge that an individual may have and that others may not have, for example in academia, law and medicine.
- Economic power through being financially well off.
- Power based on personality and the ability to lead and influence others through persuasion.
- In some contexts, an individual's gender, age, class and ethnic group may affect their power.

Classroom activity 6

Although the local politician has a degree of political power, in this context, the radio interviewer is very much a powerful participant. Initially he applies constraints in terms of content by asking a precise question *which is it*. The politician attempts to shift the focus away from the question by detailing all of his council's achievements, but is interrupted on a number of occasions by the interviewer who continues to force the question of poor public services. The politician's unease is apparent through non-fluency features such as hesitations and pauses as he again attempts to deflect the topic of conversation. His final words *these are the issues that are on mind* are then formulated by the interviewer in another interruption *right so there is no difficulty admitting that some services are not good enough*.

Classroom activity 7

You may have identified the following:

- Extensive use of first-person plural subject and possessive pronouns 'we' and 'our'. These are used to express the desire and vision not just of Blair, but of the party as a whole. The final five paragraphs mark the branching out of this inclusiveness to suggest that this is also the need and vision of the the British people, as a way of establishing a group identity.
- Abstract nouns that carry particular ideological force, for example 'solidarity', 'cooperation', 'partnership', 'community' and 'society'.
- Heavy use of negated epistemic modal 'cannot' and deontic modal 'must' to express necessity and obligation.
- Metaphorical constructions such as personification of the abstract values that Blair advocates, calling for new politics and conceptualising social and political change as physical construction work, 'we must build the strong and active society..., That is our project for Britain, we must work for it together...and we must plan for it together'.
- Use of temporal deictic terms such as 'the past' and 'today' to draw attention to the 'new beginning' that Blair is aiming to give the party and the British people.
- Extensive repetition in the final paragraphs. Here using a rhetorical device known as anaphora (beginning each line with the same word(s)) for maximum impact before the contrastive 'That is our insight'.

Language and gender

Classroom activity 11

You may have discussed the following options:

1. A member of a Police Force shall at all times abstain from any activity which is likely to interfere with the impartial discharge of *his duties*.
2. A member of a Police Force shall at all times abstain from any activity which is likely to interfere with the impartial discharge of *her duties*.
3. A member of a Police Force shall at all times abstain from any activity which is likely to interfere with the impartial discharge of *his/her duties*.
4. A member of a Police Force shall at all times abstain from any activity which is likely to interfere with the impartial discharge of *their duties*.
5. A member of a Police Force shall at all times abstain from any activity which is likely to interfere with the impartial discharge of *duties*.

Whereas options 2 and 3 seem awkward, option 4 is probably now the most widely accepted and non-sexist way of using a pronoun where the gender of the referent is unknown (although prescriptivists may argue that the sentence is ungrammatical since the third-person pronoun *their* does not agree with the singular noun phrase *member of a Police Force*). Equally, omitting a pronoun altogether as in option 5 avoids attempting to use a pronoun generically, although it might be argued that the omission of a possessive here lessens the force of the message. You could explore the use of generic pronouns further by looking at other texts (company policy documents and instructional booklets are good places to see this in action).

Classroom activity 15

The two examples use tag questions in different ways. Claire uses one to soften the effect of telling off her daughter, whilst the superintendent's tag question acts as a **boosting device**, to strengthen the force of his comment to the constable. It is clear that tag questions are not always a sign of insecurity and a lack of confidence: in some contexts they may act as supportive measures and even as a sign of an assertive speaker. To this end, Holmes suggests that the following are all possible functions of tag questions and may be used in ways other than signs of uncertainty.

- As facilitative or positive politeness strategies.
- As softeners showing support and concern for another speaker.
- As coercive devices demonstrating security and a degree of forcefulness.

Language and technology

Classroom activity 16

The opening lines or turns between John and Steve fit Schegloff's opening sequences routine. The channel of communication, *initiated* by the ringing telephone, is opened through John's 'hello', which is a conventional if formal way of answering the telephone. Once Steve *identifies* himself and is recognised by John, John uses the less formal 'hi' as a sign of friendliness. This *greeting sequence* sets up the *shared space* between them, marking the conversation as an informal one before a series of 'how are you' sequences. These are *small talk*, designed to maintain the relationship between the speakers. Both John and Steve use *informal elliptical constructions*, 'good thanks' and 'not bad...', and the relaxed humour of 'we're all sniffing at the mo' develops the focus on establishing a *social relationship* before the main purpose of the call is revealed. The speakers' shared knowledge is evident in the way the main topic is introduced 'so what's happening next week'. In line with Schegloff's model and suggestions, we can see that this routine is both a collaborative and creative enterprise between two friends.

Classroom activity 19

In terms of discourse structure, there is a short greetings sequence 'Dennis good morning to you' and 'good morning' followed by an invitation to the caller to speak in the form of a question, relevant to the topic of conversation and which allows the caller to draw on his expertise and experience of working as a teacher. Lexically, items from the field of education dominate, for example *students*, *exams* and *questions* and there are examples of an informal register despite the seriousness of the topic, for example the use of the fixed expression 'you know'. In addition, pauses, minor false starts and some fillers that are conventionally found in spoken discourse are also present, here occurring as a natural part of speech rather than as a signal of any uncertainty.

The presenter's control of the phone-in is evident in the way that he controls the topic of conversation by referring to the criticism study through an imperative contracted form 'let's look at what the critics are saying...' and also resists his attempts to interrupt him in order to force him to address his question. You could argue that this is a blatant neglect of the caller's face needs! Pragmatically, there is evidence of shared knowledge in the parallel made by the caller between qualified personnel in the teaching profession and police and nurses in the *exophoric*

reference to *police and nurses* (these professions had recently been criticised in the media) and in the caller's implication that the government is to blame for using less qualified staff. As Dennis is digressing from the original topic of conversation and beginning to move into politics, the presenter avoids a complete topic shift by reverting back to the issue of coursework. This would have been part of the originally planned sequence of questions and the more spontaneous comments Dennis makes are swiftly dismissed in favour of the topic the presenter wants to focus on. There is little that can be said on phonology from looking at the transcript, although (as you might imagine) a range of **prosodic features** can be heard in the original audio.

Classroom activity 20

You may have identified the following features:

There is a lexical field of cricket terms here such as 'swing and seam' (1), 'over' (1), 'strokes' (3), 'off side' and 'leg side' (5) that may be regarded as examples of technical language. Their use assumes knowledge on the part of the viewer, who is likely to be familiar with such terms.

The speech is fluent, although there are pauses, hesitations and fillers. These however are intentional pauses rather than non-fluency. The commentators add subjectivity through modifying phrases such as 'superb example' (1), 'controlled swing and seam' (1), 'terrific start' (3), 'ironic cheer' (4) and 'poor misfield' (6). There is also personal evaluation, as in 'that's the key' (2) and 'I think' (7), as well as some mild emotional responses 'ooh' (1) and 'cor dear me' (2).

There are a number of deictic expressions such as 'that's' (1), 'this is' (2), 'a problem here' (7) and 'is that out?' (9), which are understood to refer to what the viewer can see on the screen. Adverbial constructions such as 'from the football stand end' (8), 'Fernando bowling round the wicket' (9) also indicate place and space. Again, the fact that this is a television commentary means that these are not always necessary for the viewer to follow the action.

Grammatically, a range of elliptical constructions is used, for example where the verb is omitted as in 'Dilhara Fernando from the football end' (7) or where small functional words are not spoken, for example 'superb example of controlled swing and seam' (1) and 'fifty up for England thirteen overs' (8). Metaphor is also used, for example 'smooth passage' (4) and 'scoreboard rolling along' (5).

Unit 2, Section A Original writing

Appropriate linguistic terminology

Classroom activity 2

Linguistic term	Definition
Adverb	Word that provides information about a verb
Metaphor	The use of a term to describe something that it does not denote, to suggest similar qualities between the two
Alliteration	The use of the same initial sound in words close together
First person	Discourse that uses 'I' or 'We'
Noun	Word that names a place, a person, a thing, a feeling or an idea
Pronoun	Word used instead of a noun or a name
Adjective	Word that provides information about a noun
Third person	Discourse that uses 'she' or 'they', for example
Personification	Giving human qualities to a non-human object
Analogy	The use of a comparison between two cases, implying that if this comparison works, then the two cases have many similarities
Emotive language	Language that encourages readers to respond emotionally rather than rationally. Many words have emotive connotations and readers may respond to these rather than their denotations.
Rhetorical question	A question that does not require an answer because the answer is obvious
Second person	Discourse that uses 'you'
Colloquialism	Informal use of language
Assonance	The use of the same vowel sounds in words close together
Simile	A comparison of one thing with another, using the words 'like' or 'as'
Verb	Word that describes an action or condition

Learning from different styles of writing

Classroom activity 5

There are no definitive answers for this activity. However, you might have completed the table like this.

Task	Purpose	Possible audience	Possible genre
Creative writing	To entertain To inspire	Teenagers	Novel
Health warning about smoking	To persuade To inform	Schoolchildren	Editorial
Preparing for university	To inform To entertain	Yr 12 students	Booklet
How to survive a pop festival	To entertain To inform	Teenagers	Leaflet/flyer

Writing to persuade

Classroom activity 13

The table below shows some answers that you may have found.

Rhetorical device	Example	Effect
Analogy	'The human brain is only like a sophisticated computer...'	Humans' brains and computers work in the same way
Emotive language	'will transform the quality of our lives and cement the marriage between humans and machines.'	Our lives will be better for this change, which was meant to be
Metaphor	'cement the marriage between humans and machines'	Sounds as though humans and machines were meant for each other
Personification	'your home computer will be able understand your voice commands'	Humans won't have to make a huge effort to get used to the technology
Simile	'make decisions as easily as a photoelectric cell does today'	Makes the changes sound simple and inevitable

Classroom activity 16

You will probably conclude that the editorial has the following structure: the first paragraph introduces the problem; the second and third paragraphs present arguments that are supported with evidence; the fourth paragraph presents an opposing view, but then dismisses it with argument; the final paragraph summarises the author's point of view.

Using source material and plagiarism

Classroom activity 18

You might have made the following comments.

URL	How reliable do you expect the site to be? Why?
www.library.uq.edu.au	.edu suggests that this is a serious and reliable site
www.elsevierdirect.com	.com suggests that this site is a commercial company; it might be trying to sell you something
www.rspca.org.uk	.org indicates that this is a non-profit-making organisation, however, since it's a charity it clearly has its own agenda and is likely to want to persuade you to give money
www.diaries.co.uk/article.%	% indicates that this is probably a personal site; it may or may not be reliable
www.standards.dfes.gov.uk	.gov is an official government site; it should be trustworthy
www.gwt.edu~space.htm	~ indicates that this is a personal site; it may or may not be reliable

Writing to inform

Classroom activity 19

There are no definitive answers to this activity, but you might have filled in the table like this.

Classroom activity 20

You might have completed the table like this.

Stylistic feature	Example
1 A unique view of a place	How important it is to be able to converse with the people
2 A central theme	The instant change in language
3 First person	'I'm a little loath…'
4 Past tense	'I felt completely at ease'
5 Directly addresses the reader	'When you're speaking your native language…'
6 A hook in the opening paragraph	'it's amazing'
7 Humour	'Irritating salesmen stop being annoying and become targets for a bit of banter'
8 Something is revealed about the place	British travellers can feel relaxed in The Gambia
9 Range of register	'even more bizarre'; 'but it's amazing'; 'an almost imperceptible transition'; 'subtleties of communication'

Classroom activity 24

Each of the paragraphs begins with a topic sentence defining the content of the paragraph.

Writing to advise/instruct

Classroom activity 26

An example of instructional writing is: 'If you don't have this feature, simply delete the message.'

An example of advice writing is: 'It's a good idea to use a combination of letters and numbers for extra safety'.

Purpose	Target audience	What the target audience should know	Possible media	Most appropriate style
Information about the dangers of illicit drugs	Teenagers	Types of drugs Consequences of drug-taking	Leaflet	Informal Informative
How to save energy in your home	Home owners	Simple solutions Annual savings	Leaflet Report	Technical
Alternative guide to your school or college	School pupils	Quality of teaching. Facilities	Booklet. Flyer	Informal Humorous
How to predict the weather	Geography students	Atmosphere Clouds	Textbook	Formal Technical

Classroom activity 27

The writer addresses the reader using second-person pronouns 'you' and 'you're'. This is likely to be to set up a relationship between reader and writer so that the reader is more likely to accept the advice. The use of personal pronouns, and informal lexis such as 'But think of it this way' and 'and whatever else they get up to' suggests that the target audience is probably teenagers rather than adults.

The tone of the text is created with phrases such as 'There's one easy way you can protect yourself here…' which is advice rather than an instruction. Information writing would have been more likely to have used an imperative sentence: 'You must protect yourself…' However, there are imperative sentences such as 'Don't be one of those people', but advice is far more common. Sentences offering advice such as 'It's a good idea to use…' dominate the text.

Although there are no links between sections, each section has an internal structure. The writer starts by engaging in conversation with the reader, with sentences such as 'Sometimes it seems a mystery how spammers get hold of your address in the first place.' This implies that the reader and writer had previously been talking about spammers. The writer then moves on with the subject of the topic sentence, to advise how this problem can be dealt with.

This leaflet uses a number of non-fluency features. In the second section, for example, 'email accounts, mobile phone codes …' The ellipsis here indicates that the sentence is not complete. This suggests that the writer and the reader share the same knowledge and so the sentence does not need to be completed.

The writer chooses words from the lexical field of ICT, such as 'blogs', 'spider' and 'spam'. This shows that the audience is knowledgeable about modern technology. It might also suggest a teenage audience, as the non-fluency features and the lexical field of modern technology are appropriate for teenagers. However, at times the register is formal. Sentences such as 'Unsubscribe merely confirms that your email address is a valid one' stand out because of their formality.

Classroom activity 28

The writer has naturally taken vocabulary from the lexical field of computers. Readers might need to be familiar with this lexis to understand the instructions completely. The writer has consciously avoided the use of pronouns, giving the piece an impersonal tone.

Cohesion is achieved with the six steps to the process. References such as 'next' or 'then' are not used as often as would normally be expected in a piece of information writing. Cohesion is essential in this text as the steps need to be carried out chronologically.

The information is presented in imperative sentences – the reader is commanded. Sentences are often simple, such as 'Here is your step-by-step guide on how to use www.beatcrime.info' or compound, such as 'Either type in your postcode or click down through the maps to find the area you are interested in'. Complex sentences are rare, so the reader is not faced with subordinate clauses or relationships between clauses which might confuse them.

The process of writing

Classroom activity 29

1. There is a clear sense of the character's frustration, and his isolation.

2. The conclusion encourages the reader to speculate about the character's future. Because we are told that the conclusion is the character's secret, we know that we are not going to be told how the events happen. In addition, the ellipsis asks the reader to consider a range of possibilities.

3. Phrases such as 'but I knew it was too good to last' and sentences such as 'I knew that He would try to protect the island but would never succeed without my help' add twists. For example, if it was too good to last, what happens? Also, what 'help' does the dead father provide?

4. The use of words such as 'haemorrhaged' and 'transfusion' have been taken from the lexical field of science. However, this linguistic feature has not been used as effectively as it could have been.

5. The formal register has been used effectively to allow the main character to explore his emotions. A more informal or colloquial register would have made it more difficult for the main character to explore his emotions using metaphor. For example, a colloquial register would have made the sentence 'Here is my prison. Here is loneliness. Here is a small island off the coast of The Mainland' inappropriate.

Unit 2, Section B Writing a commentary

Style models

Classroom activity 2

An examiner's response to this commentary made the following observations:

1. This candidate has made three interesting references to her style model.

2. There is some valuable discussion of linguistic choices, and appropriate use of terminology. The candidate refers to register and associated lexis, and uses terms such as 'semantic field', 'metaphor', 'first-person narrative', 'elision' and 'ellipsis'.

3. Some of these linguistic choices have been related back to her style model. For example, she refers to Bill Bryson's use of the first-person narrative, and how her discourse structure has been influenced: she starts her text in the same way, and she links ideas in the same way as Bryson.

4. The candidate has used examples from her own writing to exemplify her analysis. Each of the points that she has made is accompanied by a quotation from her text.

5. Although the candidate has referred to her style model, and explained how it has informed her own writing, a more thorough analysis of the travel-writing genre would have been helpful.

Extension activity 2

Here is an examiner's response to Lucy's commentary.

This is a thorough analysis of the candidate's work. She has explained how her language choices and the tone of her writing have been influenced by her chosen audience. For example, she refers to her use of colloquial language with an informal sense of humour. She has made valuable comments about her use of linguistic features and the effects that she hoped to achieve. For example, she makes reference to verbs, semantic fields, sentence range, similes and personification. Further comments could have been made about the non-standard grammar of the dialogue. In addition, it would have been helpful if she had analysed the effects achieved by the range of sentence structures that she has used.

Extension activity 3

Here is an examiner's response to the commentary.

This is a thorough piece of analysis. The candidate has identified a number of non-standard features, and is clear about differences between dialect and colloquialisms. For example, she refers to 'I's goina' as dialect and 'stomach him' as a colloquialism. She has made some important comments about linguistic features such as ellipsis and elision, giving examples and explaining the effects the writer's use of these features has. A significant, but often ignored, feature of radio scripts is non-speaking dialogue. The candidate has correctly identified examples of non-speaking dialogue and commented on them appropriately.

Extension activity 4

An examiner's comments:

1. The weakest of these commentaries is B. A number of linguistic features have been identified, such as colloquialisms and imperatives, but the student has failed to provide any examples at all from their own text to elucidate the points that they have made.

2. Commentary A is slightly better. It identifies some linguistic features, but does not analyse their effects. For example, we are told that adjectives were used to improve the description, but the candidate has not taken the opportunity to discuss one or the semantic field. The comment that the candidate used minor sentences 'for variation' is shallow.

3. Commentary C is better than both A and B. The candidate has identified linguistic devices and provided examples to elucidate their comments. It is not clear whether the candidate understands the term 'cataphoric' as it has not been adequately explained. An example of how exaggeration has been used for effect would have been helpful.

4. Commentary D is clearly the best piece. Linguistic features have been identified, and examples provided from the student's own text. However, this commentary would have benefited from more thorough analysis. For example, there is no analysis of the effect achieved by the words taken from the lexical field of charities. Also, more consideration could have been given to the nature of the engagement hoped for with the rhetorical question.

The drafting process

Extension activity 5

Read the examiner's comments about the four analyses. How far did your notes agree with these comments?

1. The weakest of the analyses is clearly the analysis of the charity leaflet. Although there are references to graphology and persuasive phrases, there is no discussion to exemplify the student's understanding of these terms. While the candidate knows that colours and pictures are graphological features, they do not say anything significant about the changes that they made to these features. Examples of persuasive phrases would have given some indication of the student's level of understanding about linguistic features.

2. The analysis of the travel writing piece is marginally better. It is extremely brief but there are two references to linguistic features: declarative sentences and sentence types. However, there needed to be more evidence that these terms have been understood. The comment that declarative sentences provide information suggests some understanding, but some examples from the student's text could have been used to further illustrate their understanding.

3. Some interesting linguistic points, with references to non-fluency features, are made in the analysis of the interview. The list of non-fluency features (incomplete sentences, ellipsis and false starts) suggests that the candidate understands the concept. The candidate also understands the stylistic demands of their target audience. However, there are no examples from the student's writing to elucidate their discussion.

4. The strongest of the four analyses is the analysis of the magazine article. While the reference to placing the text into two columns does not show significant understanding of graphological features, it does demonstrate an understanding of the genre. However, the reference to cohesion, with exemplification from the candidate's writing, does suggest some conceptualised knowledge.

Glossary

A

accent: the specific way words are pronounced according to geographical region 15, 182

acronymy: the process of abbreviating that uses the first letter of a group of words but, unlike an initialism, an acronym is pronounced as a single word 99

actor: the individual or entity responsible for the action of a verb process 35, 83

actual reader: any reader who actually engages with the text 11

actual writer: the 'real' person behind the text 12

adjacency pair: two utterances by different speakers that have a natural and logical link, and complete an idea together; a simple structure of two turns 53

adjectival phrase: a phrase with an adjective as its head, for example 'very big 35

adverbial phrase: a phrase with an adverb as its head, for example 'very quickly 35

affected: the person or entity affected by a material action process 83

agency: the responsibility for, or cause of, an action 35

alliteration: a sequence of words beginning with the same sound 40

anaphoric referencing: referencing back to an already stated lexical item 25

antonymy: words with opposite semantic value 27, 28

assonance: the repetition of vowel sounds for effect 40

asynchronous discourse: discourse in which there are delays between turns that participants take 105

auxiliary verb: a verb that supports or 'helps' another; it shows tense or modality 33

B

base form: the simple form of an adjective, serving to modify 23

blogger: an individual who uses a web log 107

boosting device: a linguistic device used to intensify the force of an expression for added emphasis or power 92, 197

C

cataphoric referencing: referencing forwards to an as yet undisclosed lexical item 25

catenative: a verb that can attach to another to form a 'chain' 34

clause: a group of lexical items centred round a verb phrase 36–7

clause patterns: patterns produced by writers using certain types of clause for impact and effect 36

cohesion: a measure of how well a text fits together as a whole, its internal logic and construction 24, 126

colloquialism: an established set of informal terms used in everyday language 16, 126, 182

comparative: the form for comparing two items; adjectives inflected with -er or combined with 'more' are in the comparative form 23

complementary: truly opposite antonyms 28

complex sentence: a sentence containing a main clause with one or more subordinate or dependant clauses, often connected with a subordinating conjunction 37, 122, 168

compound sentence: a sentence containing two or more main clauses, connected by coordinating conjunctions, or sometimes just separated by punctuation (semi-colon) 37

compound-complex sentence: a sentence containing at least two main clauses and at least one subordinate clause 37

conceptual metaphor: the way in which abstract terms are mapped on to physical entities through an underlying conceptual structure 29

connective: a word, such as a conjunction, that connects words, phrases, clauses, sentences or paragraphs 158

connotation: an associated, symbolic meaning relying on culturally shared conventions 26, 122

consonance: the repetition of consonant sounds for effect 40

constituent structure: the key components of a phrase 31

constraints: ways in which powerful participants may block or control the contributions of less powerful participants, for example through controlling content or interrupting 74

context: the temporal and spatial situations in which a text is produced or received, e.g. where the producer of the text is, what he or she is doing, who he or she is talking to, what has occurred previously 11

context of production: the situation in which a text is produced and those factors that might influence its writing 11

context of reception: the situations in which texts are read and those factors that might influence a reader's interpretation 11

continuum: a way of representing differences by placing texts along a line showing degrees of various features 9

convention: an agreed or shared feature 46

conversational analysis: the analysis of the structure and features of conversation 53–4

cooperative principle: the principle that suggests that all communication is essentially a cooperative act 43

coordinating conjunctions: words such as *and*, *but* and *or* that link clauses to form compound sentences 37

covert marking: marking that is understood, for example in the antonyms young and old, young is the marked, old the unmarked term 85

covert prestige: a form of high status given to non-standard forms 90, 91

cultural model: an organisational structure based on shared and agreed criteria by groups of people within a society 45

D

deixis: lexical items that 'point' towards something and place words in context 44, 55, 112

denotation: a strict 'dictionary' meaning of a lexical item 26, 122

deontic modality: constructions that express degrees of necessity and obligation 68

descriptive approach/attitude: an approach to language study that focuses on actual language use 30

dialect: the language variety of a geographical region or social background, revealed by a variation in lexical and grammatical terms 15, 182

direct object: an object directly affected by a verb process, for example in 'I gave him the pen', 'pen' is directly affected by the 'giving' and is the direct object 36

discourse: a continuous stretch of language (especially spoken) that is longer than a sentence 2, 50–2, 55, 96, 196

discourse community: a group with shared values and approaches to reading 13, 66

discourse marker: a word or phrase that indicates a change in topic, or a return to a previous topic 55, 158

discourse strategy: strategies used in spoken and language texts 111–12, 118, 196

ditransitive verb: a verb that requires two objects to form a double-object construction 36–7

double-object construction: a clause with a verb that has two objects: one direct and the other indirect 36

dual-purpose: a text with two clear and defined purposes 12

dynamic verbs: verbs where the situation described by the verb process changes over time, for example 'he ate the cake' involves a dynamic process 21

dysphemism: a harsh, 'to-the-point' and perhaps taboo term, sometimes used for a dark, humorous effect 27

E

elision: the missing out of sounds or parts of words in speech or writing 134

ellipsis: the missing out of a word or words in a sentence 25, 55, 134, 182

epistemic modality: constructions that express degrees of possibility, probability or certainty 68

euphemism: a socially acceptable word or phrase used to avoid talking about something potentially distasteful 27

exchange structure: a series of turns between speakers 53

explicative evaluation: explaining reasons for narrative events 53

external evaluation: an evaluative comment outside the narrative sequence 53

F

face: a person's self-esteem or emotional needs 76

face-threatening act: a communicative act that threatens someone's positive- or negative-face needs 77, 93

field: the general purpose of an act of communication 14

flaming: the act of posting aggressive threads or responses to threads 106

folklinguistics: attitudes and assumptions about language that have no real evidence to support them, for example in the assumption that women are generally more 'chatty' or prone to gossip than men 89

formulation: the rewording of another's contribution by a powerful participant to impose a certain meaning or understanding 75

framing: cutting and pasting parts of an original message into a new message 104, 105, 106

functional words: words that have less explicit meaning and serve to highlight relationships between other words 20

G

gender: the differences in behaviour and roles that are a result of societal expectations 82, 94, 197

genre: the category or type of a text, such as comedy, tragedy, horror 10, 125

go off-topic: a term for posts that stray from the original topic of a thread 105, 106

gradable: antonyms that are not exact opposites but can be considered in terms of degree of quality 28

greetings sequence: a series of turns designed to initiate a shared social space 96, 97

H

hedging device: a linguistic device used to express uncertainty 55, 92

homophone: a word that sounds the same as another word or words 42

homophonic representation: the use of single letters and numbers to represent words based on a similarity in sound 99

'how are you' sequences: examples of phatic talk that maintain the social relationship before the main business of the telephone call commences 96, 97

hyponymy: the term for the hierarchical structure that exists between lexical items 27, 28

I

identification/recognition: a sequence in which speakers identify themselves to each other 96, 97

ideology: a set of belief systems, attitudes or a world-view held by an individual or groups 67

idiolect: an individual style of speaking or 'linguistic fingerprint' 13

implied reader: the kind of reader a text producer has in mind when writing and who might be expected to 'follow' the author's point of view 11, 72

implied writer: a constructed image of the writer a reader may have in mind 11

indirect object: an object indirectly affected by a verb process, for example in 'I gave him the pen', 'him' is the indirect object 36

influential power: power used to influence or persuade others 67

initialism: an abbreviation that uses the first letter of a group of words and is pronounced as individual letters 99

initiation–response–feedback (IRF): a triadic structure in speech that allows the first speaker to feedback on the response of a second speaker 54

insertion sequence: an additional sequence in the body of an exchange structure 54

instrumental power: power used to maintain and enforce authority 67

intensifying evaluation: adding detail and vividness 53

internal evaluation: an evaluative comment occurring at the same time as events in the narrative sequence 53

intransitive verb: a verb process such as 'yawned' or 'slept', that has no object 36

J

jargon: particularly specialist terminology that may exclude others 16

L

less powerful participants: those with less status in a given context, who are subject to constraints imposed by more powerful participants 74

lexical accommodation: the way in which speakers mirror each other's lexical choices as a sign of community membership 105

lexical (semantic) field: lexical items that are similar in range of meaning and properties 26, 122, 168

lexical onomatopoeia: actual lexical items that rely on a similarity between sound and meaning 40

lexical words: words that carry explicit meanings and represent the word classes that are open to new additions and derivations 20, 115

lexis: the framework that deals with the vocabulary system of a language 19, 114, 121, 160

linguistic rank scale: a system for showing the relationship between levels of language units. The movement from left to right indicates that a unit is structured from that which precedes it, for example clauses are structured from phrases 30

lurker: a user who reads a message board as a member or guest but who rarely, if ever, posts 106

M

main clause: a clause that can stand independently and make sense on its own 37

main verb: the verb that details the main process in a verb phrase 33

marked form: that which stands out as different from a norm 85

material processes: describing actions or events 21

members' resources: the vast amount of background knowledge and information that readers use in order to interpret texts and which may be explicitly drawn upon by text producers 71

mental processes: describing perception, thoughts or speech 21

metalanguage: a set of technical terms used to describe how language operates 18

metatalk: talk that draws attention to the act of talking itself 97

minor sentence: a grammatically incomplete sentence 121

mixed-mode features: features expected in printed text combined with features expected in conversation 130, 178

modal auxiliary verb: a verb that never appears on its own and is used to express possibility, probability, certainty, necessity or obligation: will; would; can; could; shall; should; may; might; must 33

mode: the medium of communication, e.g. speech or writing 9

moderator: an individual or group of individuals who run the message board and have the right to edit or delete threads and posts 105

modifier: a word, usually an adjective or a noun used attributively, that qualifies the sense of a noun. Adverbs of comment also act as modifiers, e.g. obviously 31

monotransitive verb: a verb that only requires one object 36

morpheme: the smallest unit of grammatical meaning. Morphemes can be words in their own right or combine with other morphemes to form lexical units 30

morphology: the area of language study that deals with the formation of words from smaller units called morphemes 30

multimodal texts: those that combine word, image and sound to produce meaning, for example a children's storybook that includes images to support the text 10

multi-purpose: a text with more than one purpose 12

N

narrative categories: six key categories developed by Labov which appear in a narrative – generally in a set order 51

negating particle: a small item used to show negation 33

negative face: the need to have freedom of thought and action and not feel imposed on 76

non-lexical onomatopoeia: 'non-words' that work in the same way as lexical onomatopoeia 40

noun phrases: a group of words centred around a noun 30

O

object pronoun: a pronoun that usually appears as being affected by a verb process 20

obligatory component: a necessary part of a phrase 33

oppositional view: a broad way of defining modes, which suggests that their qualities are strictly opposites, for example writing is formal, speech is informal 9

oppressive discourse strategy: linguistic behaviour that is open in its exercising of power and control 79

optional component: an additional part, not absolutely necessary 33

over-specificity: the giving of an inappropriately too specific answer, sometimes with absurd effects 29, 194

overt marking: marking that takes place through affixation or modification 85

P

parallelism: the repetition of a pattern or structure in related words, phrases or clauses 122

personal power: power held by individuals as a result of their roles in organisations 67

personification: a figure of speech where an animal or inanimate object is described as having human characteristics 122, 180, 199

phatic speech acts: turns designed to maintain a sense of cooperation or respect for the other speaker 96, 97

phonemic substitution: the replacing of one phoneme by another for a desired effect 42

phonetic spelling: a spelling that represents the sound of a word as opposed to its conventional spelling 99

phonological manipulation: the ways in which text producers play with sounds and their effects 41, 195

political power: power held by those with the backing of the law 67, 195

positive and negative politeness strategies: redressive strategies that a speaker might use to mitigate or avoid face-threatening acts 77–8, 94

positive face: the need to feel wanted, liked and appreciated 76

possessive pronoun: a pronoun that demonstrates ownership 20

post-modification: a modifying phrase or lexical item that occurs after the head noun in a noun phrase 31

power asymmetry: a marked difference in the power status of individuals involved in discourse 74

power behind discourse: the focus on the social and ideological reasons behind the enactment of power 67

power in discourse: the ways in which power is manifested in situations through language 67

powerful participant: a speaker with a higher status in a given context, who is therefore able to impose a degree of power 54, 74

powerful participants: those who hold some degree of status in a conversation and can to some extent control its direction and the potential of speakers to contribute 54, 74

pre-closing sequences: signals that one (or both) speaker wishes to end the conversation 97

pre-modification: modifying that occurs before the head noun 31

prepositional phrase: a phrase consisting of a preposition and an added noun phrase 31

prescriptive approach/attitude: an approach that concentrates on how language ought to be structured (written or spoken) and sees alternative patterns or versions as deviant and inferior 30

primary auxiliary: used to denote tense changes: *do, be, have* 33

primary purpose: the main reason a text has been produced 12

pronoun: *you* to construct a relationship between text producer and receiver 20, 199

prosodic features: paralinguistic vocal elements of spoken language used to provide emphasis or other effects 101

prototype: a 'best-fit' example of a particular category, for example for many people, an apple is a prototypical fruit 10

purpose: the reason a text is produced 12

Q

qualifier: further information to complete the phrase 31

R

referencing: when lexical items replace those already mentioned or about to be mentioned 24

register: a variety of language appropriate to a particular purpose and context 14

relational processes: describing states of being, identification or attributes 21

representation: the projection of a certain way of thinking about a particular individual, group or institution through the use of language 15

repressive discourse strategy: a more indirect way of exercising power and control through conversational constraints 79

S

script: a pre-planned and written-out speech 2, 81, 132–3, 135

secondary purpose: a secondary (and sometimes more subtle) reason 12

semantic derogation: the sense of negative meaning or connotation that some lexical items have attached to them 87

semantic deterioration: the process by which negative connotations become attached to lexical items 87

semantic or lexical field: lexical items that are similar in range of meaning and properties 26, 122, 168

semantics: the framework that deals with meaning and how that is generated within texts 19, 194

semi-auxiliary: a combination of a primary auxiliary and another verb part 34

sex: biological differences between men and women 82

simple sentence: a sentence consisting of a single main clause 37, 38–9

slang: colloquial language that is inventive and particular to individuals or groups 16

small talk: talk that is primarily interactional in orientation and is geared towards establishing relationships 78–9

social group power: power held as a result of being a member of a dominant social group 67

socialisation process: a process by which individuals' behaviours are conditioned and shaped 82

sociolect: a defined use of language as a result of membership of a social group 13

specialist register: a set of lexical items and grammatical constructions particular to an institution or occupational group 15

Standard English (SE): a universally accepted dialect of English that carries a degree of prestige 15

stative verb: a verb that describes a state of affairs rather than an action, e.g. 'know' 21

stereotyping: assigning a general set of characteristics to a group as a whole, often with negative connotations 86

stickie: a thread that is considered important and remains near the top of the message board regardless of how many times it is read or has responses 105

style: the way in which something is expressed 118, 173

style model: a text that is used as a model for original writing 115, 173, 176–83, 201

subject pronoun: a pronoun that usually occurs as the actor in a verbal process 20

sub-mode: a sub-division of mode, such as poetry, drama, conversation 10

subordinate: a 'lower' word in the hyponymic chain; a more specific lexical item 28

subordinate clause: a clause that is dependent on another to complete the full meaning of a sentence 37

subordinating conjunctions: words such as *because*, *although* and *while* that link a main clause to a number of subordinate clauses in complex sentences 37

substitution: the replacing of one set of lexical items for another 25

summons/answer: a sequence that opens the channel of communication on the telephone 96, 97

superlative: adjectives inflected with *-est* or combined with 'most' are in the superlative form 23

superordinate: a 'higher' word in the hyponymic chain; a more general lexical item 28

synchronous discourse: discourse that takes place in real time 105

synonymy: words with very similar semantic value 27

synthetic personalisation: the way in which advertising and other forms of communication use personalised language such as the second person 71

T

tag question: a group of words that turn a declarative into an interrogative, for example 'It's cold' becomes 'It's cold, isn't it? 55, 92, 113

tenor: the relationship between the participants in a conversation or between text producer and receiver 14

text: an example of spoken or written language for analysis 2, 4–9, 50, 68

textspeak: the language (in terms of both lexis and grammar) used by those sending text messages on a mobile phone 98–100

textual cohesion: the term used to describe how a text is logically structured to create a coherent sense of meaning 19

thread: a topic area initiated by a post to which others can respond 105

topic management: the control of the conversation in terms of speaking and topic 54

transcript: an accurate written record of a conversation or monologue, including hesitations and pauses 2, 57, 62, 102, 114

transition relevance point: a point at which it is natural for another speaker to take a turn 54

trolling: the posting of messages with the intention of irritating others 106

turn-taking: the sharing of speaking roles, usually cooperatively 53

type: a form of text such as a play, short story, recipe 10

typography: font type, size, colour, emboldening, italicising, underlining and any other modification to font types 45, 48

U

under-specificity: the inappropriately vague, rather general answer to a question 28, 29, 194

unequal encounter: an alternative term for *asymmetrical*, highlighting the power one speaker has over another 74

unmarked form: the measured norm, against which marked lexical items can be compared 85

user: an individual using a message board 105

username: the name chosen by a user of a message board that is known to all on that board and appears every time a post is made 105

utterance: a group of spoken words, roughly equivalent to the sentence in written terms 38–9

V

valediction: an item that acts as a farewell 97

variant spelling: deliberately non-standard spelling for effect 99

vowel omission: leaving out vowel sounds in textspeak and other electronic communication 99

W

web log: a site that is set up to allow an individual or several individuals to post frequent entries 106–7